DESCENDED FROM
HERCULES

NEW DIRECTIONS IN NATIONAL
CINEMAS   Jacqueline Reich, editor

DESCENDED FROM
HERCULES

BIOPOLITICS
and the
MUSCLED
MALE BODY
ON SCREEN

ROBERT A. RUSHING

INDIANA UNIVERSITY PRESS

Bloomington & Indianapolis

This book is a publication of

Indiana University Press
Office of Scholarly Publishing
Herman B Wells Library 350
1320 East 10th Street
Bloomington, Indiana 47405 USA

iupress.indiana.edu

Library of Congress Cataloging-in-Publication Data

Names: Rushing, Robert A., author.
Title: Descended from Hercules : biopolitics and the muscled male
    body on screen / Robert A. Rushing.
Description: Bloomington : Indiana University Press, [2016] | Series:
    New directions in national cinemas | Includes bibliographical
    references and index.
Identifiers: LCCN 2016015832 (print) | LCCN 2016027406 (ebook) |
    ISBN 9780253022509 (pbk. : alk. paper) | ISBN 9780253022462
    (cloth : alk. paper) | ISBN 9780253022585 (ebook)
Subjects: LCSH: Masculinity in motion pictures. | Human body in
    motion pictures. | Peplum films—History and criticism.
Classification: LCC PN1995.9.M34 R87 2016 (print) |
    LCC PN1995.9.M34 (ebook) | DDC 791.43/65211—dc23
LC record available at https://lccn.loc.gov/2016015832

1 2 3 4 5   21 20 19 18 17 16

Contents

Acknowledgments

Thanks first and foremost to Lilya and Sasha, for everything.

In 2007, Michael Rothberg asked me to give a lecture for the Unit for Criticism and Interpretive Theory at the University of Illinois and even let me continue when he learned that it was about campy movies starring bodybuilders. That lecture received great feedback from colleagues, both those who have since gone elsewhere (Jed Esty, Andrea Goulet, Matti Bunzl) and those who are still at the University of Illinois (Yasemin Yildiz, Pat Gill), and eventually became an article in *Camera Obscura*, where it received further excellent feedback from their editorial staff and outside readers. Around the same time, I gave a talk on *300* and peplum memory in Paris, thanks to my colleague and friend Carola Hahnel-Mesnard, and that talk, too, eventually became an article. That year was the "year of the peplum" for me, and I assumed that would be the end of it. I was mistaken.

Over the next several years, a number of talks (thanks to Pierpaolo Antonello and Robert Gordon at St. John's College, Cambridge, and to Todd McGowan and Hilary Neroni at the University of Vermont) kept me coming back to the peplum, and conferences at the Unit for Criticism and Interpretive Theory in Illinois brought me into contact with new areas of inquiry that would prove crucial for this project (biopolitics, haptic film criticism), as well as some of the major thinkers in those areas (Roberto Esposito, Jennifer Barker). To Lauren Goodlad, director of the Unit for Criticism in those years, many thanks, as well as to those who helped organize and facilitate those conferences, especially my fellow Italianists Manuel Rota and Nora Stoppino (who have also both given me extensive feedback and suggestions), and members of the Unit for Media and Cinema Studies, particularly Julie Turnock, Anna Stenport, and Lilya Kaganovsky.

Equal acknowledgment must go to another unit at Illinois that has had an enduring influence on me, the Illinois Program for Research in the Humanities. Much of my first book was written during my first term as an IPRH faculty fellow, and much of this book was written during my second. The IPRH's director, Dianne Harris, provided fantastic feedback on my chapter on the haptic, as did the other fellows in the seminar (Fiona Ngô, T. J. Tallie, Andy Gaedtke, Craig Koslofsky, Corey Flack, and Aaron Carico come particularly to mind); the IPRH in concert with the Department of Gender and Women's Studies also organized a series of amazing lectures on the topic "Body/Bodies," which was invaluable for the material in this book.

Illinois continues to provide meaningful research support (long may it last!) as an institution: the Research Board, Scholar's Travel Funds, and International Programs and Studies all provided funding for the research trips associated with this project that took me to archives in Bologna and Turin. The staff at the Cineteca di Bologna was unfailingly helpful (along with my colleague Andrea Ricci), as was the crew at the Bibliomediateca Mario Gromo and the Museo Nazionale del Cinema of Turin (Stella Dagna, Marco Grifo, and Roberta Basano in particular) in exploring the collection of silent-era Maciste films, images, and documents. Similarly, Peter Bagrov at Gosfilmofond in Moscow went above and beyond the call of duty both in providing a copy of a rare Maciste film and in finding and providing the associated documents. The American Association for Italian Studies conference in Zurich (2014) provided an opportunity to meet with Maciste enthusiasts and experts; many thanks to Ivo Blom, Francesco Pittasio, Giaime Alonge (who shared with me his delightful family, a great dinner, and a superb article on *300* that I had not yet seen), and most especially Jackie Reich, who has been a great friend and colleague (and fellow grappa drinker, along with her husband, Michael). Ivo, Jackie, Julie, and others were also generous in showing me the ropes at the Pordenone Silent Film Festival, where Ivo's selection of Italian strongman films made abroad made a notable contribution to this book's study of the transnational dimension of the peplum.

A number of reading groups at the University of Illinois also read portions of the book—thanks to Julie Turnock, again, and Rini Mehta for their helpful feedback on slow and stopped time in the peplum, and to Michael Rothberg (again) and Gabriel Solis for their thoughts on the peplum's biopolitical dimensions. Anonymous readers and the staff at *Cinema Journal* gave amazing suggestions, as did Amanda Klein and Barton Palmer, editors of *Multiplicities: Cycles, Sequels, Remakes, and Reboots in Film and Television,* who helped me think through how to give an overview of peplum history. The staff at Indiana University Press, especially Raina Polivka, has been stellar, and I would like to particularly thank David Gerstner for his extremely insightful suggestions on the manuscript, several of which were rich enough to warrant possible future articles in themselves.

Equally influential in more informal ways are the members of a fantastic circle of friends and colleagues who have tolerated my peplum obsession with amusement and good cheer (helped, no doubt, by an occasional cocktail): Michael Rothberg and Yasemin Yildiz, Jim Hansen and Renée Trilling, Nancy Castro and Gillen Wood, Brett Kaplan, Justine Murison, Dara Goldman, Carola and Philippe Mesnard, Maggie Flinn and Patrick Bray, and many more. In many ways, the most invisible but constant contributions to my thinking about the peplum have been made by students over the years: Ezra Claverie, Elysse Longiotti, Corey Flack,

Federica di Blasio, Peter Tarjanyi, Patrick Brown, Heather Gode, Dora Valkanova, and many others.

Gratitude and love to my family for their love and support.

Finally, I extend grateful recognition to *Cinema Journal* for permission to reprint portions of chapter 3, "Skin Flicks," which originally appeared in *Cinema Journal* 56.1 (2016).

Note on Film Titles and Foreign-Language Citations

PEPLUM FILMS MADE in Italy during the 1950s, 1960s, and 1980s often had quite different titles in the United States; referring to these films is further complicated by the fact that some were released with multiple English titles at different times. The 1961 Mario Bava film *Ercole al centro della terra*, for example, has been released with the fairly literal translation *Hercules in the Center of the Earth*, the slightly altered *With Hercules to the Center of the Earth*, and the radically different *Hercules vs. the Vampires*, but it is most widely known today under the title *Hercules in the Haunted World*. For Italian films from midcentury and the 1980s, I have opted to refer to them by their most popular current English-language title, giving the original title in Italian after the first appearance. Italian films from the silent period, however, are referred to by their original Italian title, with the English-language title given also after the first appearance. I generally refer to the television series *Spartacus* (2010–2013) as *Spartacus: Blood and Sand* (this is technically the title only of the first season) to avoid confusion with Stanley Kubrick's 1960 *Spartacus*.

Much of the criticism on the peplum is in Italian or French, and I cite theoretical texts in Italian, French, and German. Rather than giving cumbersome double quotations for foreign-language texts, I have translated citations into English, occasionally giving a term or a phrase from the original in brackets. In this case, page numbers refer to the original article or book in the original language. If, however, a translation is listed in the bibliography, I have used the published translation (sometimes slightly altering it for clarity), and the page numbers given refer to the translation, not the original text—but here, too, I have consulted the original and occasionally give a term or phrase in the original language where it might be helpful. I do not give page numbers for the original text, however (the awkwardness and confusion of double page numbers seemed more serious than the potential lack of scholarly rigor). For the *Standard Edition* of the works of Sigmund Freud, I give volume and page number thusly: 19:43.

DESCENDED FROM
HERCULES

INTRODUCTION

A Peplum Genealogy

THIS BOOK REPRESENTS the culmination of many years of engagement with a curious film genre, the peplum. Many readers, if they are familiar with this term at all, will think of a flap of fabric attached to a blouse or a skirt (see McDowell 1997). In fact, in classical antiquity the word "peplum" also referred to an article of women's clothing, the Greek *peplos* (later Roman *peplus* or *peplum*), a loose, draped shift or tunic for women. In the 1950s, there was a real vogue for films set in classical antiquity, many of which made use of a certain freedom imparted by their ancient settings to present filmgoers with shapely young women in revealing and silky shifts. French fans of these films (popular in both Europe and the United States) began to refer to them as *les péplums* as a result.[1] Even in the conformist 1950s, films set in the classical world (see Solomon 2001 and Wyke 1997a) allowed for representations of both virtue and vice, of great moral character and intimations of debauchery and decadence that permitted more of the body to be revealed than in contemporary settings. American studios produced a number of these epics set in Greece, Rome, or Egypt throughout this period, from *Samson and Delilah* (1949) to *Spartacus* (1960). The Italian film industry did the same, with films like Alessandro Blasetti's *Fabiola* (1949) and Pietro Francisci's *Attila* (1954, starring Anthony Quinn and Sophia Loren). Beginning with the massive success of Francisci's *Hercules* (*Le fatiche di Ercole*, 1958), however, Italy began to produce large numbers of cheaply and rapidly made peplum films that starred American bodybuilders, such as Steve Reeves or Gordon Scott, in the primary roles as mythological strongmen: Hercules, Goliath, Samson, and others.

By the early 1960s in France, the term "peplum" had found its way from provincial university film clubs onto the pages of the prestigious film journal *Cahiers du cinéma* as part of the ongoing debate about mainstream genres and auteur theory (Aziza 1998; Della Casa 1968, 312–314; Ghigi 1977, 744–746). As they did with cheap American B movies about crime from the 1940s and 1950s, which they baptized "film noir," or with Hollywood Westerns, French critics attempted to take the peplum seriously, making efforts to find peplum "auteur" directors who could successfully impose an individual vision on what was admittedly a pretty monotonous, repetitive, and narrow genre. These discussions took place as the peplum was being dominated not by its early version of pulpy melodramas filled with attractive ladies in scanty costumes but instead by Italian films filled with beefy bodybuilders in even scantier costumes, and the term "peplum" came largely to be used for these low-budget, muscular extravaganzas. It is in this more specific sense that I will use the term in this book, noting at the outset that the constant foregrounding of the muscular male body as the object of spectatorial desire and identification remains today the most distinctive and notable characteristic of these films.

The following years saw sometimes sharp exchanges between French and Italian critics, with Italians predominantly deriding the peplum and the French defending it.[2] Spinazzola (1963) refers to the "rigid hostility" (95) of the Italian critics as yet another "demonstration of Italian intellectuals' traditional contempt [*disprezzo*] for popular culture" (94). Domenico Paolella, director of several peplum films, noted that it was only in France that "for the first time, I saw a group of critics [*chercheurs*] and journalists take serious interest in this genre of films" (1965, 2), while in Italy that same genre was greeted with "dérision" and "mépris" (mockery and contempt). Indeed, Paolella's defense of the peplum appeared in French in a French journal. Likewise, English-language critics who have attempted to treat the genre seriously (Dyer 1997; Günsberg 2005) have generally adopted the term "peplum," whereas more dismissive (or simply more amused) commentaries call them "gladiator movies" or "sword-and-sandal" films. This is the case in Italy as well, where the use of the term "peplum" often signals a more serious stance (Ghigi 1977; Gregori 2009), whereas the term *film mitologico* (mythological film) indicates a more neutral or even critical one. For example, Stefano Della Casa's 2001 article "L'estetica povera del peplum" (The peplum's impoverished aesthetic) uses the word "peplum" only once—in the title—and in order to ridicule French pretensions for the genre. Instead, he calls them "film mitologici" and says that they functioned as a kind of "philosopher's stone" (306) for the Italian film industry, a phrase he takes from Spinazzola (1963, 79). Like the philosopher's stone, peplums turned worthless dross (terrible films) into gold (financial gains for the industry). Della Casa also perceives them as a transitory phenomenon (2001, 317) that would disappear when Italy completed its transformation into a modern, industrialized state by the end of the 1960s—a problematic claim, as we shall see, since Italy produced another spate of peplums in the 1980s, and the genre has thrived in highly modernized Anglophone countries since the 1980s in one form or another.[3]

In English-language criticism, the term "peplum" appears rarely, even when classicists turn to cinematic representations of the classical world in cinema. Monica Silveira Cyrino's *Big Screen Rome,* for example, covers representations of Rome from the 1950s on. Her book focuses on serious films for the most part (*Spartacus, Gladiator*), but she also dedicates three chapters to humorous treatments of Roman antiquity, including Monty Python's *Life of Brian* (1979) and Mel Brooks's *History of the World* (1981)—but no peplum films. Elena Theodorakopoulos's *Ancient Rome at the Cinema: Story and Spectacle in Hollywood and Rome* follows suit, while Blanshard and Shahabudin's *Classics on Screen: Ancient Greece and Rome on Film* includes one chapter on Francisci's *Hercules*. Maria Wyke's *Projecting the Past: Ancient Rome, Cinema and History* (1997b) stays with the usual "serious" suspects, however: *Spartacus* (1960) and *Quo vadis?* (1951). (Wyke has shed important light on the peplum in article form, however; see Wyke 1997a) Jon Solomon's *The Ancient World in the Cinema* (2001) is one of the few works that give the peplum more than a passing mention, although some recent works of scholarship on the peplum (Cornelius 2011; O'Brien 2014) indicate that the resurgence of the genre since 2007's *300* has not gone unnoticed.

Admittedly, it is sometimes difficult when one is writing about the peplum not to slip into an ironic and snarky amusement, verging on ridicule, sometimes affectionate, sometimes not. The films are often worthy of mockery: unprofessional acting, ludicrous and simplistic plots, hammy dialogue, cheap props, and, most particularly, the incongruous presence of a grinning, flexing, tanned, hairless, oiled, and nearly naked bodybuilder in the middle of every scene. Peplums are the best kind of unintentional camp in Susan Sontag's sense of the term: they appear to have been made seriously and straight, with little or no understanding of their unintentional homoeroticism and no recognition of their inherent improbability and hyperbolic, even hysterical, exaggeration of gender and bodies. The peplum has had a hard time being taken seriously, even by film scholars— Della Casa notes the "irresistible effects of involuntary comedy" (1961, 306) and focuses primarily on the genre's "aesthetic poverty," such as its use of footage recycled from other films. There have been some excellent serious treatments of the genre (Dyer 1997, who notes the genre's post-colonial and racial resonances; Günsberg 2005, who argues that the hero's muscled body works as a fantasmatic resistance to industrialization and modernization), but they are few and far between. I have tried to take the genre seriously here while not ignoring the pleasure of its campy exaggerations, because, although it is hardly the apex of cinematic art, the peplum deserves a closer look.

It deserves this closer look because, as this book argues, the peplum amounts to a century-long cinematic biopolitical intervention that offers the spectator an imagined form of the ideal male body, overflowing with health, muscular energy, and natural vitality, one that appears as a defense against menacing forms of alterity on the outside, including not only illness and degeneracy but also sexual and racial difference. Biopolitics refers to a wide variety of phenomena but is centrally concerned with how the state monitors, disciplines, and regulates the biological life of its subjects. Biopolitical interventions to promote health and life range from monitoring the stuff of life (demographic knowledge about births, health, and deaths) to direct intervention to protect and foster life (agricultural screenings at the border; blood tests before marriage) and to a host of indirect pressures intended to maximize biopower, the vitality of the nation (e.g., public awareness campaigns about folic acid, drinking and driving, and child abuse). Although scholars have already produced a significant body of work on biopolitics, relatively little attention has been paid to how biopolitical interventions are *mediated* (see, however, Väliaho 2014). What role have the media—film and television in the case of this book—played in creating, disseminating, contesting, supporting, or co-opting biopolitical interventions?[4]

Descended from Hercules shows that the peplum has functioned as a cinematic mediation between life (the vitality and health of the male body) and politics in multiple ways. It has consistently offered an ideal form of the male body for its spectators to admire and emulate, framed as the best hope for the health and vitality of the population, and it has returned obsessively to the same biopolitical themes over the past hundred years: genocide, concentrationary spaces, Giorgio Agamben's "bare life" (1998) and particularly Roberto Esposito's "autoimmune" paradigm (2011b), in which the idealized masculine body that is supposed to protect and "immunize" the community also puts that community at mortal risk. But the peplum has also spoken directly to real-world politics. From *Cabiria*'s (1914) justification of Italian colonial expansion in North Africa in 1914 to the US embrace of "Conan the Republican" as a model Cold Warrior in the 1980s, or to the even more belligerent "clash of civilizations" provocations of *300* (Iran protested the film at the United Nations) during the war on terror, the peplum has been consistently associated with right-wing nationalist politics, with colonialism and Orientalist discourses. Perhaps most remarkably, it has also repeatedly functioned as a mediating bridge between the world of the body (athletics, bodybuilding) and the world of politics. Peplum films have catapulted their stars from the world of "pure body" to political careers on more than one occasion—none more spectacularly than Arnold Schwarzenegger, but he is not the only example. All of this suggests that the peplum, far from being an easily dismissed, campy, or fringe phenomenon, has indeed secured a foothold on our fantasies of the muscular hero as a protector of the state, not only within the cinematic imaginary but also at the level of public policy.

A thorough examination of the biopolitical functions of the peplum is the aim of this book. As Todd McGowan has argued (2007, 9–10), however, cinema can capture and sway its viewers only if it manages to fascinate them. In order to be swayed by the biopolitical ideology of peplum films, in other words, viewers already need to be captivated by the fascination of moving images of the spectacularly muscled male body. As Slavoj Žižek notes, "Fantasy guarantees the consistency of a socio-ideological edifice" (2001, 89); a direct appeal to develop a muscular body would stick out as a strange and arbitrary command, but when it is inserted into a complex fantasy about a time when men were real men, defending freedom while menaced by foreign usurpers, all set within the glamorous world of Hollywood, we have a compelling story. To that end, then, this study begins by examining in some detail some of the peplum's essential fantasies, the ways in which the genre has managed to create and in turn capture the spectator's fascination with the muscular male body—and the ways in which these points of fascination ultimately mirror Roberto Esposito's biopolitical "immunitary paradigm."

In chapter 1, *"Nos morituri,"* I argue that the peplum's fascination with the muscled male body gives it an unusual relationship to cinematic time and movement. Although the action genre more generally showcases the male body in rapid and often violent movement, the peplum's concern is with the perfection of physique, the form of the body, the hero's muscles captured in a frozen pose or at most in a long, slow, strained heave that showcases his exceptional strength (a technique that emerges, of course, from the practice of bodybuilding itself). Again and again, the hero is strapped to a wooden beam with his arms outstretched, tied to a rack below a heavy weight, or otherwise immobilized to showcase his body. Many scholars (Baker 2008; Bazin 1967–1971; Bellour 2008; Mulvey 2006) have tied slowed or stopped time in film to death, and indeed, the peplum is obsessed with statues and frozen bodies, often the very menace the peplum strongman must avoid. Medusa returns again and again, figuratively or literally, from Maciste magically bound to the rocks by a she-devil in *Maciste all'inferno* (*Maciste in Hell*, 1926) to direct confrontations with the petrifying Gorgon in *Clash of the Titans* (1982 and again in the 2010 remake). In the peplum's most recent manifestations, its simultaneous horror of and fascination with slowed temporality have led to films shot almost entirely in slow motion (*300*) and to unique experiments with multiple, different (but slowed) temporalities happening on-screen at the same time (*Immortals*). Throughout, however, stopped time is both what the peplum needs and desires and what it fears; the endless time of lingering contemplation of the hero's muscled body, the apparent embodiment of health and vitality, is always also the time of the gladiators' *nos morituri,* or "we who are about to die."

In chapter 2, "Pre/Post," I look at the peplum's queer sexuality. Although the peplum has fascinated many spectators over the past hundred years, male and female, gay, straight, and other, it has ostensibly addressed a straight, white, male audience (predominantly teenage and pre-teen boys) that is clearly fascinated by the male body but uncertain about what stance to take toward it. The peplum universe, while highly sensual, has largely avoided or disavowed not only a clear sexual orientation but often sexuality itself. In the genre's midcentury appearances (as well as in the silent-era Maciste films), the peplum hero is a gigantic, muscled infant, unable to even recognize the seductive evil queen's sexual advances as such. This is a pre-sexual universe or, more precisely (following Freud's notion of infantile polymorphous perversity), a universe saturated by sexuality, but not yet an adult sexuality, and one that does not fully recognize sexual differences. In his most recent incarnations, however, the peplum hero locates himself *after* sexual desire—after the death of his beloved wife, he has nothing to live for except his suicidal quest for revenge. The peplum hero has, as Lee Edelman (2004) would put it, "no future" precisely because he is based on a renunciation of desire and the futurity it comports. His only desire is for a suicidal revenge, to die in his own way, an acceptance of the death drive. In short, the stuck temporality of chapter 1, *"Nos morituri,"* reappears in the peplum hero's sexual life: he either endlessly defers the advent of adult sexuality (and the concretizing of a sexual orientation) or appears in the twilight of desire, in a barren or bereft landscape without yearning.

In chapter 3, "Skin Flicks," I turn to recent theories of the haptic in cinema as a way of addressing the peplum's intense on-screen corporeality, its fascination with the skin, the muscles, and, ultimately, the insides of its brawny heroes. The paradigmatic instance of haptic imagery in film is the image that produces a kind of virtual or vicarious sensation of touch in the viewer. Haptic film criticism has generally been rooted in a phenomenological approach that stresses a reciprocal and mutually entangled relationship between the viewer and what is viewed, and some haptic critics have argued explicitly (Marks 2000) or implicitly (Barker 2009) that haptic imagery has a special ethical value: the reciprocity and mutualism of touch, of skin touching skin, have a transformative and positive potential. Barker divides her analysis into three layers of the haptic: the skin (the surface of the image), muscles (the movement of the image), and viscera (the secret rhythms that govern the visible image). Applying this same analysis to the peplum is extremely productive but suggests, however, two rather different results. First, while Barker and Marks privilege art cinema, as well as migrant, transnational, diasporic, and other "minority" cinemas, the peplum presents a low- or middlebrow, largely right-wing genre dedicated to the exaltation of straight white masculinity that is just as haptic—and very often just as reciprocal and mutual—as other forms of cinema. Certainly few genres are as invested in skin and muscles as the peplum, and, as I show, the same can be said for viscera. Second, the most politically reactionary peplum films, such as the enormously popular *300*, have shown a particular knack for cementing their ideological hold on the viewer (the root of "haptic" means "to seize" or "to grasp" in Greek: the audience grasps the film, but the film also seizes us) precisely through the mutuality of the haptic. In the case of the peplum, the "skin of the film" has a particular resonance for how the film successfully manages to "touch" the viewer in ways that are ideologically ambivalent. The hero's skin, muscles, and viscera work as ambiguous and contested signs of his masculinity and of his place in the world. In particular, the hero's initially impenetrable, armor-like skin (Maciste and Hercules can only ever be scratched, not wounded) is connected to a model of the masculine psyche that is superficial and reactive (body and psyche are both simple surfaces). Starting with Conan in the early 1980s, however, the peplum presents a masculine psyche based on the depth of the hero's vulnerability, a wound in his skin that eventually becomes the truth of his whole being.

Finally, I address the terrain of the biopolitical directly and at length in chapter 4, "Immune Systems." The peplum demands a discussion of biopolitics because of its content (virtually every peplum ever made recounts the story of a hero who risks or sacrifices his body in the service of the state in order to protect or restore the vital force of the people), its thematic interests (over a century of cinematic history, the peplum has been persistently obsessed with strength and health, vampirism, the just and unjust ruler, genocide, the possibility of a race of supermen, and so on), and, finally, its "extra-cinematic" uses. That is, on more than one occasion, the peplum has found itself actually mediating the world of the body's representation and the real world of politics. Arnold Schwarzenegger began his bodybuilding as a teenager, but he alternated his workouts at the gym in Graz with viewings of Italian peplum films starring his bodybuilding heroes. He then mediated his transition from bodybuilding to politics precisely through a film career that exploded into prominence with *Conan the Barbarian* (1982), the most influential peplum of the 1980s (the film recounts the movement of Conan from exploited "bare life" to ruler of the state). To bring him into politics, presidential candidate George H. W. Bush repeatedly introduced Schwarzenegger at rallies as "Conan the Republican," a metonymy I examine in some detail.

Schwarzenegger was neither the first nor the last to make the transfer from "pure body" to politics via the peplum, however. Bob Mathias had done the same decades earlier: first, a gold medalist in the Olympics; second, a peplum film star; and finally, a Republican in the House of Representatives. In the 1990s, Kevin Sorbo used his success as the star of *Hercules: The Legendary Journeys* (1995–1999) both to start his own biopolitical initiative (a not-for-profit organization focusing on children's health and fitness) and to become a motivational speaker for Republican candidates in the United States. Indeed, the history of the peplum as a biopolitical tool is a long one: the very first peplum film, the 1914 *Cabiria*, has been widely understood as celebrating and supporting Italy's colonial adventure in Libya, and its breakout character, the beefy Maciste, would return again and again to support the state with his mighty muscles. Little seems to have changed between *Cabiria* in 1914 and *300* in 2007: both films posit an imaginary threat to the West originating in the Orient, which then implicitly justifies contemporary imperialist aggression. Both films do so precisely through the mediating figure of the muscular male hero, who guarantees eventual victory, the rightness of the cause, and the inexhaustible vitality of the people—and who, as Esposito (2011b) suggests, is also a radically unstable figure, never more so than in his biopolitical dimension, apt to turn against the community and ultimately against himself. Ultimately, *Descended from Hercules* aims to show that the idealized male body of the peplum that is offered for the viewer's pleasure and admiration is a body about to die, a subject bereft of desire, a man whose virility can be measured only by the depth of his wound.

As a preliminary step to these larger arguments, however, we need to first understand the history of the genre. The peplum's history can be broken into five discrete cycles, periods in which it has flourished. The first is from 1914 to 1926, the "Maciste" cycle of films, all of which starred the same strongman, Bartolomeo Pagano, as the brawny hero Maciste. The second cycle, the midcentury peplum, runs from 1958 to 1965 and stars almost exclusively bodybuilders, such as Steve Reeves, Gordon Scott, and Reg Park, playing a wide variety of fictional strongmen from mythology, the Bible, literature, and silent film: Hercules, Samson, Goliath, Ursus, Maciste, and others. For many, this is the paradigmatic version of the peplum film. The third phase of peplum history is the "barbarian" peplum of the 1980s, such as the American *Conan the Barbarian* or the Italian-made *Ator* films, which offer a decidedly more adult and graphic vision of the peplum universe, one that is both sexual and violent but already curiously melancholy, nostalgic, and resentful. The fourth phase of the peplum flourished on television in the 1990s, from live-action series such as *Hercules: The Legendary Journeys* to animated fare like *Conan the Adventurer* (1992–1993). Finally, the contemporary wave of peplum films and television began in part with Ridley Scott's *Gladiator* (2000) but found a particularly coherent form in the slow-motion graphic violence and heroic tragedy of Zach Snyder's 2007 film, *300*, and a surprisingly complex and nuanced version in the television series *Spartacus* (2010–2013).

The Silent Era and Maciste

In the early 1910s, Italian filmmakers had significant success with epic films set in classical antiquity, aided by the proximity of actual ruins, attractive landscapes, and abundant natural light. In 1913, Enrico Guazzoni directed one of the many adaptations of Henryk Sienkiewicz's popular novel *Quo vadis?* (the film was a major international success), and it contained what is arguably the first peplum sequence: the massive, if not particularly muscled, bodyguard Ursus wrestles a bull with his bare hands. In 1913, the silent film *Spartaco* featured Ausonia, a popular bodybuilder and strongman, bending iron bars with his bare hands in an early cinematic treatment of the legendary rebel slave Spartacus. A year later, Giovanni Pastrone made the even more successful *Cabiria*, which featured a character named Maciste, a slave of the Roman patrician Fulvius Axilla during the Second Punic War. Maciste was played by Bartolomeo Pagano, a tall, broad-shouldered, muscular dockworker. Contemporary audiences particularly loved Maciste, and Itala Film put Pagano in a series of approximately two dozen Maciste films from 1915 to 1926.[5] Numerous imitators and competitors appeared as well, from Saetta (who generally emphasized acrobatics rather than mere size and strength) to a handful of female athletes (Linda Albertini as Samsonette) and strong women (Astrea, who comes closest to a female form of the peplum hero, and who was in fact billed as the "emula di Maciste," or Maciste's female imitator). All emerged from "popular adventure and romance stories in *feuilleton* and comic strip formats . . . [and] the popular tradition of chain-breaking, fire-breathing strongman shows in public squares and circuses" according to Günsberg (2005, 98), a point echoed also by Cammarota (1987, 22) and Ghigi (1977, 733). These elements were part, of course, of the "cinema of attractions" (Gunning 1986) that typifies much early cinema, and that continued in part into the 1920s.

Starting with the first Bartolomeo Pagano film, simply titled *Maciste* (1915), the producers abandoned the ancient Roman context; according to the fictional world they depict, Maciste—not Pagano—is an actor who works for Itala Film and who played a slave in antiquity in blackface, but who now appears as a modern (and white) Italian. He temporarily becomes the ruler of an imaginary country, Sirdagna, in *Maciste imperatore* (Emperor Maciste, 1924), travels to hell in *Maciste all'inferno*, and moves freely from Europe to more exotic locales, such as safari in Africa or New York City. Much of the space in Maciste films is utopian in the etymological sense of no place: vaguely defined in-between territories that are clearly "European" but less clearly associated with any real locale, as well as exotic and Orientalized fantasy terrains. Much of the action of *Maciste und die Javanerin* (Maciste and the Javanese woman, 1922, a German-produced Maciste film), for instance, is set in and around "the Grand Hotel," a typical space in films from the 1920s and 1930s that represented a crossroads for the wealthy and cosmopolitan from many different places.[6] These spaces allow the free combination and recombination of elements of the familiar and the exotic, East and West, much as Maciste moves in and out of different identities—a Bedouin, a foolish country bumpkin, an alpine mountain climber—and even occasionally appears as "Maciste," the character from *Cabiria*, but now as a role that he plays rather than himself. There is virtually no Maciste film in which he does not appear at least briefly in disguise; in *Maciste und der Tochter des Silberkönigs* (Maciste and the silver king's daughter, 1922, another German Maciste film), he goes undercover as a mustachioed fire-stoker named Jim Holmes before being sent undercover again by his new boss as a boxer named Braxton (hijinks ensue). Although the bulk of Maciste's adventures were set in the modern age, many of his silent-era imitators (e.g., Sansone, Ausonia, Ajax, Saetta) maintained the mythological and the fantastic, from orcs and lizard men to Amazons and dragons (Martinelli 1983, 37).

In *Cabiria*, Pagano's skin was darkened for the role to suggest racial difference, but at the same time, Maciste is also differentiated from "real" Africans in the film (he turns his nose up in disgust at the smell of an African woman at the inn where he is staying, for example), who are also portrayed as having much darker skin. In "The Metamorphosis of Maciste" (2013), Jacqueline Reich offers an extremely perceptive and detailed account of Maciste's transformation from an African slave to a white Italian in his first film. Even so, *Cabiria*'s racial ambiguity about Maciste (he is not Roman but not precisely African, either; Pastrone called him a "mulatto" [Usai 1986, 74]) continues throughout the rest of the films. Maciste dons blackface and a fez to pose as a colonial servant in his first feature film, *Maciste*, for example. Reich correctly points out that this works to make his whiteness more visible, but it simultaneously suggests that race is only skin deep— that "passing" is possible—since both the "real" mulatto of *Cabiria* and the "fake" African servant of *Maciste* consist of the same body.

Maciste, setting a pattern that will continue through the midcentury peplums, almost never falls in love. *Maciste innamorato* (Maciste in love, 1919) is perhaps the only significant exception, but his love is unreturned.[7] Instead, he facilitates a romance between the female protagonist and another man. Sometimes this match is what we might expect from an ideologically conservative genre (as in *Maciste contro lo sceicco* [Maciste vs. the sheik, 1926], where Maciste brings together two members of the aristocracy), but just as often, Maciste facilitates a match across some sort of barrier (see Hay 1987, 151, on Maciste moving across class boundaries). In *Maciste all'inferno*, it is that of a working-class girl to the local aristocrat who has gotten her pregnant, while in *La trilogia di Maciste* (The Maciste trilogy, 1920), it is the love between a plebeian newspaperman and an aristocratic girl. In *Maciste nella gabbia dei leoni* (Maciste in the lions' cage, 1926, released in the United States as *The Hero of the Circus*), the strongman brings together Giorgio, the wealthy (white) son of a circus owner, and Seida, a girl (in brownface) he rescues while on safari in Africa. In a telling publicity still for *Maciste in vacanza* (Maciste on vacation, 1920), Maciste simultaneously holds aloft both the man and the woman whom he is about to bring together. The woman is turned so that her face and body are more directly facing the camera, so it is only with a prolonged gaze that we notice that both the man and the woman gaze adoringly not at each other but at Maciste. Both reach out a hand to touch him: the woman caresses the bare skin of his face, and the man rests his hand just above Maciste's heart on his impressive chest. Implicit in this image is an idea that will be fully worked out in the midcentury peplum: the male spectator's desire to look at Maciste's marvelous body can be mediated by the strength of the strongman himself. Maciste will put the right two pieces together (a man and a woman). In other words, Maciste already exercises a function not only as a mediator but also as a teacher. In *Maciste imperatore*, Maciste meets with two fussy old men who work as tutors of the young Prince Otis, and they give him terrible news: the prince has run off with a woman! Maciste laughs with delight and reminds them that "it'd be worse if he'd run off with a man!" Under Maciste's tutelage (and control), Prince Otis will end up with a woman, and with the right woman.

Maciste remains excluded from the romantic plot, however, and the films convey clearly that it is from personal disinterest. Martinelli notes that this lack of interest was typical of the whole strongman genre in early Italian films—they are, in his words, "rather sexless [*assessuati*]" (1983, 41). He can maintain and order the libidinal field precisely because he stands clear of it himself. In *La trilogia*, he simply rolls his eyes when a besotted girl declares her love for him, preferring instead the company of what "has always been most dear" to him, his masculine pipe. In *Il viaggio di Maciste* (1920), this attachment to objects rather than girls becomes a running gag when Maciste's wife, with the curious name Diattolina, appears for the first time. Maciste has a wife? The film elicits the audience's anticipation only to comically deflate it: she is a car made by the Diatto firm (hence the diminutive Diattolina), which would later give rise to Maserati. "She's cute," Maciste remarks about the American girl, Miss Edith, who pursues him, "but not built like my Diattolina!" Maciste cannot take any lady friends along when he takes his road trip, since his beloved car was specially made to have only one seat (Maciste is too large for a normal seat, of course, but this also suggests a kind of structural fidelity to his car rather than any woman, since no couple can be accommodated). "A man has to support his wife," he declares before lifting the entire car onto his shoulders and carrying it into the castle bedroom where he is staying.[8] In *Maciste all'inferno*, Maciste is briefly tempted by sexuality and kisses a female demon in hell. He is roundly and repeatedly punished for this, transformed into a hairy satyr himself (again, speaking to a fundamental ambiguity in the character, not only racial, but between man and animal), and imprisoned in the nether world for most of the film. When a host of scantily clad she-demons tries to tempt him again at the film's end, he returns to the type that is so prevalent in the midcentury peplum film: a grinning, muscular schoolboy who refuses woman's sexual temptations mostly because he isn't mature enough to even understand them.

Instead, the basics of Maciste can be summed up, as Sarah Keller has noted, by the formula "eating and beating," the simple bachelor pleasures.[9] As with later peplums, Maciste performs a variety of fairly standardized set pieces to showcase his strength, such as bending bars, lifting his enemies and hurling them as a weapon, and lifting heavy objects. Martinelli attempts to list the "principal exercises of these Hercules," which are "the lifting of cast iron barbells, of persons or objects; the breaking of braces or chains with the biceps or the expansion of the chest; demonstrations of strength with the jaws" (1983, 43), and others. Maciste has a particular penchant for destroying machinery; in *Cabiria*, he breaks free of a millstone that he was forced to turn for ten years, and he smashes a water mill in *La trilogia* as the saw it powers is about to bisect his friend. In *Maciste nella gabbia dei leoni,* Maciste takes the stairs while the young man he is chasing takes the elevator, and naturally, Maciste arrives first; in these films, technology always loses out to muscle. (Reich [2015] also notes that the Maciste films present "mechanized industrialization" [152] specifically and modernity more generally as particularly problematic.)

Virtually everyone who has written about Maciste agrees that his strength, energy, and vitality are meant, and were understood at the time, as a nationalist allegory for Italy as a nation coming into its own, particularly in *Cabiria*'s celebration of Italy's recent war in Libya (see Schenk 2006). Reich writes that "no cinematic figure would better epitomize this convergence of Italian vigor, virility, and vitality than Maciste," arguing that Maciste managed to function as "a symbol of the nation" (2015, 242) throughout the significant changes that characterized Italy at the beginning of the twentieth century. Such an allegory was particularly potent in cinematic form, since Italian cinema was one of the pre-eminent national cinemas in the years leading up to the end of World War I. Dyer (1997, 168–169) and Günsberg (2005, 97) both suggest that the midcentury strongman represented a populist and proletarian fantasy that strength might still matter in an industrial age, and Reich extends this part of this logic back to Maciste as well, noting that his metamorphosis from Roman slave in *Cabiria* to modern Italian in *Maciste* is also a shift from Pastrone's lofty artistic ambitions in *Cabiria* "toward a populism, soon to be typical of the strongman films" (2015, 69; see also Hay 1987, 226, and Ricci 2008, 81–83, on Maciste's populist strength).[10] The Maciste films ended when Pagano retired, and he refused offers to return to the screen throughout the 1930s and 1940s.

The Midcentury Peplum

In 1958, Piero Francisci directed *Hercules,* one of many popular classical dramas and melodramas made in that decade. Two things made *Hercules* unusual, however. The first was the star of the film, the American champion bodybuilder Steve Reeves: Hercules was played by someone with a truly Herculean physique. The second was that it was bought, marketed, and distributed in English-speaking countries by Joseph Levine, the famous—indeed, infamous—promoter who was responsible for bringing both Godzilla and Sophia Loren to the attention of American filmgoers. Levine spent lavishly on the promotion of *Hercules,* advertising it in venues as varied as the official magazine for the Boy Scouts of America (Chapman 2002, 12), men's fitness and physique magazines, and under-the-counter magazines discreetly targeted at a gay audience (Tomkins 1967, 56).[11] Levine's promotional efforts were well repaid because *Hercules* was one of the most popular pictures of the year. As often happens when a cheap film has significant financial success, imitators rushed to make similar films, and between 1958 and 1965, audiences in both Italy and English-speaking countries appeared to have had almost unlimited interest in these inexpensive and easily digestible spectacles.[12]

Virtually all these films were Italian productions or co-productions with other countries, and by 1960, dozens of peplums starring bodybuilders had been released. Italy at the time had multiple systems of film distribution, and peplums were mostly shown in the cheapest and lowest-quality theaters, the so-called *terza visione* theaters that got low-budget films and worn-out prints, where, despite much lower ticket prices, they earned substantial sums over unusually long runs (Spinazzola 1963, 77). These theaters, as Dyer notes (1997, 166) were largely rural, and audiences would circulate and talk during screenings, less of a problem for peplum films, whose dialogue was relatively inessential and whose feats of strength were frequent and repetitive. Brunetta more trenchantly refers to the peplum's "half-illiterate and peasant audiences" (2004, 143). Peplums also made unusual inroads in international distribution. According to Spinazzola (1963, 81), while northern Europe and the Soviet bloc remained resistant, midcentury peplums rivaled and even outshone Hollywood in distribution success in the Middle East, the Far East, Latin America, South Africa, and Spain. Vitali (2010) notes the extensive influence that both the silent-era Maciste films (23–24) and the midcentury peplums (146–148) exercised on Hindi action films in India, for example. Midcentury peplum films enjoyed perhaps even greater success in the United States, the United Kingdom, and especially France, which was a frequent production partner. In addition to Hercules, Italian filmmakers recycled a number of strongmen characters from the silent period, particularly Maciste and Ursus (the burly giant of the 1913 *Quo vadis?*), whose names were often changed to the more familiar "Hercules" for the US release. Samson and Goliath made appearances, too, as well as burly titans, Romuluses, Remuses, Spartacuses, gladiators, Ulysseses, Theseuses, and others, not to mention a handful of strapping pirates. Although a few studies of peplums attempt to group them on the basis of the strongman's identity (Cammarota 1987), there is little if any difference between films starring Goliath and those starring Hercules or Maciste.

In fact, it is not much of an exaggeration to say that virtually every midcentury peplum film has exactly the same plot. A cruel, unjust, and foreign ruler has usurped the throne and oppressed the people. There can be minimal variations in this setup—for example, the unjust ruler may not be foreign but instead may be manipulated by foreign agents; he may be the proper, just ruler, but under a magic spell (cast by a foreign agent); or the unjust ruler may be an evil, seductive (often redheaded) queen—but the basic structure is always the same. Hercules must depose this cruel oppressor and free the people by restoring the legitimate ruler to the throne. The strongman is almost always a disinterested outsider with minimal or no ties to the throne in question; any suggestion that he could be a political threat or represent the forces of instability and anarchy is completely absent. Hercules acts purely out of a desire for justice and refuses any reward. Dyer has noted that the peplum's ostensible anti-fascism is belied by fascist structures of feeling, however (1997, 169): the films still promote the notion of a single charismatic and infallible leader whose integrity is guaranteed by his muscular virility (see Spackman 1996 on virility as a key term for Italian Fascism). The peplum reluctantly concedes that Hercules cannot be the king, but it still believes that the political order is both founded on and legitimated by this virile figure.

The connections between the first and second cycles of the peplum are so numerous and so well established that it almost goes without saying that the midcentury peplum is derived from the Maciste cycle; indeed, the most frequent character in the midcentury peplum is still called Maciste, and several of the midcentury titles are simply taken verbatim from earlier Maciste films (*Maciste contro lo sceicco, Maciste all'inferno*). Carlo Campogalliani directed both silent-era Maciste films (*La trilogia di Maciste*) and midcentury peplums, such as *Goliath and the Barbarians* (*Il terrore dei barbari*, 1959) and *Son of Samson* (*Maciste nella valle dei re*, 1960). So did Guido Brignone, whose career spanned the silent strongman (both Saetta and Maciste films) and the midcentury peplum.[13] These identities conceal, of course, certain important differences; the explicitly pro-colonialist nationalism of the Maciste cycle (*Cabiria, Maciste alpino* [1916], *Maciste nella gabbia dei leoni*) is in some ways toned down in the midcentury peplum, not least by having American bodybuilders (or Italian bodybuilders under assumed American names like "Alan Steel") as the strongman who rescues the oppressed people from an unjust, cruel, and foreign tyrant (see Dyer 1997 and Hay 1987). American bodybuilders playing Maciste essentially allowed these films to have their ideological cake (the superheroic figure who historically represented Italian nationalism) and eat it too: that figure is ostensibly American, as D'Amelio (2014) has argued, a potential reference to the US role in freeing Italy from German forces during World War II. Even if they eschew the explicit colonialism of the Maciste era, however, midcentury peplums are often racist in ways that are more familiar to contemporary audiences. In the peplums directed by Antonio Leonviola, for instance, Africans like "Bangor" and "Ubaratutu" immediately assume the "proper" relationship of subordinate to master once they meet the white hero, and they do so willingly, happily, and with gratitude. At the same time, more distant (and "exotic") locales reveal themselves as in-between, utopian spaces that open themselves up completely to the white man's investigation without cultural or linguistic resistance. In *Samson and the Seven Miracles* (*Maciste alla corte del Gran Khan*, 1961), the six-foot, three-inch-tall white hero, waxed hairless and oiled and wearing nothing but a bright red diaper, wanders through a crowd of medieval Chinese peasants without anyone noticing him. The strongman in the midcentury peplum is never out of place, in other words, because every place belongs to him, if not in an explicit colonialist sense. This kind of sequence is frequently repeated in peplum films set outside continental Europe, as in the midcentury version of *The Witch's Curse* (*Maciste all'inferno,* 1962), where a nearly naked Maciste with an enormous Elvis bouffant (Kirk Morris) rides on a white horse into a crowd of American Puritans without anyone batting an eyelash, or in *Goliath and the Vampires* (*Maciste contro il vampiro,* 1961), where an equally bare and pale Goliath tours a Middle Eastern bazaar without any second glances. A number of commentators (Hark 1993; Neale 1993; Tasker 1993) have noted that in most mainstream Hollywood fare, the male body may be revealed as a spectacle only in sadomasochistic torture sequences, while the exposure of female bodies goes unremarked (see Hark 1993, 152). Only in the peplum is the muscular white man's body so remarkably visible (indeed, on conspicuous display) and yet unseen within the diegesis.

The midcentury peplum follows many of the basic structures outlined in the Maciste films. Like Maciste, the strongman is a big, exuberant fellow whose essential attitude is ebullient and happy. He likes smashing the bad guys and saving the girl; these are simple pleasures for a simple man. The Italians called these figures *giganti buoni* or "good giants," and that is precisely what they are. Moreover, the sexuality expressed in the two cycles is also the same: women are definitely attracted to the strongman, but he is generally presented as a big boy who barely understands what is being offered to him. Like the silent-era Maciste, Hercules prefers arranging matches for others to finding one for himself. Unlike the Maciste films, however, these matches rarely, if ever, cross racial boundaries. Although those racial boundaries are much more sharply established in the midcentury peplums, class hierarchies are vague and ill defined. Maciste, Hercules, and the like usually appear to be soldiers, farmers, or other manual laborers who happen to be good friends with the king.

There are only a few films of the silent era in which Maciste has a real sidekick. In *La trilogia,* he is sometimes accompanied by his "good friend" Saetta (Domenico Gambino), another action star of the 1910s and 1920s, who specialized in more athletic roles. In the midcentury peplum, however, and ever since, a sidekick is almost always present. Whereas the hero is massively muscled and generally dark haired and bearded (following the model set by Steve Reeves in *Hercules*), the sidekick is only average in his musculature, a prince or a warrior, perhaps, but only a normal man. He is almost always clean shaven and often has lighter hair than the strongman; he is generally younger and sometimes a mere youth. In several films, a moody, morose, or lethargic sidekick emphasizes the strongman's optimism and energy, for example, Ilius in *Goliath and the Dragon* (*La vendetta di Ercole,* 1960) or Theseus in *Hercules in the Haunted World* (*Ercole al centro della terra,* 1961). Both have shockingly bright, dyed hair, one platinum blond, the other red. When there is a romantic plot in the midcentury peplum—and there usually is—it is generally between the sidekick and an apparently impossible love. Hercules then helps the sidekick obtain this out-of-reach woman or, if she is prohibited for some reason, persuades him to redirect his attentions to a more proper love object.

Alternatively, the sidekick may be present purely as comic relief, in which case he may be short, flabby, garrulous, and incompetent or, not infrequently, a wisecracking dwarf. More rarely still, the sidekick is African American, in which case he is fearful, passive, and absolutely dependent on the white hero, even if he is also a bodybuilder. Even these versions of the sidekick, however, seem to have a similar function and may be treated in much the same way. In *Goliath and the Sins of Babylon* (*Maciste, l'eroe più grande del mondo*, 1963), for example, there are two sidekicks, a moody, slight young man and a wisecracking dwarf. Both are united with their proper love objects at the end of the film (the princess and a female dwarf, respectively) as the strongman watches over them and smiles benevolently. In *Mole Men versus the Son of Hercules* (*Maciste, l'uomo più forte del mondo*, 1961), the hero presides over the union of his fearful African sidekick and a lovely African lady.

The visual focus throughout the midcentury peplum, as in the silent-era Maciste films, is the protagonist's body. It is his muscles that take priority—or rather, not quite the muscles themselves but their presence and power revealed through tension (the arms straining to pull chains together, to push the jaws of a torture device apart, to lift up, to press down) and in particular through the taut, oiled skin of the bodybuilder. Just as in the Maciste films, the standard and rapidly exhausted repertoire of feats of strength formed the bulk of the action in any midcentury peplum film, and any new expedient for showcasing the hero's muscles was quickly adopted. In film after film, the strongman wrestles with a wild animal (a sequence that originates in the 1913 *Quo vadis?*), turns a giant wheel (as in *Cabiria*) to showcase his shoulders (figure o.1), lifts an enemy into the air, uproots a tree bare-handed, or wraps chains around a pillar and pulls down the building that it supports. In many peplums, all these things happen, sometimes more than once. To vary the action, the evil, seductive queen may administer a magic potion to the unsuspecting hero, after which he does all the same feats of strength, but to support her side. Eventually, either the magic is reversed or the hero reveals that it was all a pretense, but either way, the final resolution of the plot can come about only through one more utterly extravagant feat of strength, almost invariably the collapse and destruction of a building or city.

This emphasis on the hero's muscles to the exclusion of all else often leads to a peculiar kind of anti-narrative spirit in the peplum. More focused on showcasing a posed body in a static tension, it delays or foregoes altogether chances for narrative or character development. Most narrative developments occur primarily to give the hero another opportunity to lift something heavy or break something hard, and they often appear without any apparent cause or motivation. *Goliath and*

Figure 0.1. The strongman, trapped between fire and enemy lances, is forced to turn a giant wheel. *The Vengeance of Ursus (La vendetta di Ursus)*, 1961.

the Vampires opens with Maciste plowing a field (is he a farmer? really?) when his plow runs afoul of a tree stump. He tears the stump from the ground with only his powerful body (long, lingering shots of his back and shoulders); as he pulls it free, he hears a cry for help: a boy (who?) in the nearby sea (are we on the coast?) has been attacked by a sea monster. Having defeated the monster, Maciste sees smoke from his village (he lives in a village?) nearby; it has been attacked by pirates (there are pirates?), and so on. There is, strictly speaking, not much narrative in the sense of a series of unfolding and concatenated events, each a consequence of what went before. Rather, there is a series of set pieces, connected primarily by the presence of the strongman's body.

As was the case with silent-era Maciste films, time and place are surprisingly plastic in the midcentury peplum. The strongman might get swept away from Greece in a storm and wash ashore in pre-Colombian South America, as he does in *Hercules against the Sons of the Sun* (*Ercole contro i figli del sole*, 1964), or go— we never learn how or why—to medieval China (*Samson and the Seven Miracles*), the Middle East (*Devil of the Desert against the Son of Hercules* [*Anthar l'invincibile*, 1964]), Africa (*Maciste in King Solomon's Mines* [*Maciste nelle miniere di re*

Salomone, 1964]), or Atlantis (*Hercules and the Captive Women* [*Ercole alla conquista di Atlantide,* 1961]). These movements in space are also movements throughout time, of course, from antiquity to the Middle Ages and even into the sixteenth century (as in *Samson and the Slave Queen,* originally titled *Zorro against Maciste* [*Zorro contro Maciste,* 1963], set during the reign of Philip II of Spain). Indeed, the peplum strongman could even move into the Western (and hence the nineteenth century), as in the singular *Hercules and the Treasure of the Incas* (*Sansone e il tesoro degli Incas,* 1964), a spaghetti Western crossed with a peplum, in which the Western elements (horses, hats, Indians chasing the stagecoach) eventually give way to the hero (bodybuilder Alan Steel) out of his shirt to reveal his muscles and all the usual set pieces (breaking chains, including the final collapse in the underground cavern). The overall effect is to suggest that heroic, white, Western (read American) masculinity was universal, de-historicized, omnipresent. This was not in any way different from the temporal and geographic elasticity on display in the Maciste films—Maciste, as the bearer of Western heroic masculinity, was everywhere, at all times. But while Maciste could exist in the present, the midcentury peplum posited a certain necessary distance between the heroic past and the viewer's present world. Greek and Roman settings suggested that this distance represented a certain continuity, but they also made the heroic past unapproachable for the modern viewer. The only two films to attempt to combine the peplum past and the present make explicit the "impossible" nature of the divide: *The Three Stooges Meet Hercules* (1962) and *Hercules in the Valley of Woe* (*Maciste contro Ercole nella valle dei guai,* 1961) both posit contemporary people making use of a time machine to return to the mythic past, where masculinity was still "the real deal." In *The Three Stooges Meet Hercules,* one of the time travelers bulks up his muscles in this "time of the real man," but even so, his body and strength still cannot compare to those of the "real" Hercules. Both films are comedies, as if there is something temporally incongruous about the epic masculinity of the past co-existing with modernity (and no film brought the strongman into the contemporary world until the 1969 *Hercules in New York,* also a comic treatment).

The Barbarian Peplum

As in the previous two cycles of peplum cinema, there were direct lines of cultural transmission from the 1960s peplum to the 1980s barbarian peplums: both Franco Prosperi (who directed the 1982 *Conan* knock-off *Gunan, King of the Barbarians* [*Gunan il guerriero*] under the pseudonym Frank Shannon) and Umberto Lenzi (who directed the 1983 peplum *Ironmaster* [*La guerra di ferro: Ironmaster*] under the improbable pseudonym Humphrey Milestone) had worked extensively on midcentury peplums. But there were other influential channels of cultural transmission as well that carried the peplum through its apparent long drought from 1965 to 1982. These indirect channels are perhaps more important in the case of the barbarian peplum, since when the peplum returned in the 1980s, it was significantly changed in many respects.

To begin with, midcentury peplums remained in the popular imagination because they commonly appeared as late-night or daytime movies on Italian television and as regular staples on American daytime television in the late 1960s and early 1970s. In the United States, films were repackaged, retitled, extensively edited, and shown as a series, *The Sons of Hercules,* as syndicated "filler" (many American viewers of the right generation still recall the series' distinctive theme song). More important, the peplum also migrated into other media, such as children's animated television. *The Mighty Hercules,* designed to cash in on the peplum craze but airing rather belatedly, ran from 1963 to 1966 but was still on American television as a Saturday-morning cartoon in the mid-1970s. In animated form, Hercules was capable of even more colossal (and improbable) feats of strength, but the show clearly drew on numerous images from the Italian films. Hercules wrestles wild animals and monsters, smashes evil statues, is paired with a weak adolescent who should become the proper king but needs help (Prince Dorian), and has a decidedly nonerotic, nonromantic relationship with an attractive blonde (Helena). The midcentury peplum's obsession with still and frozen time (see chapter 1) is clearly visible, with numerous episodes of *The Mighty Hercules* revolving around magic wands that turn people into stone, stone statues that come to life, or magic creatures (like Medusa) who can petrify with a glance.

More important, Hercules lived on in American comic books. In 1965, Jack Kirby and Stan Lee based the Marvel character Hercules directly on Steve Reeves, and he quickly acquired his own series; DC Comics had its own Hercules (Gerry Conway's *Hercules Unbound*), however, appearing in the mid-1970s with a cover that directly references Reeves's famous "pillars and chains" sequence from the 1958 *Hercules.* Like much popular culture from the 1970s, *Hercules Unbound* explored Cold War anxieties and was actually set after World War III. An even more striking example is Mike Grell's *The Warlord,* another series that began in 1975, in which Travis Morgan, an air force pilot, crash-lands in a primitive and barbaric world inside the earth called Skartaris. He is chained to and forced to row a war galley alongside a muscleman named Machiste, the English phonetic spelling of the Italian Maciste, who will become his best friend and a fellow gladiator. Machiste's name and musculature certainly recall the many midcentury films starring bodybuilders playing a character named Maciste, but his dark skin and apparently African features suggest that Grell was deliberately recalling Maciste's first appearance as a dark-skinned Roman slave. Is it possible that American comic book artists of the 1970s had a cultural memory extending back to a silent Italian film from 1914? Indeed, in his initial appearance in *Warlord* #2, Machiste

Figure 0.2. Maciste (*Cabiria*, 1914) versus Machiste (Grell, "Arena of Death," *The Warlord* 1.2, 1976). Image on the left courtesy of the Archives of the National Cinema Museum, Turin.

is clothed only in a leopard-print loincloth virtually identical to the one that Pagano wears in the 1914 *Cabiria* (figure 0.2).

Hercules Unbound and *The Warlord,* in particular, recycled the strongman in a new world that came not before but after civilization, a newly barbaric world that would find its most famous cinematic personification in another figure from popular fiction and comic books. The 1982 *Conan the Barbarian* reimagined the strongman as an action hero who is resentful and nostalgic about a past happiness that is forever lost to him (in the case of Conan, his love for Valeria as well as his family, all killed by Thulsa Doom). The preferred setting for these films was still an ancient mythological past, but one that had all the traits of a *Mad Max*–style post-apocalyptic landscape; Western civilization (especially the state) was now in disrepair and incapable of protecting anyone, even the strongman and his family (Jeffords 1994, 19). In twenty-odd films made between 1982 and the end of the decade, some in Italy, some in the United States and Argentina, the term "barbarian" appears repeatedly—*Conan the Barbarian, The Invincible Barbarian* (1982, another title for *Gunan, King of the Barbarians*), *The Sword of the Barbarians* (1982, also known as *Barbarian Master*), *Barbarian Queen* (1985), *The Barbarians* (1987), and *Barbarian Queen II: The Empress Strikes Back* (1989)—and virtually all of them position their imaginary universe outside the domain of the civilized, abandoning the Greek and Roman settings that typified the midcentury peplum.

Such films are explicitly cut off from our own history in some fashion: an opening voice-over or text positions the viewer "in a time before legend," a notion that was already implicit in the midcentury peplum film. The overall effect is to suggest that the time of heroic masculinity is over for us, and that the contemporary viewer stands on the far side of a rupture with the time in which men were men. The hero, like Conan, is sometimes the last of his kind or his tribe, giving the sense of an overall closure, the end of an era that is already remote and lost to the contemporary viewer of the film.[14] Barbarian peplums of the 1980s intimate what contemporary peplums suggest with much greater force: the era of heroic (white) masculinity is over and irrecoverably lost.

Clearly we have here another example of what Dominick LaCapra (1999) has analyzed as the ideological conversion of mere *absence* (we have no titanic, epic warriors among us today) into a traumatic *loss* (where have the titanic, epic warriors all gone?). Freud (1953–1974d) described a specific example of this dynamic, in which the male child notes an anatomical absence (women do not have a penis) but comes to imagine it as a loss (women must have had them and then lost them). The transformation of absence into loss comports a certain ideological and affective surplus value, however: these castrated beings must have done something to deserve such a punishment. This ideological surplus becomes even more powerful when another transformation takes place, according to LaCapra. This is the conversion of loss into lack: woman becomes defined, structurally, as a fallen creature, less than whole. The barbarian peplum stops short of depicting men as structurally constituted by lack, but it clearly situates modern man as a lesser and lacking version of the true hero he once could have been, and it derives from this conversion a surplus affective value: resentment. In the past, our strength was legendary; now we are weak. Although the belief that epic masculine strength was a thing of the past already subtended the midcentury peplum, it took on a new set of meanings in the 1980s. This epic past becomes a curiously idealized space, filled with everything the "true man" could want: aggressive, violent struggle and unlimited possibilities for sexual conquest. This freedom is presented as unconstrained by the nuisances of civilized, modern life in ways that range from the comical—Conan punches a stubborn camel in the face—to the horrifying, such as the 1980s *Deathstalker* films, where the barbarian hero is free from such modern annoyances as obtaining sexual consent from women. The distant past is technically a dystopia, characterized by its barbarism and lawlessness, but it simultaneously represents a utopian possibility of an intensified heterosexual masculinity released from the constraints of the civilization that holds it in check.

It is not hard to find the stereotyped features of the midcentury peplum in the barbarian peplum. There are fights with wild animals; the hero is tied to a rack, and we watch his muscular struggle to free himself; there are eroticized female dance routines; and in *Conan the Barbarian*, Conan is chained to a giant wheel he is forced to turn, a sequence that we find in several midcentury peplums (see figure 0.1): the bodybuilder Mark Forest found himself chained to a giant wheel he was forced to turn at least twice, once in *Mole Men against the Son of Hercules* (1961) and again in *Hercules against the Mongols* (1963).[15] The sequence, however, actually stretches all the way back to the original Maciste in the 1914 *Cabiria*, a film from sixty-eight years earlier—both Maciste and Conan turn their millstones for ten years. *Conan* and many of the peplum films that followed also made use of crucifixion, a pose that optimally showcases the hero's muscular physique (and that, as Dyer notes [1997, 150], alludes to the history of pain that was necessary for the creation of the ripped, muscled body). A variety of crucifixions appear, often featuring the hero tied, chained, or nailed to a St. Andrew's (or X-shaped) cross; in all cases, however, the symbol appears to be devoid of religious meaning within the diegesis. The 1980s films still depend, however, on a series of Orientalized figures—many of them feature a marauding horde that is more or less explicitly Mongolian or appears to be—and exotic locales, costuming designed to maximize exposure of the protagonist's body, and a final sequence that involves a spectacular collapse of an oppressive building, following the 1958 *Hercules*.

Even so, the feats of strength common in earlier peplums largely disappear in favor of scenes of combat, and despite his muscles, the protagonist no longer has the impossible or superhuman might that characterized the heroes of the midcentury peplums.[16] In compensation for his lost superhuman strength, the new peplum hero acquires psychological depth, especially in the case of Conan (Arnold Schwarzenegger), the only character of the 1980s peplums that was enduring and influential. Conan's life is marked by double traumas, both of which are the loss of women. His mother was decapitated by Thulsa Doom as she held little Conan's hand, and later, his lover and comrade, Valeria, was killed by Doom's magic arrow. Together, these lost women form the central absence that organizes a new masculine subjectivity: melancholy, nostalgic, and resentful. "For us, there is no spring," Conan muses regretfully late in the film after fondly recalling his childhood.[17] He may become a powerful king, destined to live forever in legend, but his character and his film are already essentially melodramatic—it is already "too late" (Linda Williams 1991, 10–11; but see also Fradley 2004) for Conan, as it will be for the heroes of the contemporary peplum. For the most part, however, the new psychological depth of Conan, such as it was, was not widely imitated by other barbarian peplums, which were largely exhausted by the end of the 1980s. The vast majority were simply ultra-low-budget exploitation films, devoid of innovation or originality; the bulk appeared in 1982 and 1983, and by 1987, the resurgent genre seemed tapped out again, at least on the big screen.

Peplum Television

Peplums were already on television in the 1980s, at least in animated form. If *Thundarr the Barbarian* (1980–1982) had limited popularity, the same could not be said of *He-Man and the Masters of the Universe* (1983–1985) and its spin-off for girls, *She-Ra: Princess of Power* (1985). Both shows are still in reruns today on retro and cartoon networks. He-Man and She-Ra portray types already familiar from the midcentury peplum: He-Man is massively muscled, clad primarily in a loin-cloth, and ebullient and cheerful (although now clean shaven and long haired, like all 1980s strongmen), while She-Ra is conventionally feminine, pretty, slight of build, and not visibly muscled despite her super strength. In live-action television series, we see a split between the classic bodybuilder with his massive musculature (see, for example, Ralf Möller as Conan in the 1997–1998 live action *Conan the Adventurer*) and a new body type as the peplum hero. Perhaps the most ideal representation of this new body is Dar of *BeastMaster* (1999–2002, loosely based on the 1982 peplum film *Beastmaster*), played by Daniel Goddard, a former underwear model for Calvin Klein. The impressive bulk of the midcentury stars and Arnold Schwarzenegger is gone, and the focus of the physical culture appears to be entirely the fetishistic attachment to "six-pack abs," in which abdominal muscles are sharply defined. Richardson (2010) has argued that the fetish of the abdominal muscles that began in the 1990s is typical of an emerging eroticized male body whose image deploys strategies of representation more associated with the female pinup, as on the covers of *Men's Health* magazine: smiling at the camera, sidelong glances, and poolside shots. Moreover, the abdominal muscles "connote less aggressive power than other muscle groups" (32). Later, Richardson differentiates between the "hyper-muscular physique" of the bodybuilder and the lithe or moderately muscled "pin-up," "male model," or "fitness model" (39). This second type becomes "canonized in contemporary culture as the masculine (erotic) ideal," and it replaced the bodybuilder in the 1990s as the typical peplum hero, although some exceptions (Schwarzenegger, Dwayne "the Rock" Johnson) remained.[18]

BeastMaster thus offered a less extreme and more mainstream version of the idealized, muscular male body. This softer, slimmer profile appeared elsewhere in the series as well. The show may have maintained the muscular white hero in colonial spaces (including a native sidekick) that Dyer takes to task in his chapter on the peplum in *White* (1997), but the message of the show was broadly tolerant, environmentalist, and pacifist—certainly a far cry from what would follow in the twenty-first century, the savage brutality of *Spartacus: Blood and Sand* or the reactionary racism and homophobia of a film like *300*. *BeastMaster*, in fact, is absolutely typical of the television peplums of the 1990s: it depicts a less massively muscled, gentler, and more ethical hero who is broadly tolerant of diversity.

Like virtually every peplum television show of this era, *BeastMaster* strongly embraced diversity, but in a curious way. The hero was white, but his sidekick appeared Asian (Jackson Raine is Australian and has played numerous "ethnic" roles, from Asians to Indians), and every village they saved was populated by a mélange of whites, blacks, Latinos, and Asians/Pacific Islanders. This is fairly obviously not supposed to represent the real demographics of the ancient world (not least because the world of *BeastMaster* is explicitly not our world); is this multiculturalism or post-racial thinking? As Dorothy Roberts has argued about the modern invention of race, the ancient world "did not partition all human beings into a relatively small number of innately separable types . . . markers of immutable distinctions" (2011, 6). Indeed, we appear to be situated in a pre-racial universe, a world ostensibly set before the recognition of racial difference.

Midcentury peplums had been unashamed of their dual assumptions that dark-skinned people were inferior and that white heroes would treat them fairly and patronizingly, as Dyer (1997) has pointed out. *BeastMaster* and other television peplums of the 1990s (*Hercules: The Legendary Journeys, Xena: Warrior Princess* [1995–2001], the various Conan series) still feature a white hero saving native peoples, but those peoples are now an undifferentiated blend of all recognizable racial types. This scenario is not simply pre- or post-racial, however; rather, it occupies an unstable terrain analogous to the midcentury peplum's attitude toward sexuality: I know very well, but all the same. It is hard to miss the colonialist outlines of this scenario, for example, or the fact that most characters with speaking roles are white while the undifferentiated "common people" who need saving are a mix of racial backgrounds; but it is equally hard to miss what we might call "tragic utopianism": these characters live in a world in which racial difference is a completely meaningless category, but the day is coming when that innocent ignorance will be lost, and someone will invent racism. The effect is to make the advent of a recognition of racial difference, like the advent of the recognition of sexual difference, appear as a tragic loss of innocence for the viewer, but also an inevitable one.

BeastMaster was also typical of 1990s television peplums in a different way: it was made in a British Commonwealth country, namely, Canada. Unlike previous cycles, Italy played no role in the production of peplums in the 1990s. The two most popular television peplums of the 1990s, *Hercules: The Legendary Journeys* and *Xena: Warrior Princess*, were both US–New Zealand co-productions, as was their little-known spinoff, *Young Hercules* (starring a then-unknown Ryan Gosling as an even less heavily muscled version of the peplum hero).[19] *BeastMaster* was entirely Canadian, while the animated *Conan the Adventurer* was a US-Canada joint venture. Only the virtually unknown animated series *Conan and the Young Warriors* (1994) and the live-action *Conan the Adventurer* were entirely made in the United States. The definitive shift away from Italy in the 1980s had little to do with a newfound Italian distaste for muscles and the classical world, however, and much more to do with the contraction in the Italian film industry that began in the 1970s (see Sorlin 1996, 118–121 and 144–164, for a description of the contraction and some of its causes). Starting in the late 1950s with genres like *commedia all'italiana* and the peplum, Italy had been a major force in inexpensive genre cinema: after the peplum, spaghetti Westerns, Italian horror, James Bond–inspired espionage films, soft-core pornography, and a variety of exploitation and shock films (*Mondo cane* [1962] and its successors up through the infamous *Cannibal Holocaust* [1980]) were major exports that gained both notoriety and audiences. Italian horror films (*i gialli*) still have an active audience of avid collectors, for example, always in pursuit of the original and uncensored cuts of the films. Since the contraction of the 1980s, however, with few exceptions Italy no longer produces much in the way of genre cinema for international consumption.

The Contemporary Peplum

Ridley Scott's classical epic *Gladiator* opened in 2000 to widespread popular and critical success, winning five Academy Awards and numerous other accolades. It was even credited for sparking what the publishing industry called, according to the *New York Times*, "the *Gladiator* effect" (Arnold 2002)—a widespread renewal of interest in the classical world, including a renewal of interest in historical epic films (both *Troy* and *Alexander* were released in 2004). A few critics were struck by the film's intense melancholy, however; Roger Ebert (2000) described a "pall" cast over the whole film and noted that virtually all the characters were "bitter, vengeful and depressed." If 1980s American action films provided a hyperbolic vision of masculinity to compensate for a masculinity in crisis (Jeffords 1994; Neale 1993), 1990s films, at least on occasion, removed the hyperbolic compensation and simply left the crisis, perhaps most famously in 1993's *Falling Down*. In that film, William Foster, deprived of his wife, child, and job, lashes out at all and sundry in a steadily escalating rampage that eventually leads him into a direct and ultimately suicidal confrontation with the state. Although Ebert referred to *Gladiator* as "*Rocky* on downers," I might call it *Falling Down* in togas. Maximus, deprived of his wife, child, and job, lashes out at all and sundry in a steadily escalating rampage that eventually leads him into a direct, suicidal confrontation with the state. In his insightful "Maximus Melodramaticus," Martin Fradley (2004) situates *Gladiator* in a line of 1990s films like *Falling Down* and *Fight Club* (1999) that posit the time of true masculinity as lost and invite the viewer to enjoy and sympathize with the male hero's suffering over this loss. Fradley's emphasis is on masochism, but I would like to call attention to the melodrama in "Maximus Melodramaticus." *Gladiator* is firmly situated in the temporal dimension of Linda Williams's (1991) version of melodrama: Maximus is too late. The empire is already incurably decadent and corrupt, and a good man doesn't stand a chance;

the game, including the games in the arena, is literally rigged. *Falling Down* and *Fight Club* suggested that aggressive, assertive "real" masculinity no longer had a place in the 1990s, and that the only way to reclaim it was through a transgression so extreme that it would eventually prove to be suicidal. It was too late. *Gladiator*, by contrast, makes the claim that it was already too late two thousand years earlier.

Gladiator's plot is familiar from the midcentury peplum film, in which legitimate state power is usurped by an illegitimate ruler, and the hero's strength and virility are the only way in which the usurper can be defeated. *Gladiator*, however, is not a peplum; it is a big-budget film with serious artistic pretensions that keeps its male star's torso covered for most of the film. The camera may admire Russell Crowe, but it is not particularly interested in his body. Even so, *Gladiator*'s popularity eventually brought its suicidal and nihilistic masochism to the peplum. The masses are indifferent to their rulers' decadence; the killing of Commodus will not free the slaves or return Rome to a republic, as Maximus hopes, and the hero's epic and astonishingly persistent struggle against the powers that be will accomplish nothing. The modern viewer will marvel at the hero's masculine persistence in the face of such odds, and indeed, the magnitude of his masculinity can be measured not by his triumph, since the quest is hopeless and suicidal, but by how long he holds out against overwhelming odds. In short, the plot of the contemporary peplum is the melancholy and melodramatic inversion of the midcentury peplum plot; the hero still struggles against an illegitimate state that cruelly oppresses the people, but the outcome is always predetermined. However far back in time we may go, we find that it is always already after the last moment when men could be real men. Once again, an absence is turned into a loss, but now it is also turned into a structural lack.

Gladiator's melancholy proved to be powerfully influential in the contemporary peplum. *Spartacus: Blood and Sand* and *300* clearly model their protagonists on Maximus. Stern, melancholy family men, both Spartacus and Leonidas find themselves betrayed by the state, bereft of their beloved wives, and locked into a suicidal struggle against odds that are not simply overwhelming but impossible. *Gladiator*'s Maximus was fictional, but Leonidas and Spartacus are not; their ends were written long before the viewer began watching. Within all three texts (*Gladiator*, *300*, and *Spartacus: Blood and Sand*), however, the principal character and his band of fellow warriors are always set against an explicitly debased and decadent form of masculinity that will survive after the hero does not. In other words, the pleasure for the viewer is not simply in the melodrama of the doomed quest for revenge that animates these characters, but in the pleasure of *ressentiment* that the viewer can enjoy: I, too, have come on the scene too late and have been denied my chance for epic greatness.

Not every contemporary peplum has cultivated this melancholy nostalgia. *The Scorpion King* (2002), starring Dwayne "the Rock" Johnson, gave viewers the massive muscles of the midcentury peplum, as well as the multicultural diversity and more cheerful (or at least less dismal) outlook of the 1990s television peplums. But for the most part, contemporary peplum films have followed the same darker and grittier tone that other franchises, particularly superhero films, have in recent years. *Immortals* (2011), for example, follows its muscled and largely shirtless hero, Theseus, through a struggle that will ultimately prove suicidal. The film's antagonist is the evil King Hyperion, who is determined to make himself doubly immortal. On the one hand, he aims to kill or castrate every man alive in order to perpetuate exclusively his own image into the future (we are given to understand that every soldier in his army is a castrato); on the other hand, he will release the Titans in the pit of Tartarus in order to destroy the gods. Hyperion will then be the only immortal in existence. The protagonist sees his beloved mother murdered by Hyperion's agents (just like Conan) and eventually realizes that he can defeat Hyperion only at the cost of his own life. Although the hero manages to procreate before he dies, the film's overall message is that the time of great men and great deeds is over, even as the hero secures the future of everyday time and human reproductivity. The child can watch the greatness of the father's sacrifice only at a distance.

The year 2014 saw four peplum films at the US box office (*300: Rise of an Empire, The Legend of Hercules, Hercules, Pompeii*), and most preserved the melodramatic nostalgia and regret that have animated peplum films since *Gladiator*. *The Legend of Hercules* directly reworks much of the material in the 1958 *Hercules*, but again in a darker key: Kellan Lutz's Hercules repeats the most iconic scene of the midcentury film, pulling down stone pillars with huge chains and killing the evil king's guards with them, but now it is because Hercules is in despair and desperation.[20] (Likewise, at the end of 2011's *Immortals*, a hunky Zeus is menaced by Titans who have escaped their long imprisonment and have killed his beloved daughter, Athena. In grief and rage, Zeus grasps two chains, each of which is connected to the pillars that hold Tartarus up, and with a superheroic effort pulls down the mountain, burying his enemies.) *Hercules* stars Dwayne "the Rock" Johnson again and dwells predominantly on Hercules's misery and bitterness over the death of his wife and children (the film does, however, offer a more positive ending). *Pompeii* chronicles the enslavement and abuse of Milo, who must fight to the death in the arena as the city is destroyed by a volcano; although he eventually flees with his beloved, it is too late for them, and they are entombed forever in volcanic ash.

The other distinctive trait of contemporary peplums is their notable aestheticism. *300* was famously shot entirely in a green-screen studio, allowing the entire environment to be computer generated; Snyder elected to create a painterly look rather than a photorealistic one, however. Colors were muted (except for red, which was left vivid to emphasize the sprays of blood and the Spartans' cloaks), and chiaroscuro effects abounded. The overall look may have been created on a budget, but it did not look cheap. *Spartacus: Blood and Sand,* produced by Sam Raimi of *Hercules: The Legendary Journeys,* reprised almost all of *300*'s formal devices (slow motion, the extensive use of ramping, computer-generated sprays of blood, de-saturated and painterly use of color and light) and, in early episodes, occasionally cultivated a surprising Maxfield Parrish or Pre-Raphaelite look, one that also appeared in *Immortals* (which also made extensive use of slow-motion effects and selectively de-saturated colors; see figure 0.3). The director of *Immortals,* Tarsem Singh, boasted before the film's release that its look would be "*Fight Club* meets Caravaggio" (O'Hara 2009), indicating that, regardless of the particular painter or painterly style being referenced, the combination of virile violence and painterly aesthetic was seen as key to the contemporary peplum, at least partially because the same combination of violence and richly aesthetic imagery is often present in contemporary video games.

Finally, the peplum has historically been associated with right-wing nationalism, at times overt (the silent-era Maciste films), at other times subtler (the midcentury peplums). Contemporary peplums have ranged from extreme and extremely coherent ideological positions—*300*'s intense homophobia, misogyny, ableism, and racism are coupled with a "clash of civilizations" narrative in which the free West is about to be overwhelmed by the decadent East—to much more nuanced and complex ideologies. The contemporary peplum is, however, populist in every case, reflecting the historical populism of the peplum. In *300,* King Leonidas stands against not only the subhuman legions of King Xerxes but also the corrupt elites in Sparta who impede his virile militarism. In both *Immortals* and the *Clash of the Titans* franchise, a humble farmer or fisherman turns out to be a man of direct action who confronts a state that is incompetent or corrupt. Moreover, both films are set in a time of the "twilight of the gods," in which these elite beings fade in power and relevance, and in both cases, this is largely seen as a good thing, since the gods do not seem either able or willing to protect mankind from divine, demonic, or mortal mischief.[21] Although its identity politics is more nuanced and open than that of most other contemporary peplums, *Spartacus: Blood and Sand* is also one of the most aggressively populist. The Roman elites are intensely corrupt, degenerate, and totally bereft of what the show presents as manly virtues, particularly loyalty; the Roman women are vapid and scheming. In contrast, the tribal identities of those oppressed by the Romans—the Gauls, the Africans, the Cilicians, the Thracians, the Celts, and the Germanic warriors— are energetic and full of vitality, and they understand the manly virtues of sacrifice, honor, courage, and loyalty. (They are also, it is understood, doomed.) Unlike the xenophobic *300, Spartacus* imagines that these racially diverse populations, which include multiple same-sex couples, could unite in their rejection of their effete, elite Roman oppressors.

Figure 0.3. Aestheticism in *Immortals*, 2011.

The muscular, populist hero of the contemporary peplum is not far removed from the brooding Maximus of *Gladiator*, who wanted nothing more than to stop being a Roman general and return to his farm, and who, in turn, was not much different from the massively muscled Gordon Scott as Goliath pulling a tree stump out of his farmland with his bare hands before going on to fight sea monsters and vampires, or even the silent-era Maciste, a man of the people who was never afraid to get his hands dirty and do a little muscular work. Much has changed in the one hundred years of peplum history, but those changes are dwarfed by the many forms of thematic, ideological, and formal continuity that the peplum has shown in its apparently endless parade of idealized masculinity. So it is that, at the end of *300*, the narrator, Dilios, can speculate about the origins of these Spartans that the film has so idealized. Where do these perfect warriors, ideal men, come from? When he muses that "the old ones say we Spartans are descended from Hercules himself," how can we not hear the title of the 1958 Steve Reeves blockbuster? These Spartans are indeed descended from *Hercules*.

Notes

1. According to the French Wikipedia page for "péplum," the first to use the term were the members of the Ciné-club Nickelodéon of the University of Liège in the 1950s after the release of *The Robe* (1953), a Henry Koster biblical epic starring Richard Burton, and the first film in widescreen CinemaScope (perhaps the title of the film also suggested the sartorial name for

the genre). The pedantically correct plural form of the Latin *peplum* is *pepla*, a form I have avoided in this study.

2. In a long footnote (1963, 98–99), Spinazzola describes how both the French and the Italian critics responded to the peplum hyperbolically, with the French claiming that Cottafavi's films were masterpieces comparable to those of Otto Preminger and Kenji Mizoguchi (a rather dubious claim for those who have actually seen, say, *Goliath and the Dragon* [*La vendetta di Ercole*, 1960]), and Italians responding with an equally polemical and scathing critique of peplums as "nullità" (rubbish or, more literally, nothings). The Italian response was not just conditioned by a cultural prejudice in favor of high art and allergic to popular culture; French critics like Michel Mourlet used the peplum as a pretext for attacking Italian neorealism of the late 1940s and early 1950s, which French critics saw as passé, but for which many Italian film critics felt nostalgia.

3. To this day, the peplum is primarily discussed by cult fans in Italy, and most of the books on it are catalogs or guides to the genre (lists of films and directors, plot synopses). To give a sense of how overlooked the genre is, in the years 1960–1964, the peplum accounted for between 8% and 15% of all Italian film production (Ghigi 1977, 736) and a much higher percentage of exports (Wagstaff [1996] claims over 40% during the early 1960s). Volume 10 of the enormous *Storia del cinema italiano* (History of Italian cinema) covers precisely the years Wagstaff discusses, but dedicates just 12 of its 730 pages to the peplum. The first page of the volume's introduction cites it as an example of "low genres [*generi di profondità*]" (3) and does not mention it again. In the United States, the peplum has rarely been acknowledged as a genre with any real historical duration or meaningful connections to contemporary films, although Cornelius 2011 is an exception. In Italy, however, even the serious books about the peplum insist on it as a stylistic, generic, and historical parenthesis. Della Casa and Giusti's *Il grande libro di Ercole* (The big book of Hercules) (2013), for example, notes the upcoming Hercules film starring Dwayne "the Rock" Johnson but insists that despite the later films, "the genre really ends with the arrival of Clint Eastwood" (46), that is, in 1966. And after two short introductory essays, the remainder of *Il grande libro di Ercole* is the usual list of peplum films and actors, along with a set of high-quality images.

4. Väliaho (2014) discusses first-person shooter video games, experimental virtual reality scenarios used to treat veterans with post-traumatic stress disorder, and experimental art video installations, but not cinema or television. Although I find much of his analysis exemplary, he equates only the "post-cinematic image" with "post-Fordist production, neoliberal ideologies, and contemporary biopolitical ways of taking charge of the life of individuals and populations" (8); the cinematic image, by extension, is associated with Fordist modes of production (almost certainly true), liberal ideologies (likely the case), and presumably older forms of biopolitics. Despite being older forms of media, however, cinema and television continue to merge with the same forms of post-cinematic images that Väliaho discusses; this is especially true of the peplum and the video game, which have enjoyed a fertile and ongoing cross-pollination.

5. There are twenty-two films in the Maciste cycle if one counts *La trilogia di Maciste* (The Maciste trilogy, 1920) as a single film (it is a feature-length film but is composed of three shorter films that were originally released separately; the three parts do, however, tell the beginning, middle, and end of the same story). Some filmographies list both *La trilogia* and the individual parts of the trilogy as separate entries. Five of the films were also produced in Germany between 1922 and 1923. For a comprehensive treatment of Maciste as an international star, see Reich 2015.

6. On Italy and the issue of nationalism and cosmopolitanism in the Grand Hotel, see Hay 1987.

7. In *Maciste und der Tochter des Silberkönigs,* there appears to be a successful romance between Maciste and Ellen Lund, the titular silver king's daughter, but the only copy I know of, in Moscow's Gosfilmofond, is missing the final reel. The archive has all the intertitles (in Russian), but the final titles are about the resolution of the mystery, not the romance.

8. See Reich 2015 for a delightful series of letters between the Diatto car company and Itala Film that continue and elaborate the jokes (180).

9. Private communication. Maciste himself very nearly uses the formula "eating and beating" in *Maciste alpino* when Austrian soldiers threaten him with arrest. Instead, he seizes the meat on the table and declares, "Arresto l'arrosto" (I'll arrest the roast). He beats the Austrians quite soundly once he has run out of food.

10. In personal conversation, Stella Dagna of the Museo Nazionale del Cinema in Turin made the point that the silent-era Maciste may be a populist figure, but that this should not be misunderstood as meaning that he is "one of the people" or an "ordinary person." Indeed, in *Maciste innamorato,* he is recognized by striking workers precisely as a celebrity, not as one of them. Even so, they perceive him as being in some sense on their side (they will listen to him, but they will not listen to management), and the film ends with a sequence that clearly marks Maciste as a man of the people incompatible with the wealthy elites: his extreme discomfort while wearing a tuxedo and gloves and attending a formal dinner.

11. On the complex connections between peplum films and beefcake magazines, see Wyke 1997a.

12. The exact number of peplum films released in the midcentury cycle is unclear, but Wagstaff says that "some 300 films of this type" (1996, 224) were released between 1958 and 1967. This number seems large but plausible: over one hundred are still available today, and there were even more spaghetti Westerns released in the next Italian genre film boom. The number will also vary depending on how one defines a peplum: any low-budget sensationalistic film set in classical or mythological antiquity, or only those that star a bodybuilder or athlete? (I have opted for the latter solution in this book.) Gregori divides the production into two phases: an initial one from 1958 to 1960 in which, after the enormous success of *Hercules,* filmmakers had access to decent budgets, and a second phase from 1960 to 1965 in which budgets fell continuously, and filmmakers had to be increasingly clever or increasingly impoverished in their filmmaking (2009, 229). Gregori gives one of the best histories of the midcentury peplum I have read, especially considering that her article is actually about the promotional posters for peplum films.

13. Monica Dall'Asta (1992) reports that Campogalliani tried in 1941 to get Bartolomeo Pagano to return once more as Maciste for a new generation of spectators; Pagano, in very poor health, said no. Campogalliani had to settle for bodybuilder Mark Forest in the 1960 Egyptian-themed *Son of Samson,* whose Italian title was *Maciste nella valle dei re* (Maciste in the valley of the kings). In directing the 1961 *Ursus,* starring bodybuilder Ed Fury, the following year, Campogalliani reached even further back into the peplum's past, to the strongman-versus-bull sequence in the 1913 *Quo vadis?* As Dall'Asta points out (137–140), Campogalliani's connection to the peplum and to the figure of the strongman was personal: he had cast himself as Maciste's companion and alter ego, the weak sidekick who needs help romancing the girl, in *La trilogia di Maciste.*

14. See Wall 2013 on how Conan fan cultures are also organized around nostalgia for a masculinity that is lost in the past and cannot be recovered.

15. The "wheel of pain" in *Conan* appears to based specifically on the wheel in *The Vengeance of Ursus* (*La vendetta di Ursus,* 1961): both wheels feature three slaves chained to each spoke and a grimy urchin who squats atop the device to watch them. Figure 0.1 shows precisely that wheel, but in a later sequence, minus the other slaves and the grimy urchin.

16. Notable exceptions to all these changes are the two Lou Ferrigno Hercules films from 1983 (*Hercules*) and 1985 (*The Adventures of Hercules*), both of which were Italy-US co-productions and drew heavily on the 1950s Steve Reeves Hercules films. Ferrigno's strength is depicted as superhuman (ludicrously so: in one infamous sequence, he hurls a bear that he is wrestling into outer space), and unlike most 1980s peplums, his films are quite tame, without the graphic sex and bloodshed common in the barbarian peplum.

17. The "crisis of masculinity" narrative suggests that this constellation of affects (nostalgia, regret, resentment, melancholy) is a way of expressing anger over the loss of traditional male prerogatives in a world where it was not really socially acceptable to do so; one is supposed to think that modern gender and racial equality, for example, are good things. At first glance, it might seem curious that so many of these films base the hero's nostalgic melancholy on the loss of a woman if feminism and women entering the workplace were indeed crucial factors in provoking a crisis in masculinity. But the deaths of Conan's mother and later his lover, Valeria, and the death of Maximus's wife in *Gladiator* all create an all-male world in which strength and courage are paramount.

18. Richardson's larger argument is beyond the scope of this book, but he situates the emergence of the fitness-model ideal in a dialectical opposition to the changes in bodybuilding as a sport and practice. During the 1980s, bodybuilding began to embrace a new ideal of an exaggerated, unbalanced, and even grotesque muscular development, abandoning or eschewing any attempt at larger cultural acceptance. Bodybuilding had always been potentially understandable as a practice that resisted dominant gender norms, but from the 1990s on, it was declaredly so, and bodybuilders use terms like "grotesque," "gross," "mutant," and "freaky" to describe themselves with pride.

19. Solomon (2001) noted that *Hercules: The Legendary Journeys* was "the most popular syndicated television program in the world" (323), even if it garnered less critical attention than its two female competitors, *Buffy* and *Xena*.

20. The film is somewhat uncertain about its tone and affect, especially at the end; Hercules appears to save the girl, have a son, and win a kingdom, but there are foreshadowing hints of their tragic end (in mythology, Hercules kills his family in a mad rage), and the film's final shot is of Hercules alone at night.

21. As one of my graduate students, Dora Valkanova, has suggested, implicit in this description is a neoliberal critique of the state and a concomitant affirmation of a need for individual action and responsibility.

1 NOS MORITURI

Time in the Peplum

> The great assemblage had gathered to see the strong man. . . . The lights were turned down throughout the building, to shine with doubled radiance upon the proscenium. A moment later the curtain curled upwards. . . . Upon a small red pedestal stood Sandow himself . . . bared to the waist. Slowly the red pedestal began to revolve, and the living statue with it.
>
> —*The Age*, September 8, 1902

> . . . *homo sacer* is, so to speak, a living statue, the double or the colossus of himself.
>
> —Giorgio Agamben, *Homo Sacer*

The Ballerina and the Biceps

Most genealogies of the peplum point back to the 1914 film *Cabiria* as the origin of the genre.[1] We might also acknowledge the many previous traditions that contributed parts of the peplum, from the classical or mythological epic adventure to vaudeville and circus traditions of the strongman. Still, *Cabiria* was the first time at which a significant number of the elements that would eventually become the peplum's standard features appeared together, in one image, on film. Although the entire film is classical and fantastic, arguably the very first peplum image in *Cabiria* is the first time we see Maciste, the physically dominating strongman played by Bartolomeo Pagano, who would eventually parlay his minor role in *Cabiria* into approximately two dozen spin-offs in the 1910s and 1920s (Usai calls his character "epidemic" [1986, 62] in its spread and longevity). Maciste also had his competitors and imitators—Saetta, Ajax, Ercole, Sansonia, and others—but, as Steven Ricci argues, Maciste remained not only the standard by which these other characters were judged but also distinct in his reliance on pure physical strength, in his de-sexualization, and in his populist, working-class/laborer origins (2008, 81–86; see also Bertellini 2003, 259–261). Almost without exception, Maciste's competitors exemplified a very different kind of body, one that is perhaps more fundamentally cinematic. Willemen (2009) calls this body "the athletic body" and distinguishes it from "the Hercules body," emphasizing the speed and kinetic dynamism of the former and the ideological/political valence of the latter:

> The athletic body is part of the discourses of expertise, speed and geographical displacement, while the Hercules body is part of a discursive constellation emphasizing the static expenditure and management of labor power. The statically filmed muscle body is a figure in fantasies about primitive accumulation, that is to say, the transformation of agricultural laborers into factory laborers, valued for the quantity of labor power at their (and therefore the factory owner's) disposal. (276)

Luciano Albertini, for instance, was a competing figure whose promotional shots featured him shirtless and flexing his muscles. Like Pagano, he went to Germany in the 1920s to make action and adventure films, but in films like *Mister Radio* (1924) and *Der Unüberwindliche* (The invincible, 1928), Albertini's body always remains covered, and he amazes with his Fairbanks-like rapidity and coordination and performs impressive stunts that showcase his climbing and leaping abilities in particular (he was a former circus performer).[2] By contrast, Maciste's body is regularly exposed to the viewer's gaze, even in circumstances where there is no plausible motivation to expose it. In *Maciste alpino* (1916), for example, we see Maciste, after having joined the Italian alpine soldiers in World War I, washing himself in the snow. He strips to the waist amid the snow- and ice-covered Alps and, grinning hugely (the strongman always takes enormous pleasure in his strength and endurance), rubs snow all over his bare torso. We find here again a confirmation of the link between admiration for the spectacularly muscled male body and a certain slowing of cinematic time. While Albertini's lithe, gymnastic body lends itself to the kinetic dimension of cinema (not only in his astonishing, rapid movements but also in fast-paced editing and a preference for medium and long shots), Maciste's muscular bulk brings the camera up close to slowly linger over his pecs, abs, and biceps.

In her famous "Visual Pleasure in Narrative Cinema," Laura Mulvey (1987) noted in passing that certain kinds of cinematic attractions that are regular features of narrative films (she specifically cited musical and dance numbers, a point I will return to later) had the curious tendency to retard or even temporarily freeze the forward movement of the narrative. More recently, she has expanded that reflection into a book-length meditation on cinema's inherently "kinematic" character (they are moving pictures, after all) and its simultaneous reliance on the still image (cinema's "hidden past" is both still photography and the individual frames on the strip of film, a "secret . . . that might or might not find its way to the surface" [2006, 67], but a past that might be cinema's digital future as well). In this chapter, I argue that the peplum has had, since its very first film—indeed, since the very first peplum image—a curious reliance on the still image, on a variety of visual registers that are in fact opposed to the normal and normatively kinetic register of the moving pictures. Slowed time and stopped time are part of the genre.

The first image of Maciste in *Cabiria* consists of him not in motion but standing still, performing what will be a central necessity for the principal actors in the peplum from 1914 to the present day: striking and holding a pose. He holds the pose for several seconds while two characters in the background speak animatedly, then moves briskly to block the camera's view of the more distant figures and strikes and holds another pose. His body language conveys a dominant physicality and assertiveness, quite surprising for a character who is supposed to be a slave (figure 1.1). As Oksana Bulgakowa points out in *The Factory of Gestures* (2008), gesturality and posture have always been primary ways in which spectators have understood a character's class, background, education, attitude, and other attributes. Other servants in *Cabiria* (Croessa, the nurse, or Bodastaret, the innkeeper) feature the bent back and slumped shoulders that Bulgakowa argues indicated subordination and social inferiority.

Figure 1.1. Maciste the slave in a dominant posture next to his master, Fulvius Axilla. *Cabiria*, 1914. Courtesy of the Archives of the National Cinema Museum, Turin.

No character in the film stands as upright as Maciste does, however. He is broad shouldered, powerfully built, and possessed of a raw physicality, as well as a kind of lightness and grace. Critics have long noted (see Dalle Vacche 1992, 27–28) that his appearance seems designed to evoke not a body in action, but the idealized and static forms of the classical statue.[3] The title card that precedes Maciste's first appearance simply reads, "Fulvius Axilla, a Roman patrician, and his slave Maciste, live incognito in Carthage." What we see, however, activates a variety of contradictory visual codes. We expect to see a Roman aristocrat and a slave, and what we see mostly corresponds to our expectations: in the foreground, a magnificent and dignified statue-like figure clad in a flowing, wind-swept toga draped dramatically over his arm; in the far background, a small man in a belted tunic and cloak, hunched over. The figures, however, are reversed. The slave is the dignified, toga-wearing figure in the foreground, and the aristocrat is the distant man in the cloak.

This first appearance of Maciste has precisely the quality of a still image, a tableau; as Dalle Vacche notes, Pastrone frequently allows "spectacular tableaux to slow down causal narrative development" (1992, 31), although this is perhaps not fair to films of the 1910s, which did not yet have a coherent dedication to linear narrative development, what Tom Gunning (1986) famously called a "cinema of attractions."[4] Regardless of whether the film's action is slowed down here, however, the viewer is invited to enjoy the still image, letting the eye wander across the strongman's body to appreciate muscles, proportions, and a bodily tension held in check. The actor's impressive body asks for, and receives, a lingering gaze. Mulvey notes that when "film is delayed . . . , the spectator is able to hold onto, to possess, the previously elusive image. In this delayed cinema the spectator finds a heightened relation to the human body, particularly that of the star" (2006, 161). Again, it is perhaps anachronistic to think that this reliance on the still body was unusual for a film from 1914, but it does establish a link between slow time and the body that was visible in early cinema, long before Mulvey's digitally slowed time. Indeed, as Guido (2012b) notes, between the influential philosophy of Bergson, the futurist experiments of the Bragaglia brothers' photography, and the vitalist thinking of early film theorist Ricciotto Canudo, the Franco-Italian context for early cinema (precisely in the years leading up to *Cabiria*) was very markedly interested in the question of motion and stopped time. Bragaglia, influenced by Bergson, found the truth of cinema in its movement, rejecting its reliance on the single image, while for Canudo, "notions of immobility and fixation assume a positive role" (Guido 2012b, 12), but both found the relationship between stillness and motion a fundamental and highly charged question for cinema of the 1910s.[5]

Before moving pictures, still photography was famously used to slow movement down or to stop it, as with Eadweard Muybridge's famous 1877 photographs of a galloping horse, so that we could see what motion had previously obscured.

But Muybridge's photo series could also be used as a form of proto-cinema, projecting the still images one after the other and flipping through them so that the still horse would begin to gallop. This is precisely the effect the peplum strives for again and again—not so much a return to the still image or the frozen pose, as the rhythmic oscillation between cinema's essential paradox: moving pictures and their simulacrum of life, on the one hand, produced from a series of still images, on the other. As Freud writes in *Beyond the Pleasure Principle* of the death drive, it arises "from the coming to life of inanimate matter, and seek[s] to restore the inanimate state" (1953–1974a, 18:44). This is, for Mulvey, the essential uncanniness of slowed and stopped cinematic time: a return to the still photography that pre-exists the advent of cinema, as if there were a "daemonic" drive to "restore an earlier state of things," as Freud says (18:36). We can begin to see that slowed and stopped time might exert an uncanny fascination or pull—a fatal attraction, if you will, for film. In direct reference to the peplum's pre-history, however, Wyke also notes that Muybridge was already in 1879 photographing athletes posing as classical statues (1997a, 56). Chapman notes at several points (2006, 77, 97–98) the connections between Sandow's emergent discipline of bodybuilding and early cinema, connections that I hope this chapter's epigraph showcases: the strong man bared to the waist, the lights, and the slow movement of the "living statue."[6]

Certainly the peplum's central pleasure is precisely that of savoring the elusive image of the spectacular male body, and Bartolomeo Pagano positioned himself in advance as the film's star by stepping in front of the protagonist in his first appearance on screen, offering himself as a frozen image to be savored. Maciste is not the only character in *Cabiria* to be associated with the slow or still image, however. The film's major female characters also strike and hold poses, create frozen tableaux, and provide the viewer the pleasure of pure contemplation. The cinematic construction of woman as a still rather than a moving image is true of the Carthaginian princess Sophonisba (played by the diva Italia Almirante-Manzini). The figure of the diva was a staple of early Italian cinema; these were some of the earliest "stars" in cinema, names guaranteed to pull in an audience. Arguably, the entire institution of the diva was predicated on a kind of cinema of stopped time since divas specialized in melodramatic (and often gothic) stories of illicit sexuality, public women, and the like, all of which culminated, almost invariably, in an extended death sequence after the diva consumed poison to end her tragic and immoral life. The diva is always, in some sense, *moritura*, "about to die" (see Dalle Vacche 2008). Her death sequences—and the one in *Cabiria* is no exception—are rooted in an acting style that is now (rather anachronistically) seen as theatrical rather than cinematic since it consists precisely in striking and holding a series of poses and emotional gestures.

Cabiria (Lidia Quaranta) herself is literally frozen as a still image; when Fulvius and Maciste escape from prison but end up trapped in an underground

Figure 1.2. The still image is reanimated into a kinetic (implicitly masculine) register. *Cabiria*, 1914. Courtesy of the Archives of the National Cinema Museum, Turin.

storage room, Fulvius draws a life-sized image of her bringing him water in prison, in a chalk outline on the wall, so that he can reminisce (and enjoy the pleasure of the male gaze). Maciste, in turn, turns Fulvius's purely static fetishism of the image into motion by adding motion to the eternally frozen Grecian urn the drawing of Cabiria carries: he draws wine emerging from the spout, then mimes drinking the liquid, and finally puts his storyboard into reality by actually drinking from the similar wine jug he carries. What Maciste draws on the wall here is not a thing, a pro-filmic object, nor is it in any way reducible to a still image; what he draws, to be precise, is not wine or water, but motion lines that signify the flow, the movement, of liquid.

Here we have to pause—to stop and linger over precisely the image—because this is a particularly important moment in the history of the peplum. The film seems to suggest to Fulvius that he is in a kind of danger in his rapt contemplation of the still image, and this idea will return again and again in and around the peplum. The still, adoring gaze is a pleasure to be indulged, but not for too long, and not without certain kinds of risk. We have to note, for example, that there is an implicit feminization of the still image and a concomitant masculinization in the return to cinema's kinetic character. Maciste says, in effect, "Enough with the staring at the girl, Fulvius—it's time to return to masculine camaraderie and carousing." Indeed, one might argue that Maciste's mark on Fulvius's drawing is a kind of masculine defacement, a stain, but one that points toward movement. In lingering over this image from *Cabiria,* it is also useful to compare it to Rosalind Galt's (2011) discussion of the gendering at work in "The Origin of Outline," an image from Walter Crane's turn-of-the-century handbook for artists (40–45). Crane's image shows a toga-clad caveman drawing, in rapt admiration, the outline of a submissive maiden; the image is remarkably similar to Fulvius's image of Cabiria. In Galt's terms, Fulvius's inclusion of decoration on the vase and on Cabiria's dress is already perilously close to the "pretty," an aesthetic category she finds to be rigorously excluded from classical film theory, and Maciste effectively defaces that pretty image, allowing it to be masculinized (and returned to a more properly filmic register).

Mulvey, along with many others, associates the still image with the stillness of death. Raymond Bellour (2008) notes that the still image in cinema has a long and rich history that is "reflexive, mortifying, and nostalgic" (258)—that is, the still image is a way of commenting on cinema itself and its relationship to still images and motion (it is reflexive); it is a "source of obsessive fear" (258), consistently linked to death. Guido (2012a) offers a compelling synthesis of the various theories (he mentions Mulvey, Bellour, Stewart, Bazin, and Barthes) that associate the still image in cinema with death: essentially, the flash of light that freezes the past is always, at least potentially, a traumatic memory or, in Barthes, the anticipation of what will one day be a traumatic memory (235–236). Again, Freud would argue that the still image is cinema's pre-history, "an initial state from which [it] has at one time or other departed" (1953–1974a, 18:38) but to which it is tempted to return, like a salmon returning to its spawning grounds in order to die. I am generally disinclined to think that any formal technique has one specific and inherent meaning (such as "slow time = death," what Guido calls "the frequent equation of photography to the 'dark side' of cinema" [2012a, 225]), and indeed, I argue in chapter 3 that slow time often has a quite different and more positive meaning in action films, but it is not a stretch to note that slowed and stopped time in film is often *correlated* with death; certainly the peplum makes this correlation consistently.

So the peplum, already in the time of *Cabiria,* and certainly up to the present, develops two ideas in tandem. The frozen body is the primary source of pleasure in the peplum film, but it also represents a frequently feminine death for both the film's characters and potentially its spectators. We must ask ourselves: If Maciste warns us against becoming lost in the contemplation of the still image, then why is his own body perpetually used to invite the spectator to gaze at that same still image? And if staring at the image of a woman puts the male spectator at risk of forgetting about his male companions, then isn't there a different, more narcissistic risk for the putatively heterosexual male spectator in contemplating the image of an idealized male body instead? (I note in passing that this sequence with Maciste and Fulvius is also the first time we see what will become the standard pairing in the midcentury peplum: the strongman is partnered with a less manly, weaker sidekick who, unlike the strongman, is interested in women.)

The image of the male body in motion, in contrast, is a safe image for the male spectator; it conveys virile (and often violent) action and is understood as offering a target for the spectator's identification rather than his desire. The strongman grabs one of his opponents in a fight—Maciste does this in *Maciste* (1915), the first film that followed *Cabiria*—and hurls him across the room into a whole group of enemies, knocking them over; he grabs another man in his way, lifts him into the air, and stuffs him through the top of a nearby table. Such scenes seem designed to offer a model of forceful, kinetic action. But something happens when the pace of movement slows down, and the moving image begins to approach the still image: slow motion effectively forces the viewer's gaze to become fetishistic, since we have nothing else to do besides gaze lingeringly at the details. Identification becomes increasingly more difficult as we approach the still image, and it becomes harder and harder not to see the camera's gaze as an expression of desire. This is particularly the case when the camera's gaze is focused not on an object, not even on a face, but on a body.

I should be clear that I am not arguing that the peplum had a special role in developing the role of the still image in cinema, or that the peplum has more static cinema than other genres (although the latter might be true). Bellour (2008) and Mulvey (2006) both give accounts of the long presence of a static dimension of cinema, present at least from Dziga Vertov through classic Hollywood films of the 1950s and 1960s, and both also claim that cinema has been, in Bellour's words, "increasingly innervated by . . . the photographic" (2008, 260). I am, however, claiming that the peplum has a special relationship to the still or slow-moving image, and that it has developed this register of cinema in unique and influential ways. As a genre, the peplum is necessarily connected to cinema's desire to slow movement down and explore the visual (and other) pleasures afforded by the lingering gaze, since its single most fundamental characteristic is its fascination with spectacular male bodies. From that very first shot in which Maciste appears, the focus is on the play of muscles and drapery that both conceals and reveals the physicality of the body, on the pose and the figure's physical presence.

Maciste projects its star into "real life" and the modern day. The film opens at evening with a young Italian woman on the dangerous outskirts of the city, fleeing from mysterious pursuers. She takes shelter in a movie theater showing *Cabiria*—or rather, some of the sequences that star Maciste. Indeed, the few moments of *Cabiria* we see in *Maciste* are edited in such a way as to suggest that

Maciste was the principal character in that earlier film, and they focus on his more kinetic sequences, such as forcing open the iron bars that imprison him and Fulvius (who is hardly visible in this new version). The young woman decides that only Maciste can save her and so writes him a fan letter begging for his help. The film ignores entirely the confusion between the actor and his role, between the ancient past (*Cabiria* is set in the Second Punic War, 218–202 BC) and the present day.

The Maciste films in general have fairly conventional melodramatic plots that offer the filmmakers the widest possible latitude to include sequences that show-case Maciste's remarkable physical strength and physique. But these are two different categories: on the one hand, strength is best shown by kinetic displays, while the body as the object of our gaze is best suited to the still image, the slowed motion of contemplation. Such sequences are present in virtually every Maciste film, even if they are less frequent than kinetic displays of strength, in part because of the difficulty in finding a good reason for Maciste to remove concealing cloth-ing, which interferes with the viewer's fetishistic appreciation of his physique. In most Maciste films, however, an expedient is found.[7] In *Maciste nella gabbia dei leoni* (1926), Maciste is originally introduced to the viewer wearing safari clothes (he works for a circus as a strongman but sometimes hunts animals for it as well), but an adversary tears Maciste's shirt off during a fight in order to permit the viewer to more readily contemplate the strongman's body. For the later portion of the film, however, Maciste generally wears clothing more typical of a circus strongman in order to perform some of his usual feats of strength. In one tell-ing sequence, Maciste performs with the young orphaned woman he discov-ered on his African safari, a big-eyed, dirty gamine who cleans up well. In an impressive spectacle, he lifts her up, and then she stands *en pointe* on the palm of his outstretched hand. They hold this position for a moment, and then, in close-up, Mimi the gamine begins to dance ballet on Maciste's outstretched biceps.

Once again, let us pause and linger over this sequence. The peplum's essen-tial focus is on eliciting the viewer's admiration. Admiration as an emotional state suggests both an enthralled gaze—it etymologically means "gazing at"—and a certain distance between the person who is being admired and the one doing the admiring. This distance is both horizontal (we are not allowed to approach our heroes too closely) and vertical (the objects of admiration are superior to us; hence the title of the highest naval rank). These forms of adoration are precisely reproduced in the theater itself, where we gaze up and out at our cinematic heroes.

The sequence is remarkable not only for how it activates the viewer's sense of wonder and admiration, however. Maciste strikes and holds a pose here, inviting the viewer to turn to that other register of cinematic temporal pleasure: slow contemplation, the lingering gaze. Any narrative movement slows down or stops, and the kinetic turns static. When, however, the girl begins to dance *en pointe* on Maciste's arm, we see that the sequence unfolds simultaneously across two very different temporal dimensions, kinetic and static.[8] The two do not interfere with each other; on the contrary, one is very much in the service of the other. The presence of a young woman dancing on Maciste's outstretched arm amplifies the viewer's wonder and admiration for Maciste's exceptional body. As Gunning has noted, "Most early films can be viewed as contemplations of the event of movement" (2012, 27), and he specifically mentions the "trained bodies" of dancers and acrobats, but this sequence uses the "event of movement" precisely in order to facilitate our contemplation of the still body. Why is this sequence not charged with the same potential anxiety that characterized Maciste and Fulvius trapped in the underground cellar in *Cabiria*, however? In sharp contrast to that earlier sequence, Maciste is overdetermined in this film as free; he is not a circus employee but rather a free agent, presumably a man of independent means, certainly presented throughout the film as the social equal of prominent citizens (and tuxedo-wearing capitalists) like the circus owner. The actor Pagano needed to pose his still body for the audience's enjoyment, but the character Maciste does not; he may walk away whenever he likes (indeed, the lion's cage of the title is one he will enter voluntarily, to save the girl).

In *Maciste all'inferno* (1926), Maciste is trapped in hell by a female demon's kiss and is himself transformed into a demon. Even so, his heart is good, and he causes continuous trouble and foments rebellion. Hence, at the end of the film, he is magically bound to the rocks by the she-demon who tempted him in the first place, bound in a posture that both suggests a Christ-like suffering and permits the spectator's unimpeded vision of his body. This scenario will be repeated countless times throughout the midcentury peplum: the hero is caught by a temptress in a "frozen time" in which nothing can happen. I will examine the "frozen time" of the midcentury peplum, which often takes absolutely literal forms, but I first pause to consider what happens when Maciste is imprisoned, arrested, and held still.

Such sequences are part of the long continuity in the peplum. They appear regularly in the Maciste cycle of the 1910s and 1920s and continue to the present day.[9] In a spectacular sequence in *Maciste,* the hero is knocked unconscious by ruffians and tied up so thoroughly that even he cannot break free of his bonds. Such a sequence offers both advantages (Maciste is brought to a physical standstill so we can contemplate his body freely) and a problem: the story's forward movement would appear to be blocked. Such sequences function according to a rigorous logic that faithfully follows an elementary law of physics describing a body in oscillation. If one imagines a swinging pendulum as it arcs downward, it expresses kinetic energy, the energy of an object in motion. As it reaches its lowest point and begins to arc back upward, that kinetic energy is converted into potential energy: the mass at the end slows and even stops. For a brief moment, we can see it suspended in the air, fully charged with the potential energy that fills an object at rest, before it returns to expressing that energy kinetically.

In other words, we should not make the mistake of thinking that sequences of slow or still time in the peplum are simply static, frozen, or dead. They are part of a larger pattern for the film and its protagonist that seesaws between masochistic moments (the hero is imprisoned, trapped between spikes, or tied up) and sadistic moments (he bursts free, beats up the guards, or lifts a man in the air and throws him away). I will dwell at greater length on psychoanalytic readings of the peplum in chapter 2, but for now, we might note along with Cowie (1997) that there is a general tendency toward "the reversal into the opposite . . . the change of the drive from active into passive" (181), what Lacan (1991) calls the "see-saw of desire" (169) that can freely invert subject and object. Moreover, Lacan goes on to suggest that this tendency to move back and forth between the one who hits and the one who is hit is related to the body and its feeling as a body. "It is within the see-saw movement," Lacan writes, "the movement of exchange with the other, that man becomes aware of himself as body, as the empty form of the body" (170).[10] Indeed, part of the pleasure of slow time lies precisely in the way it can express a certain kind of haptic sensation that is intermediate between masochistic pleasures and sadistic ones: the tension of the muscle getting ready to spring into action. The bound body offers a superb stage for this muscular and temporal state of frozen excitation; Wyke (1997a) calls bodybuilding "the display of static moments of extreme physical tension" (53). It is, if you like, the temporality in which nothing has happened, but something is about to.

The inevitable outcome of such sequences is the pleasurable conversion of potential energy into the spectacular display of kinetic energy, precisely how Freud defines the pleasure principle—the shift from high levels of excitation and tension to lower levels (see especially the last two chapters of *Beyond the Pleasure Principle*). Maciste may not be able to break his bonds, but that does not stop him from kicking his guardian into unconsciousness and then, in a truly magnificent scene, stacking a small table on a larger one by lifting it with his teeth and climbing onto first one and then the second table, unable to use his hands. Finally, he stands atop the table on a table, high enough to brace his head and shoulders against the ceiling so he can push his head through the ceiling and the floor of the room above where the damsel is imprisoned; in a last burst of kinetic energy, he chews through the ropes that tie her. (The sequence consists of only two uninterrupted shots; the break comes when the camera must be moved from the ground floor to the floor above.) If this kind of threat was not terribly important in early films, less structured by narrative drive, its persistence indicates that it provided an increasingly pleasurable anxiety as narrative became more and more the rule rather than a suggestion.

Such sequences depend for their tension on the possibility that Maciste might not get free. In *Maciste contro lo sceicco* (1926), he is also tricked, knocked unconscious, and tied up; will he escape in time to save the girl whom the other, wicked sailors plan on selling to the sheik for his harem? The fact that every viewer knows already that he will does not change the fetishistic fact that we must also believe that he might not. We know very well (that Maciste will break his bonds in time), but all the same . . . In fact, in real life, many of our most common fetishistic beliefs exist primarily to sustain simple anxieties and neurotic behaviors (I know very well that air travel is safer than driving, but all the same . . .). This is the power of the logic of the fetish; as long as we fail to recognize that it produces pleasure, it will seem nonsensical. I cling to my anxieties precisely because I enjoy them (as in Žižek's [2001] imperative, "Enjoy your symptom!"). Our enjoyment of these totally conventional sequences depends, in fact, on our ability to sustain a phantom anxiety. Without the anxiety, the sequence falls flat and appears as what it really is: a rote recitation, an arbitrary and mechanical gesture.

The time of narrative cinema has always been understood to be complex. The pro-filmic event was captured by the camera in the "now" of the actors in the front of the camera, but it is long lost in time, definitively past. On the other hand, as a viewer, I experience that lost past in my now. Virtually everyone has found something uncanny in cinema's reanimation of the dead (Barthes 1981; Bazin 1967–1971; Mulvey 2006; Stewart 1999); Guido (2012a) calls the "deadly dimension of the photographic instant in film" a "leitmotiv of [its] historiography" (235). Bartolomeo Pagano died in 1947, but over and over again, I have reanimated his image, a spectacularly healthy, strong body, on the walls of my classroom. After teaching *Cabiria* for many years, I learned that Pagano died frail and weak, wasted by diabetes, confined to a wheelchair, unable even to stand; watching him effortlessly lift and toss smaller men about like toys in my own present, how can I now avoid this knowledge of his future, now long past? It was Roland Barthes, in his beautiful *Camera Lucida* (1981), who noted that the still photograph possesses this quality in an intensified form, however. In analyzing an 1865 photograph of Lewis Powell (aka Lewis Payne), a convicted killer waiting to be executed, Barthes realizes that Powell is both dead and yet about to die (95–96). The image tells us both, simultaneously, forever. Every photograph is an uncanny *memento mori*, or in the language of this chapter, a *memento morituri*: in freezing life and holding it still, it speaks to the fact that one day, this will be the distant past. Effectively, every time cinema approaches the still image, it is also approaching its most uncanny temporal dimension: the time of being dead and about to die. In contrasting film's static and kinetic dimensions, we should recognize that it is only the kinetic dimension that holds the uncanny death of the still photograph at bay (and simultaneously, that the risk of that death creates a kind of fetishistic enjoyment for the spectator).

In the next section of this chapter, I will argue that these two sources of anxiety appear continuously throughout the history of the peplum but take on particularly clear forms in the midcentury cycle. Before I do that, however, I want to try to clarify a theoretical point. Mulvey's extremely influential early work posited that there were sources of visual pleasure in narrative cinema, but also sources of anxiety—and in the case of beautiful women on screen, they were one and the same source. Mulvey argued that classic Hollywood cinema had developed an ingenious plan for keeping the visual pleasure while eliminating the anxiety (investigate these beautiful women and find them guilty), and I have so far sketched a very similar situation. But although Mulvey understood that there was something enjoyable about the whole process (and dedicated herself for a time to the "destruction of pleasure" in cinema), she perhaps did not appreciate that the anxieties produced by narrative cinema are themselves a source of pleasure for the viewer. Anxiety and pleasure are not at all inimical but indeed produce each other. Attacking the viewer's visual pleasure as a political maneuver was guaranteed to fail, as was the Godardian de-mystification of the cinematic apparatus; it simply created cinema that very few people wanted to see, and that could be experienced only as a chore (McGowan 2007, 9–10).

The more effective tactic would have been to take the source of anxiety—woman as a source of symbolic castration, an image of historical marginalization and socioeconomic disempowerment that potentially threatens men—and intensify it, make it the affective focus of the film. Arguably, this is precisely what film noir did, reaching its apotheosis in intensely masochistic and hysterical films in which the male protagonist is not at all released from anxiety by the investigation of the woman, but rather the opposite: in films like *The Maltese Falcon* (1941), *Detour* (1945), or *Sunset Boulevard* (1950), the male investigator (who is presumably the target of the putatively and normatively male spectator) is traumatized, scarred forever, or even exterminated by the femme fatale. Perversely, this intensification of the genre's organizing anxiety is probably the natural progression of narrative cinema in general, since intensifying anxiety also increases the viewer's pleasure. Certainly this would explain why the peplum has over time intensified, not mitigated, its principal sources of spectatorial anxiety. This intensification is perhaps most spectacularly visible in its movement from a latent homoeroticism to a manifest and explicit one, but it is equally true of the peplum's constant attraction to a cinema of stopped time, its reliance on the still image (produced by its fascination with the posed male body) and on the uncanniness produced by the mortuary character of the still image.

The Bodybuilder as Statue

The first film in the midcentury peplum cycle was Pietro Francisci's *Hercules* (1958), starring Steve Reeves. It set up the typical traits of the peplum films that came after it (e.g., the exotic dance sequence, the consultation with the oracle, the political restoration plot) while retaining from the Maciste films the constant use of set pieces that showcase the physique of the hero (in many cases, the actual set pieces are the same, such as the bare-handed combat with a wild animal or picking up an adversary and hurling him against other opponents). The camera loved Steve Reeves—like Pagano, Reeves had a natural and dominating physical presence. He was not a gifted actor and rarely conveyed an emotion with any success, but his body convinced where his voice and face did not. But the camera also seemed to love him in a different, metaphorical sense—it looked at him constantly, adoringly, often photographing him from below. These sequences were, not surprisingly, shot in the slow, static time of the admiring gaze discussed earlier, but they were much slower, more lingering than similar sequences in the Maciste films, a trait that was characteristic of all the midcentury peplums. As Paul Willemen (2009) notes, "The Italian peplums often filmed the Hercules-body . . . with a static camera showing the muscleman straining while performing an act of strength. The camera tends lovingly to caress the body with slow pans and tilts detailing the sweating torso, arms, biceps, thighs, and so on. The actor, if he moves at all, does so slowly" (275). The adoration of Hercules's body is a source of anxiety within the film, too; the fathers of Thebes worry that their sons are forming a "cult," a "fanaticism" out of their adoration. It is suggested that this might pervert them in some fashion and turn them against their fathers (see chapter 2 on the peplum and Oedipal sexuality). It was, however, in the sequel to *Hercules, Hercules Unchained* (*Ercole e la regina di Lidia*, 1959), that the thematic anxiety over stopped time was most fully developed.

This film added another enduring trope to the peplum world: the evil queen (a reincarnation of the diva of early cinema, openly sexual, ultimately doomed). The queen is often linked to a magical or supernatural power, generally one that allows her to control the minds of men by making herself an object of total, hypnotic fascination. The men bewitched by her lose all awareness of their surroundings—in particular, their male comrades. All they can do is gaze in rapt fascination at their mistress. In *Hercules Unchained,* this is the power of Queen Omphale, the queen of Lydia in the original Italian title. Omphale has multiple sources of magical power. The first is the magic water of Lethe, which makes Hercules forget his former life (and wife). In his new existence, Hercules is of course entirely captivated by the beauty of the queen and forgets his former companions. Naturally, his kinetic life of virile deeds disappears, and we see him exclusively reclining on couches, snacking, and being massaged by servant girls. Bundled together with this package of sedentary activities is, implicitly, making love with the queen. Lest the viewer find this image—and it is indeed a static, unchanging image—appealing, we learn that there is a consequence for Hercules: he loses his fabled strength and becomes an ordinary man (albeit with an extraordinary physique).

But the anxiety about fascination with the still image emerges also in a different direction. Hercules is simply a beautiful image for Queen Omphale, something to be cleaned, made up, dressed, and decorated. Throughout this middle portion of the narrative, it is clear that Hercules is a more or less literalized form of the boy toy. In its most extreme form, he is not only static but also explicitly feminized: he lies recumbent on a couch while servant girls rub him with fuzzy feathers and place garlands of pretty flowers around his head. Literate viewers (and Italians have traditionally had very strong classical educations) will probably recognize in these sequences echoes of an even more explicit feminization of Hercules, in which Hercules was forced to become Queen Omphale's slave for a year; indeed, in some sources, such as Ovid, Hercules not only performs women's work but also does so while dressed in drag.

But Omphale possesses another magical power besides forgetfulness and fascination, one even more profoundly connected to the cinema of stopped time. Hidden within the royal palace is a sequence of special chambers, the queen's trophy room. After she tires of her boy toys, she has them immortalized by a team of Egyptian sorcerers who embalm these men in largely athletic and sporting poses, in undying stasis. They appear undead, clearly living men, but pasty, lit with lurid lights, as Hercules's companion, Ulysses, wanders about them. Once again, the static and the kinetic registers co-exist within the frame. Note that Omphale's two magic powers correspond precisely to the two anxieties about the contemplative gaze I discussed earlier: a concern about a hypnotic fascination produced by film's slow time and the uncanny life-in-death of the still image itself. Writing about the intersections between moving cinema and photography, George Baker (2008) refers to the stereotypical sense of the photographic image as a "frozen fullness. . . . Its devotion to petrifaction or stasis has seemed for so many to characterize the medium as a whole" (179). Likewise, Bazin (1967–1971) counterposes still photography, which "embalms time" (14), to cinema, although the uncanny persists in cinema, which is "change mummified, as it were" (15). In short, the connection between still cinema and death, petrification, and embalming seems to have been abundantly made in theory. Indeed, Queen Omphale and her Egyptian mummifiers appear to have read Bazin, who begins the first essay in *What Is Cinema?* with a reflection on Egyptian mummies, finding two basic tendencies in art. The first captures the inner essence or truth of what it represents, while the second preserves the exterior appearance. Omphale speaks to her Egyptians about precisely this issue:

"You Egyptians are truly so clever that almost certainly you'll find the way of even preserving life."
"Life is different. We can't create the soul of man."
"Still, it must be exciting, your work. To fix for eternity a man's character. Just the man: the way he looks, the way he stands."
"When can we expect to get to work on Hercules?"

The uncanny undead take the form of the athletic body, arranged and carefully posed to give the impression of a frozen moment of a body in motion. When Hercules regains his mind and escapes the palace with the aid of his companions, they traverse this gallery of still images, their own frozen doubles. As they leave, one of them gestures at an empty pedestal: Hercules's name is already written there. It is a space prepared in advance for that narrative and cinematic possibility that ends up never being realized: the strongman trapped, frozen forever, the camera left unmoving on a beautiful body, strangely still. But the film nevertheless ends with Hercules and his wife, Iole, in a frozen embrace, standing next to a statue (see figure 2.2). Wyke (1997a) notes that already the nineteenth-century circus increasingly featured still spectacles for the strongman, tableaux drawn from classical statuary and paintings, and that Eugen Sandow, widely considered the first bodybuilder, generally posed in imitation of classical statuary rather than performing more typically vaudevillian feats of strength (53–54). She concludes that "classical statuary, rather than classical athletic practice" (69), is the ultimate aesthetic and rhetorical basis of bodybuilding in popular culture, and it appears to guide the aesthetics and rhetoric of peplum films as well. When Hercules fights his way out of the Queen's palace, he uses an Egyptian funerary statue as a weapon, but in the midst of that kinetic act, he must pause and pose, a statue himself (figure 1.3).

Figure 1.3. Statue lifting statue. *Hercules Unchained*, 1959.

Goliath and the Vampires (1961) begins with Maciste plowing a field and encountering a tree stump, which he then proceeds to uproot by hand. This task speaks powerfully to the intended Italian audience (who would view these films in cheap, third-run theaters called *terza visione* and were largely rural, working class, and familiar with agricultural labor), but also to the peplum's willingness to engage in dead, nearly static cinematic time. The sequence lasts for over a minute, almost all of which is spent in the camera dwelling on Maciste's nearly motionless but powerfully straining, muscular body, shot from behind to showcase the actor's heaving shoulders.[11] If such an unengaging opening hardly seems to suggest the uncanny quality of cinema's approach to the still image, there is plenty of evidence that the film is indeed anxious about slowed time and frozen bodies. Maciste's village is soon after razed by pirates who are led by a vampire master named Kobrak, who seems particularly interested in the blood of maidens (preferably blonde, even more preferably Maciste's fiancée). Kobrak is opposed by a kind of double, the ultimately good-hearted but nearly as creepy alchemist, Kurtik, who has a penchant for mummifying Kobrak's victims in the hope of later restoring them to life. Here everyone is at risk of being turned into a frozen image of what he or she once was. "They look like statues!" Maciste exclaims in horror. Later, Kurtik explains that Kobrak turns his victims into "creatures without souls . . . robots with blood . . . slave robots . . . puppets," and that his own mummies are simply these same creatures half-restored to life. "As yet, they remain just statues," he sighs. "I must restore life!"

We see these automatons later on; where Kurtik's loyal servants have bright blue skin and communicate telepathically, Kobrak's are exceptionally pale, are entirely silent, and wear inexpressive, blank white masks. All these "others"—the mummified statues, Kobrak's "robot slaves," Kurtik's kindhearted but strangely blue soldiers—are either frozen or move in slow motion, automata, puppets, as if they are mindless or hypnotized. Queen Omphale's servants could not restore the soul, but *Goliath and the Vampires* promises that there is a return from the stopped time of the undead (a masculine and scientific cure; Kurtik talks of "chemistry" and a "missing element" and is surrounded by boiling beakers and steaming retorts). While it holds out this promise of a cure for the trance-like time of static film, however, it also multiplies the number of statues and slow-motion automata. They belong to men and women, to the good guys and the bad guys; they are the enemies, as well as Maciste's fellow villagers, mummified and then restored. The film ends with the people of the grateful kingdom, now free, erecting a statue of Maciste in the center of the main plaza. The posed bodybuilder, frozen in time, is unavoidable in the peplum.

The image of the statue as the enemy of the peplum hero returns again and again. In the original *Hercules*, the statue threatens to destroy the ship in the storm, while in *Goliath and the Dragon* (1960), the statue of the God of Vengeance topples on the hero after persecuting him for years. At times, the enmity is more tenuous or symbolic: in *Son of Samson* (1960), Maciste's friend, the new Pharaoh Kenamun, is ensorcelled by the evil Queen Smedes. While Maciste is forced to erect a massive stone obelisk, Kenamun whiles away his dreamy, trance-like time by sculpting a bust of his now-beloved queen. Both are stuck working on stone. Even the slapstick and deliberately camp comedy peplum *Colossus and the Amazon Queen* (*La regina delle Amazzoni*, 1960) opens its obligatory exotic dance sequence with three frozen metal statues that are then revealed as male figures wearing silver loincloths and with their bodies and faces covered in silvery makeup. This image is particularly inflected in the film since its comedy is based on the gender reversal in Amazon society, and these slender but muscular young men are clearly intended as objects of desire for a female gaze (really a campy male gaze in drag). *Hercules in the Haunted World* (1961) is filled with characters that are hypnotized automata (Hercules's wife); robotic oracles wearing Kabuki masks; slowly shuffling but ambulatory rock men bent on cutting Hercules's companions down to size (Procrustes, whom Hercules destroys while shouting "Of stone you are made, and by stone you shall be destroyed," which now reads like the self-fulfilling prophecy of every peplum); the zombies that emerge from stone sarcophagi to kill Hercules, which he in turn destroys by hurling stone monoliths at them (again, of stone and by stone). According to Gabriele d'Annunzio, the author of the intertitles for *Cabiria*, the name Maciste means "born from the rocks," and countless peplums suggest that he might also die that way. He is chained to the rocks in the silent-era films *Maciste* and *Maciste all'inferno*, but he is also trapped underground in the midcentury peplum *Mole Men against the Son of Hercules* (1961); in *Samson and the Seven Miracles of the World* (1961), he is buried alive.

One final example, from near the end of the midcentury peplum cycle, is *Hercules against the Moon Men* (1964). Coming late as it did, *Moon Men* faced an additional temporal problem: by 1964, it was becoming apparent that the time of its genre was running out. Like many late peplums, it used recycled footage, plots, and costumes (Della Casa 2001). Giacomo Gentilomo repeated much from *Goliath and the Vampires:* the semi-mummified heroine, vampirically drained, who must be saved by the strongman, and the general appearance of Kobrak, now the Moon Man Redolphis. Much of the film's time consists of nonnarrative action, including an infamously monotonous fifteen-minute sequence of the characters lost in a sandstorm. Even narratively important sequences are unbearably slow: the evil Queen Samara is ordered by her Moon Man master to kill Hercules and elects to do so by placing him in the vertex of a giant wooden V internally lined with spikes. Teams of slaves pull the sides of the V shut while Hercules strains to keep them open. This *vagina dentata* torture sequence lasts for over four (exceedingly slow) minutes, during which there is virtually no movement by anyone: the queen

Figure 1.4. Over four minutes of Hercules's straining pectorals. *Hercules against the Moon Men,* 1964.

watches rapturously, getting more and more turned on as she anticipates Hercules's imminent penetration. Hercules strains to resist. Almost the entire sequence is simple shot and countershot between the strongman and the queen, the camera slowly moving closer and closer to Hercules's body. Eventually, it is so close that we can no longer see even the movement of his abdominals as he pants for breath, but only the tautness of his tanned, smooth skin stretched across a muscular frame (figure 1.4).

That slow buildup of potential energy eventually leads to the anticipated explosion of kinetic activity: Hercules bursts free, breaking the machine. Once again, everyone and everything in this film risks being turned into static, dead time, into statues, automatons, mummies. The queen administers (or so she thinks) another magically hypnotic drug to Hercules, in order to turn him into her boy toy, an obedient puppet. Billis, one of the damsels in distress, is slowly drained of her blood to reawaken Selene, the goddess of the Moon Men. For betraying her people and handing the earth over to the Moon Men, Samara is promised that her "beauty will never fade"; she too will be made into an unchanging and static still image, fit for the interminable rapt adoration that the end times will produce. Or not: she is killed by Redolphis's Rock Men, more men turned into stone.

Unlike most conventional genres, for most of the peplum's history, the body in motion has been the woman's body. One of the most fixed and repetitive elements of the peplum is the exotic dance sequence, which appears already in typical form in *Maciste imperatore* (1924), for example, seductive and Orientalist. However, the sequence became absolutely obligatory, appearing in virtually every midcentury peplum film and in almost all peplums since. Almost all are exotic, featuring women in silken, Orientalist garb (more or less chaste variations on the theme of the dance of the seven veils) or occasionally a single woman in an imitation of Middle Eastern belly dancing. More rarely, they may feature a single dancer or a troupe of dancers who are mixed men and women (as in *War of the Trojans* [*La leggenda di Enea*, 1962, also known in English as *The Avenger*] or the campy *Colossus and the Amazon Queen*), or the dance may be "tribal" and African in inspiration (see the 1961 *Triumph of Maciste* [*Il trionfo di Maciste*] or the Stone Age peplum *Fire Monsters against the Son of Hercules* [*Maciste contro i mostri*, 1962]). Occasionally, they are extravagantly weird, race- and gender-bending spectacles in which all these possibilities are combined, as in *Giant of Metropolis* (*Il gigante di Metropolis*, 1961), a science-fiction peplum (hence the reference to Fritz Lang's 1927 *Metropolis*) in which a female belly dancer is accompanied by two men, one black, dressed in a pink-feathered and bejeweled headdress and boa, the other white, wearing a leopard-print loincloth and matching bracelets and sporting a mop top and long antennae protruding from his shag. They cavort ineptly (except for the black dancer, who appears to be a professional) to a chaotic, modernist, science-fiction sound collage under the intent but inscrutable gaze of the ruler of Metropolis. Almost all peplum dance sequences fall into one of two types: either a dance to seduce the hero (and his men, if any) or a dance to entertain the ruler, who is always wicked and illegitimate. The ruler, male or female, almost never expresses any interest in the dance, in sharp contrast to the torture of the strongman, in which the ruler takes an avid and often clearly sexual interest.

These dances continue into the modern era of peplums: the tribal dance sequence of mixed men and women appears in the 1982 *Ator, the Fighting Eagle* (*Ator l'invincibile*), while a sexualized, topless dance appears in 1984's post-apocalyptic science-fiction sword-and-sorcery romp *The Warrior and the Sorceress* (to showcase the post-apocalyptic mutations, the dancer has four breasts). The belly dancing and the group dance to entertain the corrupt sovereign continue absolutely without change in *Gor* (1988) and *Outlaw of Gor* (1989). In the once-again chaste films and television shows of the 1990s and in the more graphic contemporary era, the dance has not gone away; instead, it has been coupled with the female prophet. In *300* (2007), King Leonidas climbs a remote tower to consult the oracle, a beautiful maiden in breast-revealing translucent fabric, who dances yet another slow-motion, rhythmically ramped sequence (shot underwater to give the otherworldly appearance of zero gravity) before whispering meaningless, drug-induced ramblings into the ear of her translator. The narrator, Dilios, frequently self-referential, comments that these oracles are "remnants of a senseless tradition."

The peplum's anxiety over the male body being slowed down and petrified, however, appears everywhere in the genre. In the American animated children's series that cashed in on the peplum craze, *The Mighty Hercules* (1963–1966), more than one episode features the menace of being turned to stone. In "Medusa's Scepter" from 1963, Hercules manufactures a statue of himself to convince the evil magician that he has already been turned into stone, and two episodes from 1964, "The Sinister Statue" and "Wings of Mercury," feature uncanny statues that come to life (the question of the frozen image that comes to life is perhaps of particular significance for the field of animation). In the 1985 *The Adventures of Hercules*, a rather dim-witted Hercules (Lou Ferrigno) wonders at the exquisitely carved statues in the evil queen's cavern. "There is nothing more beautiful than the human form caught in a moment of tension," she explains, as if defining the peplum's central premise, before continuing menacingly, "and sculpted forever in stone." But, of course, there is no real difference between the costumed extras pretending to be frozen statues and bodybuilder Lou Ferrigno striking muscular pose after muscular pose, the human form caught in a moment of tension. The inaugural episode of *Hercules: The Legendary Journeys,* "The Wrong Path" (1995), turned to territory already well trodden in the midcentury peplum: a seductive female demon who lures men to her, only to then turn them into statues. But this Hercules would also be duplicated by a statue built by the blacksmith Atalanta (played by female bodybuilder Cory Everson) that would be brought to life by magic in the 1998 episode "If I Had a Hammer"; obviously the uncanny statue must be destroyed, ensuring the triumph of narrative time over static time once more. In the Norse-mythology-themed episodes "Norse by Norsevest" and "Somewhere over the Rainbow Bridge" (1998), Hercules is encased in stone, and even the Norse gods are frozen in an endless static time that must be defeated but that also represents one of the peplum's chief anxieties—and pleasures. For the hero to survive, he must move, break out of his stone coating that keeps him "frozen in moments of maximum tension" (Dyer 1997, 167). At the same time, this frozen time is precisely what affords the viewer the peplum's chief pleasure, namely, the contemplation of the idealized male body. The midcentury peplum's solution of this problem is to structure the film according to the alternation of the two times: first, the kinetic and narrative time in which the rebel army charges the castle in, say, *Samson and the Seven Miracles of the World;* then the frozen time of Samson, imprisoned underground, straining against the rocks; then back to the kinetic energy of the attacking forces; then back again, and so on. Is this not what Freud, in *Beyond the Pleasure Principle,* described as the "vacillating rhythm"

(1953–1974a, 18:49) of the two kinds of drives when he first theorized the death drive? One rushes forward while the other seeks compulsively to return to the time before birth—in the case of cinema, the stopped, lingering, contemplative time of the still image, or the slowly revolving pedestal of the living statue.[12] This vacillating rhythm is only one solution to the central paradox of peplum time (kinetic time versus static contemplation), however, and contemporary peplum films have made extensive use of modern technology to provide the viewer with other ways to see the male body both in virile action and in admiring contemplation, sometimes even in the same frame. Lest this narrative seem overly teleological and Hegelian, as if the peplum were inevitably marching toward the simultaneous kinetic and static registers of a film like *Immortals* (2011), it is worth recalling the ballerina dancing on Maciste's biceps in 1926. There are many ways to satisfy these two demands, even at the same time in the same frame.

We Who Are About to Die Salute You

Like the midcentury peplum, *300* was understood as relatively lowbrow popular entertainment aimed at young men; like the original *Hercules,* it was critically panned, hugely popular, and widely imitated. Its flaws are evident even on a first viewing (historically inaccurate, unabashedly racist, homophobic, misogynist, ableist, deliberately linked to a failed neoconservative foreign policy, and more), and perhaps as a result, its formal and aesthetic coherence has sometimes gotten second billing.[13] Zach Snyder drew on a number of important sources (the midcentury peplum, video games, and principally Frank Miller's graphic novel of the same name), but the film succeeded in creating an entirely new look and feel.[14] This was true on almost every formal level; the color, for example, is selectively de-saturated throughout, generating scenes that appear painterly and graphic or ultimately resemble tinted black-and-white films (the one color that is never de-saturated is the red of the Spartans' cloaks).[15] Although Snyder carefully re-created specific panels from Miller's graphic novel, the many new sequences in the film also have the same character. Virtually every shot in the film was performed in front of a blue screen, and the environment was later added digitally, generating a further layer of cinematographic consistency. And in one of the film's most widely imitated touches, the spatter of realistic blood was eschewed in favor of computer-generated blood that appears to have been lifted from the pages of a graphic novel rather than a crime-scene photo.

Just as influential as the film's visual appearance, however, was how *300* handled time. Its stance toward history is obviously the creation of a free-form anachronism, certainly no more (but probably no less) accurate than the average midcentury peplum, for all that the core story is based on what is probably a true event—the ancient past is used principally to give a nostalgic and resentful gloss on the fallen masculinities of the present day. This is not Fredric Jameson's post-modern nostalgia (7–10), since neither Miller nor Snyder was interested in using popular images of the past as a way of conveying pastness. Rather, they were interested in the present. Xerxes, for example, is an eight-foot-tall, shaven-headed, and multiply pierced metrosexual; Queen Gorgo quotes Bush/Cheney rhetoric ("Freedom isn't free") when she appeals to the cowardly city council to fight against the menacing hordes coming from Persia; Xerxes's troops deploy primitive hand grenades against the Spartans; and so on. The film is serious, however, about fidelity to cinematic history. Numerous sequences (some of which are in Miller's novel, some of which are new) recuperate traditions from the midcentury peplum: using an opponent's body as a weapon; the ritualized fight against a wild animal; the consultation of the oracle; the exotic and erotic dance sequence; the Greek setting; the bearded, dark-haired hero set against his blonde sidekick; and, of course, the comically revealing, S&M-like garb worn by the well-muscled heroes. It should come as no surprise, then, when Delios, near the end of the film, tells his assembled listeners about their genealogy: "The old ones say we Spartans are descended from Hercules himself." One can almost hear the italic type: the Spartans are descended from *Hercules*.

  300 had good reason to establish a genealogy that goes back to *Hercules* rather than *Gladiator:* like the midcentury peplum film (but quite unlike the Russell Crowe film), *300* is intensely fascinated by the muscled male body. The fitness of the male body is, of course, a major thematic concern in the film, which opens with the baby Leonidas held over a pit of infants' skeletons; if he is less than perfect, he will be tossed below. He and his companions are constantly juxtaposed to bodies that are different (virtually all the other inhabitants of Sparta are old men or women); Leonidas confronts the leprous and rotting ephors, who guard the oracle; and of course, he rejects the deformed and hunchbacked Ephialtes for not being able to hold his shield as high as the other men.[16] As a result, the film is able to extensively indulge in a fetishistic and lingering gaze that looks admiringly not only at these superb male bodies but also at everything else: the beautiful Gorgo, the dancing oracle, the magnificent costumes and masks of the Immortals, and the landscapes suffused by uncanny but lush computer-generated lighting.

  In fact, *300*'s preference for the lingering gaze is applied so rigorously in the film that one can safely make the following claim: outside sequences with dialogue and fight sequences, virtually the entire movie is filmed in slow motion. This is not an exaggeration. The Spartans cresting a hill, rejoicing over Xerxes's fleet being destroyed by storms—slow motion. Leonidas and Gorgo have sex in slow motion, as we might expect; but Leonidas also sets his helmet down in the snow in slow motion. Leonidas's son runs through the wheat fields in slow motion; the Oracle dances in slow motion. The Persians sound the charge to attack in slow motion, ride out to meet the Spartans in slow motion, and fall into the well in slow motion. Someone might object to my earlier caveat about fight sequences, noting correctly that almost half the film consists of such sequences. These sequences, however, are shot with high-speed (overcranked) cameras, allowing Snyder to develop a temporal register that has become almost inseparable from the contemporary peplum: rhythmic ramping. Most of the film was shot at speeds between 24 and 100 frames per second, using cameras that could freely vary their speed, and the most extreme slow-motion shots were done at 360 frames per second (D. Williams 2007, 62). This allows the director to compose a shot not only in space but also in time, moving smoothly from time that has nearly come to a halt to time that moves forward at a normal tempo (in fact, however, Snyder—or his director of photography, Larry Fong—rarely lets the camera come all the way to normal speed even in fight sequences; it oscillates rhythmically between slow motion and ultra-slow motion).

Let us also slow down for a moment to appreciate what is happening here at a theoretical level. Obviously, rhythmic ramping makes it possible for the viewer, at long last, to experience both registers of filmic time (static and kinetic) within the same shot. Time is slowed, allowing the viewer to gaze in rapt admiration at the beautifully muscled body poised to strike, and then smoothly ramps up to nearly normal speed so the viewer can admire the kineticism of the movement as it uncoils. It is Maciste's rigid muscular pose and a ballet dance one right after the other; Turner (2009) claims that it turns the film's "scantily-clad protagonists . . . into nothing less than living statues" (130), language that has been employed to describe the muscled body of the classical male since Sandow invented bodybuilding at the end of the nineteenth century. Rhythmic ramping permits the viewer to see that both temporal regimes are always at work in every shot: the screen as a canvas to be admired and the forward movement of time whose kinetic impetus can be seized by the eye. It does not simultaneously present both regimes, but the rhythmic alternation between them leaves the viewer in no doubt that they are always both present.

Even so, the uncanny quality of slowed time in cinema does not seem to have gone away at all. More than ever, in fact, slowed time is the time of death. Turner notes (2009, 139–140) that certain scenes of death, particularly the death of young Astinos, evoke not only the "living statues" of the bodybuilder but also the motionlessness of true death. Her point is that the film's reliance on the register of the "statue" is a way of negotiating the "underlying contradictions of the male nude itself" (140), which pivot around the question of vulnerability. The superb male body is never more heroic and athletic than when he is depicted as nude, but he is simultaneously most vulnerable, both to the weapons of his enemies and to the potentially castrating gaze of those who look on him. (For more on vulnerability, see chapter 3, which addresses the vulnerability of the peplum hero's skin.)

Turner's point about the vulnerability of the male body in *300* is also true in a more literal way, however. As Leonidas severs an opponent's leg, the camera slows to a crawl; as the Spartans drive their opponents off a cliff en masse, we move from the live time in which dialogue and speech are still possible to a funereal slow motion; we switch to a long shot and gaze rapturously at the beauty of falling bodies. One might even argue that so much slow time is needed in *300* and its most direct follower, the television series *Spartacus: Blood and Sand,* because all time in these productions is the time of death. The slow-motion Oracle is effectively foretelling Leonidas's death by withholding the Spartan army from him; the child running in slow motion through the wheat field is about to learn of his father's demise.

Rhythmic ramping is used almost identically in *Spartacus: Blood and Sand.* The primary difference is that it is generally confined to fight sequences (which also borrow Snyder's soundtrack—heavy metal mixed with Orientalist music [often a combination of Middle Eastern and Indian scales]—and computer-generated graphic sprays of blood), and there is relatively little use of slowed time outside the gladiatorial spectacle. Since *Spartacus* is a television serial, however, it has more time in which the spectator can gaze at the muscled male body, even without slowed or stopped time, and it uses other techniques to make certain that those bodies are visually comprehensible to the viewer. The gladiators depicted in the show wear almost nothing as a general rule and indeed appear completely naked on occasion—it is not unusual to have sequences of dialogue in which one or more of the men are presented with full frontal nudity. More often, their bodies are held still, at attention, in order to be inspected in minute detail (also by the viewer) as they are trained or even exploited sexually (figure 1.5). As with *300,* however, the slowed time of ramping is also invariably the time of death. Indeed, like *Gladiator, 300, Immortals,* and other recent peplum films, the television series' overall orientation is toward death. This is true not only because we already know that the story of Spartacus ends tragically with his defeat, both historically and cinematically, but also because of a curious extracinematic fact: the actor who played Spartacus in the first season, Andy Whitfield, was diagnosed with cancer as the series was originally airing in 2010 and died the following year at the age of thirty-nine (about the same age at which the historical Spartacus died).[17] Legend has it that those who were fated to die in the arena would salute the emperor by saying "Ave Imperator, nos morituri te salutamus" (Hail, Emperor: We who are about to die salute you). The time of the peplum is the time of the *morituri,* literally Barthes's "going to die" (1981, 96) of still photography, a future without a future. But I mean this reference to Roman custom rather more literally: the male body on display, prepared for inspection as a passive object of the gaze, is a source of anxiety indeed, one that no amount of honorable and manly kinetic violent action to follow can fully erase.

Because the star of the show was replaced for its second season (*Spartacus: Vengeance*), flashback sequences were limited to those in which Andy Whitfield's

Figure 1.5. The body about to die, ready for inspection in *Spartacus: Blood and Sand*, 2010.

face does not appear. Although the new actor, Liam McIntyre, resembled Whitfield, the resemblance is not close enough to permit more than a fleeting glance, apparently preventing the lingering gaze. But one sequence is an exception to the impossible flashback. A Roman lady, Ilithyia, constantly fantasizes about her one sexual encounter with Spartacus; the sequence can be shown because Spartacus was presented for her visual inspection (and sexual use) covered in gold paint and wearing a mask, appearing as a statue. The result is an image that seems to concretize all of the peplum's temporal anxieties: the halt of narrative time (Ilithyia returns to the image obsessively); the man turned from active viewer into an object to be admired, a boy toy; the frozen statue of cinema that has come to a halt; the still image as a metaphor for death (here completely literalized, since this is the only image of Whitfield that the show can use).

I argued earlier that *300* manages, for the first time in the peplum, to consistently offer static or slowed time and kinetic time within the same shot; indeed, it shuttles smoothly and balletically between the two different temporal registers, suggesting that all moments, all perspectives, could be viewed either way. Sometimes, for example, the fight slows down so that the killing blow can be delivered in ultra-slow motion. This way, the spray of blood, the severed limb, or the hero's muscular body can be fully grasped by the audience. At other times, the emphasis is on the sudden and dramatic release of static energy, the slow-motion buildup as the thrust is readied and muscles bunch and then a sudden return to near-normal speed as the spear pierces the body. The technique is fundamentally psychoacoustic in character (finding a rhythm in the pulses of slow time). A different approach, however, would be to have the two registers appear simultaneously, allowing both the lingering gaze to apprehend the play of muscles and the kinetic gaze to seize the pleasure of speed and motion.

This technique was realized in *Immortals* (2011). The film relies on certain techniques from *300*, including slow-motion battle sequences filmed directly from the side, with all movement progressing from left to right (such as the battle in the tunnel), selective de-saturation of the color palette (gold and red, especially, are left intact), and a reliance on green-screen filming to produce painterly backgrounds. It also recuperates numerous images and tropes from the midcentury peplum: the consultation of the oracle; the oracle's exotic dance; the dark-haired, muscled hero paired with a blond, wisecracking sidekick; the hero chained or tied to a huge wooden beam carried across his shoulders; the fight with an animal or monster; outfits that consistently reveal the hero's chest and abdomen; and a final sequence in which the muscleman wraps chains around pillars and pulls them down, provoking a catastrophic collapse. Singh also locates his film within peplum history in a different way. *Immortals* presents the viewer not with the usual twelve Olympian gods, but with a mere six: Zeus, Athena, Apollo, Poseidon, Ares, and Hercules. Hercules has been bodily assumed to the ranks of the divine, canonized, if you will. Singh has his hero, Theseus, bodily assumed into heaven at the end of the film, suggesting a continuity—even an eternity—in this peplum genealogy while clearly establishing that Hercules belongs to an earlier generation of peplum heroes than his own. (For the record, Hercules fights in this film as he does throughout the midcentury peplum, ever since Steve Reeves did it in *Hercules:* swinging heavy iron chains.)[18]

Singh's solution to the problem of having both static or slowed time and kinetic time in the same frame is ingenious. It appears when the gods battle lesser beings, Titans or ordinary men. The Titans are not only locked up underground but also appear to emerge from, be made from, the earth itself: they are nearly black, with crackled skin. Befitting their lesser status and their statue-like character, they move primarily in slow motion, while the gods move in real time; the trick is that these two registers interact with each other, and they do so naturally and believably. More precisely, both move at normal speed until they interact; then, as if by magic, the Titans' speed is ramped down while the gods ponder what to do with their opponents. Poseidon, for instance, kicks a Titan in the chest; as the Titan flies back, he slows to a crawl and hangs suspended in the air. Poseidon contemplates the Titan's body and then spears him with his trident. The tines enter the flesh, and then, phenomenally quickly, Poseidon flicks the body free, sending it flying into a group of Titans. As they, in turn, are knocked off their feet, they slow down and again hang in the air. Poseidon leaps up, turns his trident sideways, and uses the long handle to decapitate all three of them as he comes down. Their blood sprays and the heads separate, all in ultra-slow motion, the time of death. Poseidon has already moved on. It would be easy to imagine that slowed, static time would be the time of death, while kinetic time would be associated with forward-moving narrative, but in fact, both registers seemed destined to end blocked, collapsed, at a dead end.

Immortals is set in two different registers of the end time as well. In one, the end of the divine reign of the Olympian gods appears to be at hand.[19] The Titans, the ancient enemies of the gods, are soon to be released by the evil King Hyperion (Mickey Rourke) in order to destroy the Olympians. Hyperion plans on effecting a different kind of end time, however: the elimination of all genealogical lines other than his own. He will do this by conquering the earth and killing or castrating all males (again, the film redoubles what would seem to be the anxieties of its primarily straight male spectators: the male Olympian gods are beautiful young men wearing gold lamé loincloths; the audience watches one character being literally castrated by having his testicles smashed with a hammer). As in much contemporary cinema directed at primarily male audiences, the message seems to be that the time of real men is past, here literalized: there was a time when men were heroes, literally godlike, but now they are literally castrated. The appeal is both ideological, reinforcing an already exaggerated sense of white male *ressentiment,* and melodramatic: by placing us in a time in which it is already too late to hold off the coming (literal) apocalypse, the film suggests that our worth can be measured by how well we maintain our manly virtues in the face of certain doom.[20] Although one of these masculine and temporal apocalypses can be avoided—Theseus defeats Hyperion and foils his plans to bring human genealogical time to an end—the other cannot be. The time of gods and heroes proves surprisingly vulnerable; they are more mortal, if anything, than the humans whose time can be saved. Zeus alone survives, taking the dead Athena back to Olympus with him and sealing the Titans once more underground by collapsing the entire mountain of Tartarus.

Theseus's time is destined to come to an end, too, but here he, like Hercules, finds a sort of immortality that appears more durable than that of the gods. Singh follows the Greek mythological convention of placing heroes in the sky as immortal images, and this is how we see Theseus at the end of the film. His son has been taught about his father's great deeds, which have been carved in marble in a series of frozen high reliefs (similar to the metopes of the Parthenon). The scenes are simply the sides of a pedestal that supports a marble statue of Theseus in his epic fight against the Minotaur; once again, our hero is frozen forever, one of the immortals of static cinematic time. We might also note that in all the scenes, Theseus is completely naked, with only a windblown piece of cloth or a strategically placed sword concealing his genitals; we can indeed admire his body freely for-ever. His son looks up into the sky and sees his father engaged in a floating, end-less, celestial battle. As the figures rise up away from the camera, we see more and more battling figures emerge into the frame, eventually forming a painterly trompe-l'oeil vaulted ceiling (the film was intended for 3D screenings). It almost goes without saying that this eternal combat is shot with an overcranked camera and so appears in the slowed time of death. We have a choice here, but only between the truly stopped time of the statue and the slow motion that can put off the definitive demise of the muscular hero, always and forever about to die.

Throughout Guido and Lugon's volume on still and moving pictures (2012), they stress repeatedly the connection between the appearance of the still image in film and psychoanalysis. One of the contributors, Mireille Berton (2012), help-fully lists the many ways in which images of photography and cinema pervade psychoanalysis and discussions of mental illness, with photography having a privileged place in discussions of memory or the idée fixe, while cinema serves as a metaphor for the flow of images in dreams. Guido himself particularly stresses the connection between the disruptive value of the still image in film and "trau-matology" (2012b, 18; but see also 2012a, 231), a way of registering the shock of modernity, drawing on Benjamin's language of "unconscious optics." In "The Work of Art in the Age of Mechanical Reproduction," Benjamin (1968) writes specifically about the use of slowed time:

> With the close-up, space expands; with slow motion, movement is extended. The enlargement of a snapshot does not simply render more precise what in any case was visible, though unclear: it reveals entirely new structural formations of the subject. So, too, slow motion not only presents familiar qualities of movement but reveals in them entirely unknown ones. . . . Evidently a differ-ent nature opens itself to the camera than opens to the naked eye—if only because an unconsciously penetrated space is substituted for a space con-sciously explored by man. Even if one has a general knowledge of the way people walk, one knows nothing of a person's posture during the fractional second of a stride. The act of reaching for a lighter or a spoon is familiar rou-tine, yet we hardly know what really goes on between hand and metal, not to mention how this fluctuates with our moods. Here the camera intervenes with the resources of its lowerings and liftings, its interruptions and isolations, its extensions and accelerations, its enlargements and reductions. The camera in-troduces us to unconscious optics as does psychoanalysis to unconscious impulses. (236–237)

Like Žižek's apparently impossible "unknown known" (2004)—the thing you know but do not know that you know it—that turns out to be the unconscious, Benjamin's "unconscious optics" are the "unseen seen." We have seen these bod-ies and their movements all our lives, and yet there is something else in them we have seen but do not see that we have seen it-—or we do not see it until the slow, lingering camera of the peplum forces us to see it. In chapter 2, I explore the psychoanalytic dimension of the peplum, concentrating on the traumatic element that the slow temporality of the *morituri* has begun to open up for us: the death drive.

Notes

1. Farassino begins his essay "Anatomia del cinema muscolare" (Anatomy of muscular cinema) by noting that "it is not required to begin with *Cabiria*, even if everyone has always started there, but it is not forbidden either, and it is quite useful to do so" (1983, 29).

2. It was not the case that Albertini's body was never made visible to the viewer on film; in epic films set in the past, like *Spartaco*, or in his role as Samson (Sansone), the viewer was more likely to see the muscled body. But Maciste's body is constantly put on display in all his films.

3. Dalle Vacche (1992) argues that Maciste embodies a comedic and athletic body in contrast to the even more statuesque and operatic registers evoked by a character like Scipio in the fascist propaganda film *Scipio Africanus*. In this chapter, however, I am arguing that within the context of his own films, slow or stopped time represents a point of anxiety; Maciste is often (but not always) aligned with slowed time because it best showcases his body, his muscles, and the tension of potential energy that is a source of the spectator's pleasure. Monica dall'Asta (1992) more clearly aligns Maciste with the statue, noting "the static and heavy iconography of the strongman since his origins" (99).

4. Gunning (1986) notes that the notion of a "cinema of attractions" dominated until about 1907, but certainly its influence continued long afterward, and the Maciste films are unusually indebted to this essentially exhibitionist model, one that aims simply "to show something" (64), in Gunning's words.

5. Although most of the theorizing and writing of futurist manifestos was done by Anton Giulio Bragaglia, all the Bragaglia brothers contributed to futurist photography experiments (the movement called Fotodinamica); Carlo Ludovico Bragaglia later directed four midcentury peplum films, two starring American bodybuilders.

6. Deleuze (1995) argues that after World War II, a new organization of time became increasingly visible in cinema, what he calls the time-image, in contrast to the movement-image. Instead of time being measured by a sequence of movements and actions (the "sensory-motor" scheme), the increasing presence of these time-images (the "pure optical-sound" scheme [20]) in cinema endows the art with a self-consciousness about time. Deleuze notes that the time-image has always existed in cinema, of course, even in the silent period. It is clear how Deleuze's categories might work for an analysis of the peplum (we might, for instance, read the oscillation between images of muscular action and images of posed stasis as a dialectical movement between the sensory-motor movement-image and the optical-sound time-image). Indeed, more generally, few theorists have elaborated so many different ways for thinking about time in cinema. I remain dubious, however, about how applicable such notions are here for a number of reasons. Deleuze does not appear to be including trash cinema, cult films, or even popular genres under the rubric "cinema." Is the image of Maciste, or Hercules, or King Leonidas, replete with bulging muscles, slowed and posed to permit the viewer's lingering gaze, a "pure optical image" that might "break through [*percer*] the cliché" (21), leading to visionary, messianic, or auratic places? Already in the language of "breaking through" (*percer*, to pierce, penetrate,

drill through), we see that Deleuze presupposes the essentially unproductive emptiness of the cliché, here figured as a restraint or a closed space, perhaps a wall. The logic of popular culture, however, is a logic of repetition, of flat, stereotyped, and clichéd images; rather than exploring by means of a poetic, divine image that fractures our subjectivity and carries us to a truth as unexpected as it is sublime, it explores precisely through variation and repetition, and its truths are more often carried on the surface (which does not, however, make them any easier to see) than buried underground. Deleuze thinks through the question of the body, time, and cinema as well (see 189–203, for example), but he does so to get at thought. If my project in this chapter shares something with Deleuze, it is his critique of the "disastrous" (271) idea that the cinematic image is necessarily in the present. Instead, he argues, its time looks to the past and, crucially for this chapter, to the future.

7. Reich (2011) is quite right to note the importance of Maciste's clothing as contributing to a presentation of a modern and idealized Italian masculine identity, but we should not lose sight of the fact that this fully "civilized" and modern European image is not fully compatible with the genre's visual logic, which is the revelation of the muscled body. In *Maciste all'inferno* (1926), for example, the transformation is magical, from a schoolboy-like suit to a muscled, hairy satyr.

8. There is in fact a bewildering variety of different "times" in cinema: the mechanical time of the projection, the time of the film's reception (which was generally identical to that of the projection until the advent of home video), the time of the narrative (as short as minutes, as long as centuries), the subjective time of the spectator (action passing in an instant, dead time crawling by), and others. Doane (2002) notes that even as cinema captures actions in the act of unfolding, there is also a time of filming that never changes, allowing film to become dated (143), both because of technology (e.g., silent film, black-and-white, Technicolor) and because of the mise-en-scène (costumes, hairstyles, and props all reveal the time of the filming). Historical films add yet another temporal register: the Olivier *Pride and Prejudice* (1940) is a distinctly 1940s take on the late 1700s, a take inevitably contrasted for today's viewer with that of the canonical 1995 BBC miniseries, a distinctly mid-1990s treatment. It is Deleuze, however, who suggests that multiple temporal registers are at work even within the same images. A mirror image (what Deleuze also calls the hyalo-sign) is never simply my reflection now (the actual) but inevitably a projection of my past limitations and my future possibilities (the virtual), just as the time of Michelangelo Antonioni is "torn between an already determined past and a dead-end future" (24). Deleuze writes that for Antonioni, "all illnesses are chronic" (my translation), punning on both Antonioni's well-known assertion that "eros is sick" and the sense of "chronic" as related to Chronos, the god of time.

9. In *Cabiria*, Maciste is chained to the giant stone wheel of a mill and forced to turn it endlessly, for years, a task normally given to animals. Modern peplum fans, however, will recognize this as the prototype of the same sequence in *Conan the Barbarian*, the montage that transforms the young boy Conan into the mature, hugely muscled Arnold Schwarzenegger. In both instances, this endless turning appears as a kind of minimal kinesis, or a sort of static movement, from which the hero must eventually break free.

10. I am indebted to David Gerstner for this connection to the seesaw of desire, to which I return in chapter 2.

11. Cecilia Gregori (2009) notes the tendency of the peplum's promotional posters to re-create both what we expect (the muscles in action) and the "other dimension" of slowed time, both potential and kinetic energy: "The action is caught in its central phase, blocked in the moment in which the characters prepare the blow, the muscles already under tension, ready to unleash their restrained power" (238).

12. One might think here of the Lacanian "seesaw of desire" cited earlier, the rapid alternation of sadism and masochism displayed in the mirror stage as the subject teeters on the brink of a new psychic organization. Cowie (1997, 292–297) has suggested that this oscillating movement is not unlike the rhythm of narrative. Citing Barthes's *The Pleasure of the Text,* she argues that there are moments that disrupt the pleasures of the standard Oedipal narratives in favor of bliss, or *jouissance;* she not only mentions "narrative delay" and "the halting of narrative" (292) but also goes on to argue that there is a bliss or *jouissance* in loss that is "the work of the death drive" (293).

13. See A. O. Scott's review in the *New York Times* (2007) for a fairly standard list of complaints about the film's ideology, or Chemers's (2007) perceptive comments on the film's (shockingly retrograde) representation of disability. O'Brien (2014) also notes that the film subscribes "unconditionally to reactionary and fascist depictions of white masculine potency and authority" (172). In a more nuanced article, an anonymous member of the Italian writing collective known as Wu Ming (in this case, Wu Ming[1]) (2007) analyzes unflinchingly both the film's pleasures and its political pitfalls, as well as its critical and popular reactions, in both the United States and Europe. (Wu Ming is both a pseudonym and a collective. When individual members of the collective write, they maintain both anonymity and individuality by using a superscript number along with "Wu Ming." Hence Wu Ming[1], Wu Ming[2], Wu Ming[3], and so on.)

14. Time in video games is no doubt worthy of its own book. Still, it is worth pointing out how common slowed time is in video games. *Prince of Persia* (which was made into a peplum film as well), *Jade Empire, Fallout 3, Mirror's Edge, Timeshift, GUN, Stranglehold, F.E.A.R., Max Payne,* and many others allow the player to temporarily stop, slow, reverse, or otherwise manipulate the flow of time in the game. The idea is usually that because the protagonist is so fast, everything else appears slow. This is true in cinema as well: the first time Neo dodges bullets in *The Matrix* (1999), we see him move in ramping, snaky slow motion. Afterward, Trinity tells him that he moved "so fast," making certain that the viewer takes away the right idea. One might even recall here the 1970s television series *The Six Million Dollar Man,* in which all the sequences showcasing Steve Austin's superhuman, bionic speed were presented to the viewer in slow motion.

15. See David E. Williams (2007) for a thorough discussion of the film's visual and formal techniques, including selective de-saturation, blue-screen filming, "morph" zooming, and extensive use of slow motion, including precise frame rate figures.

16. See Chemers's review of the film (2007).

17. See Späth and Tröhler (2013) on the problem of the *corp en trop,* or "a body too many," of Jean-Louis Comolli, a French critic who wrote about historical film; Späth and Tröhler address the problem of the proliferation of bodies playing Spartacus, who had, of course, a historical body of his own.

18. This connection between Hercules and chains carries over into other media, including professional wrestling. Raymond "Hercules" Hernandez began to bill himself as just Hercules in the late 1980s, building up a more muscular body, adopting a beard, and carrying a chain that he would fight with, all clear references to Steve Reeves's Hercules.

19. This plot is also taken up in the 2012 peplum *Wrath of the Titans.*

20. On the temporality of melodrama as "too late," see Linda Williams (1991).

2 PRE/POST

Sexuality in the Peplum

> *A hill, something like an open-air latrine: a very long bench with a large*
> *hole at its end. Its back edge thickly covered with small heaps of excrement, of*
> *different sizes and levels of freshness. A bush, behind the bench. I urinate onto*
> *the bench; a long stream of urine washes everything clean; the bits of excrement*
> *come loose easily and fall into the opening.*
>
> Why did I feel no disgust during this dream? What at once [*sofort*] came
> to mind in my analysis were the Augean stables, which were cleaned by
> Hercules. I am this Hercules.
>
> —Sigmund Freud, *The Interpretation of Dreams*[1]

Before: Some Birds

The blockbuster success of the 1958 *Hercules* guaranteed a sequel, and indeed, the
following year saw the release of Francisci's *Hercules Unchained,* which reunited
virtually all the cast of the first film in new adventures. After the credits roll, we
see Hercules and Iole, now married, taking their leave of the rest of the Argonauts
and preparing to return to Hercules's hometown, Thebes. We learn that the young
Ulysses is being entrusted to the care of Hercules and Iole, and Laertes, Ulysses's
father, gives Hercules a birdcage filled with homing pigeons (figure 2.1).

I use the Dell comics adaptation of the film (1960; penned by Paul S. Newman,
with art by Reed Crandall and George Evans, all uncredited) here for a number
of reasons. First, it is a reminder of the fact that midcentury peplums were marketed primarily to children and young adolescents. The comic places itself in loco
parentis—like Hercules and Iole—giving at the end the "Dell Comics Pledge to
Parents," which promises "only clean and wholesome entertainment." The Dell
code "eliminates entirely, rather than regulates, objectionable material" to ensure that "when your child buys a Dell Comic you can be sure it contains only
good fun." Even in a film as wholesome and kid-friendly as *Hercules Unchained,*
there is such objectionable material that must be eliminated, ranging from the
sexual (Iole's rape is eliminated, as is Hercules's role as boy toy/love slave) to the
authoritarian (the negative elements of Hercules's character that appear in the

Figure 2.1. Ulysses and his homing pigeons. Dell Comics, 1959.

film—laziness, gluttony—are also eliminated). Some aspects, however, are, strictly speaking, regulated: in the film, Ulysses refers simply to Penelope by name, while in the comic her status is made more official and more socially (and sexually) acceptable and clear: she is Ulysses's "betrothed." And in the film, Laertes entrusts Ulysses primarily to Iole, but in the comic, exclusively to Hercules. Overall, the effect is to intensify the authoritarian character of the scene, subordinating Ulysses in the first panel ("I will treat Ulysses as my own son"), as well as its pedagogical value, as in the fourth panel, where Ulysses is again enjoined to follow the teachings of Hercules.

In between these reminders of social hierarchy and the necessity to teach young men to ensure that they turn out well, we find a bird, or a pair of them. In the midst of all this paternal authority, however, something about these birds doesn't quite sit right. Laertes gives the birds to Hercules, but they are not his to give. They belong instead to his son, who appears to object to their usurpation (an objection not censored by Dell nor, properly speaking, answered by Laertes). Why has the father taken over control of the birds? Why does he give them, along with his paternal authority, to Hercules rather than to their proper owner, Ulysses? Finally, what lesson is being taught here to Ulysses, and perhaps most important, to the young, putatively male reader of the comic book?

To answer that question in particular, I want to say a little about the role of pedagogy in the peplum more generally. A few years ago, when I taught a course on Jane Austen fan cultures, a student told the class that her sorority house kept a DVD of the 1995 BBC adaptation of *Pride and Prejudice* running in a continuous loop in the living room—a gesture of devotion surprising only in its degree, since Austen is often perceived as an exemplary introduction to conventional heterosexual femininity and traditional gender relations. That same year, I gave a talk about the contemporary peplum at the University of Vermont, and a student told me afterward that his fraternity house also kept a video running in a loop on the living room television: the intensely violent and frequently homoerotic peplum television series *Spartacus: Blood and Sand.*[2] In each case, I think that it is safe to say that the video functions as a sort of badge and affirmation of gendered identity, but in the context of the fraternity and sorority houses, and within the university more generally, one is almost compelled to add a pedagogical value to the video as well. These are texts that are also supposed to teach young women how to be (heterosexual) women and young men how to be (heterosexual?) men. As I will argue later, this already indicates that there is a surprising amount of work involved in doing something that is supposed to just come naturally, as well as indicating that film and television have a role, albeit an intriguingly complicated one, in that naturalizing of the process of acquiring a gendered and sexually oriented identity. Moreover, as tempting as it might be to describe that role as simply oppressive, imposed from the outside, this anecdote also indicates that some spectators, at least, seem to find the enjoyment worth the price that they may pay.

Let us take as a preliminary hypothesis the somewhat curious idea that the peplum is essentially a pedagogical text, intended, despite its homoerotic content, precisely to teach young men about heterosexual adult masculinity.[3] This sexual pedagogy appears at times in the Maciste films of the 1910s and 1920s. In *Maciste imperatore* (1924), for instance, we meet Prince Otis, a young man, perhaps in his late twenties, who lives abroad in hiding, where he is schooled by two tutors. He generally finds the tutors bothersome and boring and would prefer to chase women; in short, his behavior and his situation are rather more like those of an adolescent, resistant to his education. Maciste, however, appears as the true teacher, unlike Otis's tutors: he rescues Otis from his unwise attachment to a dancing girl who means to ensnare him and directs him to a proper erotic/romantic object. When Otis's tutors express dismay that he has run off with a young woman, Maciste jokingly reminds them that it could be worse: he could have run off with a young man. Maciste models the proper behavior of a ruler (and a man) by briefly pretending to be Otis himself and becoming the king (despite his evident lack of interest in the ladies at the court). Finally, Maciste's physicality inspires even the boring old tutors, who see the error of their bookish ways and begin exercising in a (futile) attempt to emulate the strongman. In many other films of this cycle, however, Maciste is simply an amazing figure, better than all the other men but imagined as a figure to be admired by younger men rather than emulated by them; we are also to understand him as embodying a "desexualized muscularity that signifies . . . national might" (Reich 2015, 62), an identification that might be troubled by individual and personal attachments.

From its beginning, however, the midcentury peplum presented the strongman as a teacher and a role model. The 1958 *Hercules* repeatedly places the strongman in the position of teacher of young men. This was true even outside the film: as O'Brien notes (2014, 30), contemporary newsreels showed images of Reeves working out and young Italian men in the background imitating him. Within the film, Hercules comes to the city of Iolcos in order to tutor Iphitos, the son of the current (and illegitimate) ruler. Iphitos is clearly the "bad" teenager—moody, surly, resentful, lazy, uninterested in study, and ultimately fatally foolish. King Pelias, Iphitos's father, is explicit about Hercules's pedagogical role, and that his task is to make boys into men: "With his guidance," he says to his son, "I'll make a man of you, worthy to reign." There is a recognition here that Pelias himself is weak, an inadequate father figure for the needed pedagogy. All Iolcos, in fact, seems concerned about the adequacy of father figures, and what will happen to them when this idealized symbolic father appears—one of the city elders wonders out loud whether their own sons might turn against them out of their love and admiration for Hercules (he is reassured that Hercules would never allow such a thing). There would appear to be a desperate, even frantic, need among the young men of the city for such a father figure, since they turn out by the dozens to train like Hercules: wrestling, javelin throwing, running, and other physical activities. Iphitos, unfortunately, proves to be unteachable; he fails to understand that Hercules is his teacher and master, a symbolic father to be imitated; instead, he treats Hercules as a rival, and his attempts to match or outdo the heroic strongman ultimately cause his death.

A different model is also exhibited to the audience, however: the young Ulysses. From his first appearance, in the training-camp sequence, Ulysses is marked as special. He is the only individual other than Hercules. All the rest form masses (the city elders, the mass of young men, even the twins Castor and Pollux). As the young men of Iolcos labor below to imitate the strongman, Hercules stands high above them, flanked by Castor and Pollux (the iconography of the three male figures is a clear recall of the Olympic medal platform), surveying them while they look up at their hero.[4] Suddenly, Hercules jabs his finger out and bellows, "Look!" One of the athletes has separated from the masses and runs directly at them before pole-vaulting his way to join Hercules. He is a slender boy on the verge of manhood, and his voice is high pitched and gushing: "I wanted you to notice me! I want to become like you, Hercules!" Ulysses is immediately contrasted with Iphitos: the good student and the bad student. Iphitos and Ulysses compete in an archery contest, and naturally, Ulysses wins, following Hercules's advice.

There is in all of this a certain libidinal component, of course. Hercules is not only a model to be emulated (identification) but also something to be looked at: "Look at him!" Orpheus cries. The cut to Hercules, flanked by the twins, all three of them oiled and clad only in loincloths, never fails to make modern audiences giggle at its campy appearance.[5] In the Greek mythology that furnishes the outlines of the film's story, there is much that is recognizable—Hercules really did accompany Jason and the Argonauts on the quest for the Golden Fleece, and Pelias, Iphitos, and Iole really were related to the stories of the labors of Hercules—but Ulysses is from a different time and a different story. Ulysses has clearly taken the place of a different character, Hylas, a young man who accompanied Hercules on board the *Argo*. Hylas, of course, was Hercules's squire and *eromenos,* or younger male lover. The relationship between the *erastes* (older man) and the *eromenos* (younger man) was understood, perhaps even primarily, to be pedagogical rather than sexual, but the two roles, as in the peplum, are not entirely distinguished, so our subtext, only partially erased, is both pedagogical and homoerotic. Ulysses's initial exclamation to Hercules appears to present both elements as well: "I wanted you to notice me! I want to become like you, Hercules!" The first exclamation clearly speaks to a kind of boyish crush ("I wanted you to notice me!") or desire, while the second expresses a desire for pedagogical emulation ("I want to become like you!"). Same-sex desire is acknowledged here, even explicitly, but it is placed in the past and as something that happened and is done with.[6]

In all of this, temporality is key, and the temporality of both the silent-era Maciste films and the midcentury peplum is the time of before. The viewer is taken to be a young man who is not yet finished or finalized, a work in progress; after will be a different story. As Maggie Günsberg (2005) perceptively notes of the midcentury peplum, "Heterosexuality is constantly put on hold, denied and ultimately postponed until the final cursory moments of closure" (108). Heterosexuality is constantly deferred, but to what end? The viewer and his stand-in, Ulysses, will have changed; something will have been done to them over the course of the film. We might return to suture theory (as articulated by Heath

1977–1978, Mulvey 1987, Oudart 1977–1978, Silverman 1983, and others) here, which suggested that a particular position or vantage point (metaphorized as a gap or hole) was prepared for the viewers in the film, and that various operations (editing was particularly important) would "suture" us into that position. In this sense, the world of the peplum is, metaphorically, "pre-op," set before that surgical operation that would be more or less definitive. Daniel Dayan (1974) used a specifically pedagogical metaphor for this process of suturing the viewer into a particular position in one of the seminal articles on suture theory, "The Tutor-Code of Classical Cinema." This place prepared for the viewer is the place of identification—it is how I am taught or tutored to identify "me" within the filmic text.

For the young male viewer in the theater, waiting to be schooled in sexuality and cinema, there is a half-acknowledged nod at previous same-sex desire, but a pedagogical instruction that, after he leaves the theater, it will have turned entirely to same-sex identification. In his initial, gushing speech, Ulysses moves from past tense to present tense ("I wanted" to "I want"), but Hercules completes the movement by turning to the future tense; in fact, he gives Ulysses a prophecy. After Ulysses hits the center of the target in his archery competition with Iphitos, Hercules tells Ulysses that "someday, your destiny will be decided by an arrow." This destiny to be decided by an arrow is explicitly the destiny of heterosexuality, an arrow shot straight, not bent or deviated in any way. Penelope, Ulysses's future wife, will give herself to whichever man can shoot an arrow through twelve axe shafts, a daunting task of phallic penetration that only Ulysses will successfully complete at the end of *The Odyssey*.[7] The viewing subject thus has a complete trajectory from an initial same-sex desire to a present-day identification with the beefy strongman and eventually to a future heteronormative competence. Hercules appears here as a necessary pedagogical mediator on the way to that predestined future. Heterosexuality must be gotten to, and it will require a Herculean labor to get there—much as Freud must labor mightily to avoid the evident homoerotic content (the intromission of penile fluid into an anal aperture) of his dream in the epigraph of this chapter, a task facilitated by his literal identification with Hercules ("I am this Hercules").[8]

Now we can return to the curious birds that appear at the beginning of *Hercules Unchained*. We know that the homing pigeons at the start of the film will inevitably be used later to carry a message back home to Ithaca; that is, like the arrow that Ulysses will one day shoot to reclaim his faithful wife, their orientation at some future point will be infallible. At the beginning, however, they represent an uncontrolled libidinal vector that appears to run directly between Ulysses and his girlfriend (but could perhaps fly elsewhere), not subject to parental supervision. Laertes appears to have disrupted this circuit ("He will bring [the message] to me!") and has decided that the safe place for young Ulysses's birds is in the hands of Hercules. It is perhaps worth mentioning at this point that the word for bird in Italian, *uccello,* is a common (and euphemistic) slang term for the penis.

An Oedipal Allegory

Hercules Unchained begins in medias res with a sequence that cannot make any sense to the viewer: a young man is carried on a stretcher (we will later learn that he is unconscious, not dead or wounded) to a royal palace in the jungle; a redheaded woman whose face we cannot see inspects the man on the stretcher while her lover looks on; she gives a sign to her soldiers, who kill the lover. The opening credits roll. Then we watch as Hercules, accompanied by Iole, now his wife, and the young Ulysses, takes his leave of the Argonauts and prepares to return to Thebes, his home. After some brief banter, they drive off; they are rudely passed on the road by Argive soldiers; when Hercules gives chase, Ulysses reminds him that he must drive carefully now that he is married. They tease Hercules, who abruptly decides to go to sleep while Ulysses drives. Iole sings a song (inexplicably, music of the 1950s) while (again inexplicably, and only in the Italian version of the film) a bevy of beautiful girls appears on the beach and waves at Ulysses. As soon as the song stops, the travelers see human bones scattered all over the road. The giant Antaeus appears and demands tribute. Hercules fights and eventually defeats him. Then they arrive in a beautiful wood where Hercules promises that they can rest; he also casually mentions that the gates of hell are said to be in this forest. It begins to rain; they run to a cave, passing the Argive soldiers from earlier, and in the cave they discover . . .

I pause here for a moment before continuing my plot summary to address a potential concern. To readers who regard psychoanalytic explanations with a measure of suspicion, I point out that it is not strange to think that these films would be concerned with the transition from child to adult, since this demographic (older boys and young men) was the dominant audience for peplum films, the same audience that consumed comic books and read *Boy's Life* (both venues where Francisci's *Hercules* films were advertised). Members of this demographic were very much invested in the question of how and when they would pass from the one side to the other. Moreover, the 1950s and 1960s saw an enormous flowering of interest in psychoanalysis, especially in film (witness Alfred Hitchcock's *Spellbound* [1945], *Vertigo* [1958], and *Marnie* [1964], among others), even in Italy, where Freud had long been viewed with some suspicion. Indeed, we know that at least one peplum director, Domenico Paolella, understood his peplums precisely in psychoanalytic terms, and that he understood the peplum as addressing the "infantile stage" (1965, 6) of both the hero and the general audience. Paolella conceived of his peplums, which included *Hercules and the Tyrants of Babylon* (*Ercole contro i tiranni di Babilonia,* 1964) and *Samson against the Sheik,* as a kind of Marxist psychoanalysis for the poor, and he recounted the story of how a psychoanalyst who met him at a cocktail party overlooking the Villa Borghese in Rome informed him that he recommended Paolella's peplum films to his patients. Paolella went on to note specifically the curiously pre-sexual character of the peplum:

> Several people have noted that, in peplum films [*les films mythologiques*], love stories are negligible. Often the action unfolds with a view toward the liberation of a captured woman. . . . When the hero finally manages to free his lady, the story ends. This is a trait that confirms again the infantile character of the peplum world. . . . It is only at the *climax*, at the end, that the protagonist encounters a new problem: sex. But on this question, typically attenuated by the "happy ending," the film comes to an end [*le film s'achève*]. (6; emphasis in the original)

Peplums have at most a perfunctory interest in love (Günsberg memorably called it "tokenistic and sketchy" [2005, 107]), and most of the films appear infantile, even puerile; on the other hand, they invariably and relentlessly feature erotic and Orientalist dance sequences performed by groups of scantily clad women and frequent insinuations of homosexuality (sometimes intentional, sometimes not). In other words, the peplum displays a curious (even queer) hybridity and undecidability about its sexuality. In *Hercules, Samson and Ulysses* (*Ercole sfida Sansone*, 1963), a beautiful woman, skinny-dipping in a pool, archly asks the muscle-bound hero if he would like to join her for a swim; he responds by brandishing a dead bird: "I just caught this chicken!" he exclaims, grinning. There are two registers of psychic life here, both made visible to the spectator. The spectator is clearly enlisted on the side of the one who does not see or sees but does not understand, namely, the strongman, even as the film makes visible the disparity between the situation and his reaction. This is truly curious: the viewer is urged to recognize a dramatic irony (Jeez, he doesn't realize she's coming on to him!) but then also to *identify with that ignorance*. The constant presentation, in other words, of adult sexuality that is to be seen but not recognized, not acknowledged, calls out for psychoanalysis.

In the case of *Hercules Unchained*, I begin with the figure of Ulysses. Of all the characters in the first film who also appear in the second, he is the only one singled out for special treatment. He is the sole character who accompanies Hercules throughout the film, but more important, his position as Hercules's symbolic son and student is cemented in the opening sequence after the credits, as I mentioned. Hercules, Iole, and Ulysses all appear next to one another driving what amounts to a covered wagon, arranged from left to right as father, mother, and child. Hercules remains largely distant and uninterested (that is, traditionally paternal) in his relationship with the young man. It is with Iole that Laertes insists on a particular bond: "You're so young, but I especially entrust him to you, like another mother. Ulysses, stubborn boy, thinks he's already as grown up as a man."[9] Laertes is clear on a number of points here, but particularly that Iole is both like and unlike a mother in her relationship with Ulysses. She will function as a mother despite her youth, and Ulysses will be a boy to her despite his near-manhood. The two form a bond that excludes Hercules at once; they tease Hercules about his excessive love for his hometown, Thebes; they exchange complicit glances throughout; Hercules goes to sleep and leaves the two of them alone for both Iole's romantic love song and the menace of Antaeus.

We must wonder now about the beautiful women on the beach whom Ulysses sees, and who wave to him while Iole sings her love song. There are ten of them, clad in silky, pastel shifts that leave little to the imagination—their skirts fall just to the top of the thigh, and at least two have their tops sliding off their shoulders, revealing scandalous amounts of décolletage. They pose and wave, and after a moment Ulysses smiles and waves back. His gesture and face are ambiguous: certainly he does not leer or respond with a look of desire or a knowing grin. He returns to driving the wagon without apparent regret, only turning to look and smile at Iole. If their goal was temptation, he was not tempted. It is impossible to watch this sequence and not understand it as a rewriting of a very famous scene that will take place much later in Ulysses's life and again will involve a crowd of tempting women, a song, the edge of the water, and Ulysses guiding a vessel he might wreck: namely, his attempt to hear the song of the sirens without perishing. The same elements appear here, only diffused and scattered. The erotic temptation appears on one side, the siren song on the other; but even more important, Ulysses appears here as one who is too young to be tempted, even though he is on the verge. All the elements of adult, male, heterosexual life are present but not yet congealed into the clearly recognizable figure of the perfect girl or the femme fatale.

This seems to speak to the position of Ulysses (and the spectator), who has a special relationship already with the beautiful (and equally skimpily dressed) Iole, who is both mother (nurturing and kind) and not mother (young and complicit). In other words, the women on the beach and Iole's song, both of which are realistically inexplicable, make perfect sense when they are seen as a young, pre-adolescent fantasy, that of the imagined and idealized spectator of the film. Adult sexual desire is visible but is not recognized as such (a friendly wave rather than the fatal seduction by the sirens); Iole appears as a transitional object who is no longer the mother but is not precisely the available young girls on the beach, either. Ulysses finds himself exactly in between these two spaces, both erotic and both de-eroticized. Neither of them really is accessible (and hence both can be enjoyed in a strictly Lacanian sense) by the young man on the verge of adulthood because both spaces are mediated by the sleeping Hercules, a father who is both more and less than an actual father. As long as Ulysses behaves, Hercules slumbers in back.

There are other elements of the film that suggest that the transition from boyhood to manhood is what is at stake, and that a significant investment of energy is necessary to ensure that this transition takes place in a normative (i.e., heterosexual, post-Oedipal) way. Already in the first Francisci *Hercules,* there were concerns about sons rebelling against fathers, and they appear in *Hercules Unchained* as well. In the opening leave-taking sequence, Ulysses manifests a certain independence, a surpassing of the father, that Laertes objects to. When Laertes entrusts his son to Iole, the young woman first frowns with worry but then turns to Ulysses and reminds him that he has to behave himself. Ulysses grins impudently and says, "Well, if you're going to listen to what old men say." Laertes, offended, turns in anger to his son, who immediately temporizes: "Oh, pardon me—I meant *men of a certain age*" [*uomini di una certa età*]. Ulysses uses his ready wit to offer a euphemism (but one that equally suggests that his father has outlived his usefulness) that cannot be objected to. "Do you hear how he speaks to his father?" Laertes grumbles.

This complicity that verges on intimacy between Ulysses and Iole certainly suggests a kind of ambiguity in their relationship: Iole is beautiful and young but just a little too old for Ulysses. Speaking to Iole's transitional character (between mother figure and potential lover) is a moment in the film when we cut away from the Kingdom of Lydia, where Hercules and Ulysses are held captive, to a young female figure back in Ithaca, weaving and waiting, her face hidden behind her work. Anyone acquainted with *The Odyssey* will immediately think that this is Penelope, who famously weaves in Ithaca while she waits for Ulysses to return, but as the camera moves to the left, we see her face and discover that it is Iole.

If at this point, halfway through the film, we see the young man caught in a transitional state between the two kinds of objects (pseudomother, potential wife), how are we to ensure that he makes the proper kind of psychic investment in the proper object? How are boys to be turned away from their initial love object, the mother, and directed instead to objects that are like the mother but not identical to her, in accordance with the impossible Freudian imperative: you must be like the father, you cannot be like the father? In psychoanalytic terms, what we are talking about here is, of course, the Oedipal crisis and its subsequent working out. So it will perhaps not come as a surprise when I resume my plot summary of *Hercules Unchained* where I left off: It begins to rain; Hercules, Iole, and Ulysses run to a cave, only to discover in this cave Oedipus himself, chastising his son Polynices. As recounted in Aeschylus's *Seven against Thebes,* Oedipus's two sons were supposed to alternate annually their rule of the city, but after the first year, Eteocles has refused to step down (again, the high classicism of Italian culture assumes that viewers will be familiar with most of this). Here Ulysses can see another old man whose son speaks to him without proper respect. Oedipus explains why he has left Thebes to his sons: "The time always comes when one must step down.

And even when it hasn't come, your sons impose it on you." Throughout both Francisci peplums, one catches again and again the idea of the young man revolting against the old, seizing his power; here, too, Hercules stands as the mediator who would prevent such an unjust or immoral action. But, of course, Oedipus also stands for a quite different prohibition, namely, the incest taboo.

In this sequence, and indeed throughout the movie, no mention is ever made of Oedipus's most famous adventure: sleeping with his own mother. It is, of course, a literally unspeakable crime, particularly for the supposedly conformist youth of the 1950s who were watching the film, but it has not been fully erased. It has been disavowed; it is visible without being recognized, seen without acknowledgment, for Oedipus is blind. No mention is made of how or why he became blind, however, and when Hercules has finished speaking to him, Oedipus is led into the abyss of the underworld and vanishes from sight. His blindness and his curse are made visible, and then he disappears from the film. We have here a sort of partial memory, or a recollection that is invoked only to be disallowed. It is, again, like the moment when Ulysses declares, "I wanted you to notice me! I want to be like you, Hercules!" The possibility of same-sex desire ("I wanted you to notice me!") is admitted but instantly relegated to the past and obscured by the present and active desire for identification ("I want to be like you!"). Oedipal desire, the desire for the mother, is seen and not seen all at once, as is sexual desire in general—Iole is like a mother but not a mother; Ulysses is tempted by sirens, but unthreatening ones; Oedipus's crime is alluded to but never specified.

In "The Dissolution of the Oedipus Complex," Freud begins to wonder how this fundamental structure (he calls it "the central phenomenon of the sexual period of early childhood") is dissolved. Strachey's notes (Freud 1953–1974b, 19:173) in the *Standard Edition* inform us that the title of the work uses the term *Untergang* (downfall, destruction, dissolution), but elsewhere Freud even used the term *Zertrümmerung* (shattering, splintering, demolition). Loewald notes how overcharged the term *Untergang* is in German: it "literally means a going under, going down. It is used for the sun's going down in the evening [*Sonnenuntergang*] as well as for the 'destruction' of the world [*Weltuntergang*]" (2000, 239). It would appear that Freud was prepared to do considerable violence to get beyond this phase, and that its passing, dissolution, or destruction was in some way crucial— as crucial and inevitable as the loss of baby teeth (1953–1974b, 19:173), he tells us. Freud writes that the experiences that will lead to its dissolution "are inevitable," that they "must in the end lead the small lover to turn away from his hopeless longing," that the Oedipus complex "must collapse," and that it is "bound to pass away according to programme when the next pre-ordained phase of development sets in" (19:173–174). Both the inexorability of the complex's end ("inevitable," "must lead," "hopeless," "must collapse," "bound to pass away," "according to programme," "pre-ordained") and the curious violence ("dissolution," "destruction," "disintegration," "collapse"), to which Strachey also calls attention in his first note, might appear to be somewhat overstated or fraught. If this destruction is both total and inevitable, then why do we immediately think of the many instances—not least Oedipus himself—in which this complex appears to resurface in ordinary adult psychic life? So many self-help relationship books about men with "mommy issues," so many productions of *Hamlet* that insinuate an overly intense attachment to the mother and hostility to the father—in the world of popular culture, at least, the Oedipus complex is not inevitably obliterated. Indeed, for the Oedipus complex to be interesting, or even visible at all, it must leave a lasting sign or imprint on later psychic life; hence Loewald's preference for the term "waning" rather than "dissolution" (2000, 240). As is often the case in Freud, there is something of a struggle between a fairly static model of phases or stages that simply succeed one another, each one canceling out the preceding one, and a more dynamic Hegelian view akin to *Aufhebung,* or supersession, in which what comes after both abolishes and continues what came before. Even in this introductory passage, there is a clue that this second view is also present in Freud's thinking: he declares that the Oedipus complex is "bound to pass away" (*vergehen muß*). *Vergehen* in German suggests passing away (which, as in English, can also refer to dying), time passing by, wearing away, fading, but all these phrases suggest a prolonged transition rather than an abrupt and catastrophic end.

Indeed, once Freud has analyzed the exact mechanisms by which the boy child is induced to give up the father as a love object (retaining him as such would entail accepting castration and taking the mother's position) and the mother as a love object (retaining her as such would also entail accepting castration, since it is prohibited and so will be punished), he can then declare that this loss of love objects amounts to a repression (1953–1974b, 19:177). But repressions, of course, are eternal; they do not simply fade away but rather return. Freud holds out hope that normal subjects will experience more than a repression here; instead, they will experience "a destruction and abolition of the complex" (19:177). But it is clear that the destruction of the complex is not, in fact, inevitable. This curious mixture of inevitable destruction and possible continuation is nicely summed up in Freud's phrase "destruction and abolition," or, in German, "Zerstörung und *Aufhebung*" (my emphasis)—total obliteration and Hegelian supersession, an overcoming that is also a continuation. We might return to Lacan's "seesaw of desire" from chapter 1 here and note in general that it is precisely the oscillation between two terms (masochistic and sadistic, homosexual and heterosexual, obliteration and preservation) that characterizes the particular psychic moment in which the peplum is invariably set; and as Lacan notes (1991, 169), this oscillation appears at moments of transition between one more or less stable organization of the psyche and another that is on the horizon.

Whether it is a destruction or a preservation of what comes before, Freud suggests that castration is the key to the passing away of the Oedipus complex.

The boy effectively needs castration anxiety in order to renounce his original attachment to the parents. If he wishes to take the father's place and possess the mother, he must directly confront the threat of paternal punishment. If, on the other hand, he wishes to take the place of the mother, he accepts castration "as a precondition" (Freud 1953–1974b, 19:176) of the union with the father. The boy's narcissistic attachment to his own bodily integrity trumps, for Freud, his libidinal investment in his parents—he turns away from his parents and instead turns to forming identifications, particularly the image of the stern father that will become the nucleus of the superego. Readers familiar with Lacan's mirror-stage essay (2007) will recognize that this is, in part, the source of that later essay: bodily integrity (or, in Lacan, the image of bodily integrity) is purchased with a series of identifications, idealized portraits of the self that structure the later psychic life of the subject. Lacan's version was particularly congenial for film theory because it focused on the images and the passive viewing subject who discovered his or her idealized image on a screen (initially a mirror). To return to Freud's language, however, identifications that would have been introjected [*introjizierte*] into the ego as an internal image take visible and externalized forms in film.

If ever an idealized form of the adolescent or pre-adolescent boy, one with a massively greater bodily integrity, has appeared on-screen, it is surely the figure of Hercules as personified by Steve Reeves. Lacan, in other words, would be very pleased with the peplum for offering an absurdly exaggerated image of the "ideal I," one whose physical strength in comparison to that of ordinary adult men must appear very much indeed as the power and strength of an adult does to a child. In both *Hercules* and *Hercules Unchained,* Steve Reeves's body appears in precisely this way. At the same time, Hercules has another, more Freudian, function as the authority or severity of the father image; in particular, he polices the sexual life of the younger men around him. In *Hercules,* Jason presses the queen of the Amazons on what happened to the men of her island, and she responds with vaguely threatening intimations (the dramatic irony of the scene depends on the viewer knowing at this point that the Amazons kill their men once they have mated with them), eventually asking, "Would you be willing to risk death to possess a woman of this island?" Jason's reply is cut off by the arrival of Hercules, who is chasing away three of the Amazon guards, who wave their tiny swords ineffectually at him. The camera cuts to a tight medium shot of Hercules, grim faced, his massive chest heaving with each breath. "With him here, I'm quite prepared to take that risk!" Jason finishes triumphantly, grinning. Sexual contact is explicitly seen here as needing to negotiate the threat of castration (the men will be killed after their dalliances without Hercules to protect them), and it is precisely the image of the stern and severe father figure who will permit (and hence protect) or forbid the later sexual life of the young male subject—but also who will, in some sense, guarantee or validate it as legitimate.

Later in the same film, a group of men who have been forced to remain on board the ship by Hercules, who wishes to punish their laziness, try to sneak onto the island to experience the delights they have been denied, "girls and wine." They are met by Hercules wielding a massive club, who puts them right back to work. In other films, the strongman may arbitrarily deny the young man access to women. In *Goliath and the Dragon* (1960), Goliath has prohibited his younger brother, Illis, from seeing the girl he loves, Thea. When Illis sneaks into her chambers near the start of the film, the two teenagers stand forlornly in front of her bed. "Goliath doesn't want me to come here. He's forbidden it, as you know." Thea sits on the bed and holds his hand. "I want nothing to happen to my darling," she replies. Again, the matrix at work here is quite clear: sexual contact represents a threat ("I want nothing to happen to my darling") that can be mediated only through the Herculean paternal figure, who may arbitrarily withhold or confer his consent. In *Hercules in the Haunted World* (1961), Hercules must stand between Theseus (his weaker, blond sidekick) and the woman Theseus loves, Persephone (here the daughter of Pluto, god of the underworld). Theseus knows from the beginning that Hercules will say no, so he stows Persephone away on their ship. When Hercules explains later that the love between Theseus and Persephone is forbidden, Theseus grabs a sword and fights, an act of rebellion against the symbolic father that both understand is tantamount to suicide ("This is no duel, Theseus. You're only trying to kill yourself. You know very well that your love for Persephone has no future"). Once Persephone decides to renounce this impossible love, she places herself in an explicitly maternal relationship to Theseus, an Oedipal relationship that will then be forgotten: "Our love has run its course. Look at him: he's sleeping like a little innocent child. I've given him forgetfulness. And when he wakens, I will be gone." In a sign of the midcentury peplum's always incomplete Oedipal trajectory, however, Theseus will find a new woman at the end of the film, a young woman incredibly named Jocasta.

In *Hercules Unchained*, Ulysses seems initially well placed for a working through of the Oedipus complex: both original parental objects have been replaced with what are effectively images. As transitional objects, they manifest qualities that are typical of the parental figure they replace (severe authority on Hercules's part, comforting solicitude from Iole) while also retaining traces of a pre-Oedipal attachment: love and admiration for both, a desire both to be them and to have them. But even before their encounter with the blinded Oedipus in the cave, there is a sign that not all is well: Hercules leaves Ulysses and Iole to take a nap, and he initially refuses to get up when Antaeus attacks them. This is part of a long (classical) tradition of portraying Hercules as very much a figure of the body, strong, yes, but also lazy and gluttonous (many scenes of Hercules in the peplum feature him eating, and this was also true for Maciste in the silent-film cycle). Wasn't laziness precisely the crime for which Hercules deprived the sailors of access to women in *Hercules*? One is left with a nagging suspicion: What if all this talk about justice is simply a way for the strongman to get all the enjoyment for himself as Freud's primal father: all the women, all the food, all the sleep?

Such a fear has some foundation in *Hercules Unchained*. Hercules is magically drugged by the queen of Lydia, loses his memory, and becomes her lover. He also sprawls on couches, chases serving girls, gets massages, sleeps all day, and spends his few waking moments feasting—in short, he conforms to the image not of the symbolic primal father, but of what Žižek calls the "anal father," the father who is "ridiculously impotent" and who appears as a "nauseous debauchee" (2001, 127). Hercules is certainly ridiculous in these scenes. "The night is made for love!" he declaims, watching the serving girls preparing another meal with sleepy eyes. "This is living! Waking up with nothing to do and no worries!" he says while ogling the giggling girls and digging into the food. But is he also "impotent"? He certainly is, at least in the sense that he is no longer exceptionally strong. Ulysses hands him a cast-iron torchère to bend, and Hercules cannot do it.[10]

Here we have a problem that is as much theoretical as narrative. Without an effective paternal threat, there is no dissolution of the Oedipus complex: the boy could simply take the place of the father and actually enact the Oedipal fantasy. This fate would prevent the boy from proper immersion in a heterosexual matrix since he would not cathect to women (or better, images of women) who resemble the mother, but instead would remain cathected to the mother herself. For the remainder of this portion of the film, Ulysses labors mightily to restore Hercules to his position as the proper symbolic father of prohibition.[11] His activity is almost frenetic: sending messages by carrier pigeon to obtain help, disrupting Hercules's supply of magical water, breaking out of his cell, making a trick lock, exploring the palace, and learning the queen's wicked plot to turn Hercules into an eternally frozen mummy, all the while pretending to be mute. This kind of activity adds a valuable dimension to Freud's account, one that is not immediately obvious: heterosexual masculinity is difficult and fraught. In Freud's account, there is a visible struggle within the text between the absolute, pre-ordained inevitability of the destruction of the Oedipus complex and a repressed acknowledgment of the radical contingency of that dissolution, of the possibility that it might *not* happen. In this view, heterosexual masculinity looks not only difficult and fraught but also not, strictly speaking, entirely natural. This position, which Freud would like to represent as the only possible choice for men (and superior to any possible female position), turns out to require a great deal of energy, activity, social support (all the Argonauts, in fact), and props in order to maintain itself.

But maintain itself it does. The last time the homing pigeons appear is on board the *Argo*, summoned by Ulysses' earlier message. Hercules, restored to himself, and the rest of the company turn back toward Thebes to take care of the dire political situation in that city. Ulysses takes the last pigeon and sends off a message under the approving eyes of his father. "Your mother will be reassured this way," Laertes says, manfully clasping his son on the shoulder. "My mother? No, she's a brave woman, she won't worry. Penelope is another story!" Ulysses responds with yet another grin. The English-language version is even clearer: "Mother's so courageous, she won't be upset; I sent it for Penelope!" The putatively unformed adolescent male viewer is similarly expected to have worked through his original ambiguous attachment to the mother, first through the transitional object of Iole and eventually by sending his *uccello* in the proper direction—not to the mother or to a transitional object who might resemble the mother, but to his teenage girlfriend.

This fits the overall pattern in the peplum, already visibly articulated in Freud's account of the Oedipus complex, that heteronormativity will be presented after the fact as having been inevitable and natural; what is exceptional about the peplum is how frequently it admits that before the fact, it was not inevitable or particularly natural. A whole array of sexual identities and stances are paraded before the peplum audience: the sexually aggressive and active woman (Omphale, the queen of Lydia), the passive and sensual man (Hercules), the man who fails to dissolve his Oedipal complex (Oedipus), and the boy who admits same-sex attraction but turns first to transitional maternal figures and then to more conventional heterosexual attractions (Ulysses). After the fact, the heteronormative results will be naturalized and made inevitable: Omphale's suicide marks her path as unsustainable, even unbearable; Hercules behaved this way only because he was drugged; and Ulysses will have definitively relegated his same-sex attraction to the past. What becomes evident here is that a fixed sexual identity requires an enormous amount of work, including a long series of what Freud calls *schmerzhaften Enttäuschungen,* or "painful disappointments," as the boy's "natural" desires are stalemated again and again by this rather massive undertaking that produces heteronormativity—a transition that cannot openly acknowledge that it was not inevitable and smooth (Butler's "heterosexual melancholia" [1993, 234]). Film, however, deals as much with the unspoken as it does with the spoken, and it finds its own ways to mark what cannot be explicitly acknowledged. In the final shot of *Hercules Unchained,* for instance, one sees the reunited heterosexual couple, strangely unhappy and disconnected (Hercules has been unfaithful, and it is strongly implied that Iole has been raped by one of her captors). One cannot help but notice, in addition to this visible, if unspoken, melancholia, in the lower left corner, almost out of sight, the chain that binds these figures to their traditional symbolic positions, a regretful marker of a structural rigidity that cannot be openly acknowledged (figure 2.2).

Figure 2.2. A rigid norm, to which the couple appears bound by a chain. *Hercules Unchained,* 1959.

Post(-apocalyptic)

Let us take this pattern as typifying the midcentury peplums: The recognition of sexual difference and sexual desire is presented with surprising clarity and yet consistently deferred, blurred, and contested. Likewise, heterosexual desire is clearly shown to be difficult and contingent and yet is presented as inevitable after the fact. Although midcentury peplum films emerged from the conformist culture of the late 1950s, the end result is surprisingly queer in its most authentic sense of "uncategorizable": the psychic universe of the peplum knows that more clearly defined and oriented sexual universes await, but it prefers to remain in the "innocent" time of infantile sexuality, undefined and unstructured. Later iterations of the cinematic peplum, however, such as the barbarian films of the 1980s and the quite graphic peplums of the contemporary period, follow a pattern that at first glance appears very different: relentlessly heterosexual and at times offensively misogynist. The hero of the barbarian peplum conquers kingdoms and women with ease and is an old hand at both. The hero of the contemporary peplum has an even more stable heterosexual identity: he is married, settled, monogamous, and dedicated to his one true love (Maximus in *Gladiator,* Leonidas in *300,* Spartacus in *Spartacus: Blood and Sand,* and others). I will examine these cycles of the peplum in more detail later, but I can say at the outset that later peplums are no less queer in sexuality; in some ways, they are more so. If the Maciste films and the midcentury peplums (as well as, for the most part, the television peplums of the 1980s and 1990s) essentially featured muscle babies who lived in a universe steeped in sexual imagery but who were not yet sexually mature, a world before sexual difference, a surprising number of later peplums chronicle the opposite end of psychic life: an equally uncategorizable world after sexual desire. These films are easily assimilable to the "crisis of masculinity" model—Conan is no different from Rambo or John McClane or other heroes of the Reagan era whose exaggerated masculinity appeared to many as a kind of bluster or bravado indicative of a profound underlying anxiety. But while Rambo is a classic lone wolf who never has a clear romantic or marital attachment, and McClane spends most of the *Die Hard* movies separating from and getting back together with his wife, Conan's narrative in *Conan the Barbarian* is one of tragic and decisive loss. Where Maciste and the midcentury strongman are defined by their queer pre-sexual sexuality, there is an equally strange "after" attached to the protagonists of more recent cinematic peplum heroes.

The twenty or so peplum films of the 1980s share a number of common features. They begin with *Conan the Barbarian* and show a particular interest in the figure of the barbarian warrior. This is not exclusively because of the extraordinary influence of *Conan,* however; it is also because much popular cinema of the 1980s was generally fascinated by post-apocalyptic thinking, from *The Road Warrior* (1981) and *Escape from New York* (1981) to *Blade Runner* (1982), *The Day After* (1983), and *Night of the Comet* (1984). This was true in Italy as well, which produced numerous knock-offs that experimented with the scenarios from such films, such as Enzo Castellari's *I nuovi barbari* (released as *The New Barbarians* and now under the title *Warriors of the Wastelands,* 1982) and *1990: I guerrieri del Bronx* (*1990: The Bronx Warriors,* 1982) and Sergio Martino's *2019—Dopo la caduta di New York* (*2019: After the Fall of New York,* 1983).[12] Such movies generally (especially in their cheaper and more exploitive forms) depict the dissolution of the restraints of civilization, along with a rather cheap and adolescent pleasure at the bad, anti-social behavior that follows, such as theft, rape, murder, piracy, and wanton destruction. In detective fiction, Slavoj Žižek referred to this as the "real of desire"—the way detective fiction gratifies the anti-social violence felt by everyone (who hasn't wanted to kill someone?) but projects it onto a scapegoat, permitting readers or viewers to have their forbidden desire but escape the blame for it (1992, 48–66). In the barbarian and warrior movies of the 1980s, these anti-social and destructive acts are attributed to a horde (as in the *Mad Max* films) composed of sexually degenerate mutants who appear to have been coiffed and costumed by punk musicians with a penchant for S&M. The key to understanding these films, however, is that these are not the barbarians.

The barbarian is instead the hero, a man whose flowing locks tie him more closely to 1980s heavy-metal and hard-rock culture. Rather than part of the degenerate horde, he is invariably a loner, tied to the nascent neoliberalism of the Reagan/Thatcher years. The key to the ideological sleight of hand at work in these films is that the same apocalypse that destroyed the constraints of society (and killed the hero's wife and children) has also freed the hero for the life of unrestrained violence and vengeance that valorizes and affirms his masculinity. The post-apocalyptic film, in other words, is not about working through fears and anxieties; it is a wish-fulfillment fantasy. The barbarian is entirely a positive figure; his bare chest and long, undyed hair indicate that he is "natural," while the horde's dyed hair, tattoos, and masks are signs of their degenerate, corrupt, and politically rebellious punk culture. If the connection between Cold Warrior and road warrior is fairly straightforward, it is perhaps odd at first glance that the conservative ideology behind these films might attach itself to the figure of the barbarian. It did so, however, not only at the level of the film but also in political discourse. President George H. W. Bush proudly introduced Arnold Schwarzenegger as "Conan the Republican" at political events, and right-leaning audiences were pleased by the metaphoric substitution of "Republican" for "barbarian." It was part and parcel of the 1980s identification of virility with the Right, set against a left-leaning counterculture seen as sexually ambiguous and unmanly (this identification has different nuances in contemporary American culture today, but the Right continues to equate the Left with a failed form of masculinity). In both the post-apocalyptic world of Mad Max or "Snake" Plisskin and the ancient world of Conan or Gor, a man could finally be a real man, but only insofar as modern civilization had already been destroyed.

Where the midcentury peplum could simply assert masculinity as a given and as something whose essence was known (even if it was confined to a singular exemplar), masculinity in the 1980s peplum is strangely historicized. I say "strangely" because it can emerge only under certain conditions (the Hobbesian state of nature), conditions that have a certain temporality. Agamben has convincingly argued the Hobbesian state of nature is in fact a state of exception in which the political subject is reduced to "bare life" and can be killed with impunity—but crucially, for Agamben, this state of exception is not to be found in the past before the implementation of the law, but increasingly emerging in the future. The appearance of unrestrained violence in a lawless no-man's-land is not a regression "toward outdated forms," but rather, "premonitory events . . . announcing the new *nomos* of the earth" (1998, 38).

Even for Agamben, however, this temporality of the state of nature is something of a secret that has been concealed, always depicted and understood as belonging to the remote past; in the peplum, the viewer understands it as a time radically separated from the present, a time either before or after a rupture of some kind. Where *Hercules Unchained* depicts a lightly veiled version of 1950s sexuality in development, the barbarian peplums of the 1980s depict an impossibly ancient time that comes "before" (*Conan the Barbarian, Ator the Fighting Eagle* [1982], *Gunan, King of the Barbarians,* aka *The Invincible Barbarian* [1982], *Ironmaster* [1983], *Conquest* [1984]) or a time outside time in some alternate world (*Gor* [1988], *Outlaw of Gor* [1989]) and occasionally mixing past and future in a way that suggests that they are the same (*She* [1982], *Yor, the Hunter from the Future* [1983]).[13] *She* (an Italian sci-fi peplum directed by Israeli director Avi Nesher and starring largely Americans, including the midcentury peplum hero Gordon Mitchell), for example, begins with a series of images suggesting an apocalyptic destruction, perhaps a rain of fire, before showing us a primitive past. Titles inform the viewer that it is the year 23 "after the Cancellation." The great delight of the film is this constant, forced anachronism. Virtually every shot mixes the mythical past of the peplum and the ruined remnants of our present in the far future. The title character, She, engages in a sword fight with a Roman gladiator and a knight in chain mail, for instance, all against a backdrop of dented, rusty car parts and television sets with busted screens.

Yor, the Hunter from the Future, an Italian-Turkish peplum directed by Antonio Margheriti (who had also directed midcentury peplum films), takes the same idea but separates the two elements in order to create a revelatory twist for the viewer. The first half of the film appears to be a caveman exploitation film (hunky men in loincloths with stone axes kill dinosaurs and save former or future Playboy Playmates in leather bikinis), but eventually Yor's Stone Age world is revealed to be the result of a devastating nuclear apocalypse (robots wearing Darth Vader helmets, lasers, teleportation). What films like *Yor* and *She* demonstrate is that these two fantasies of the 1980s that appear rather far removed from each other (*Conan the Barbarian* and the *Mad Max* films, let us say), have in fact both correctly intuited Agamben's understanding of universal bare life akin to the state of nature as our future, a "new *nomos* of the earth, which ... will soon extend itself over the entire planet" (1998, 38). This fantasy about biopolitics is also, however, in a cinematic context, a fantasy about sex and gender: masculinity unchained.

That said, it is perhaps also a fantasy as defined by Žižek: "Fantasy is usually conceived as a scenario that realizes the subject's desire. This elementary definition is quite adequate, on condition that we take it literally: what the fantasy stages is not a scene in which our desire is fulfilled, fully satisfied, but on the contrary, a scene that realizes, stages, the desire as such" (1992, 6). Indeed, what marks these scenarios is the structural rupture that divides them from the world the viewer lives in. *Conan the Barbarian* begins by locating the "Hyborian Age" in which the action of Robert E. Howard's Conan novels were set: "Between the time when the oceans drank Atlantis and the rise of the sons of Aryas, there was an age undreamed of." The age of Conan, in other words, is set not simply in the remote past (Howard fans set the Hyborian Age at about 15,000–10,000 BC) but quite literally in the nontime after mythology but before history.[14]

An exemplary case here might be one of the texts that bridge the gap between the midcentury peplum and the 1980s barbarian peplum. As the midcentury peplum craze was ending, Jack Kirby immortalized Steve Reeves's portrayal of Hercules in a comic-book adaptation that began in 1965; the comic-book character still sports Reeves's trademark beard and chains today. In 1975, the character was used by Gerry Conway (writer) and José Luis García-López and Wally Wood (artists) in *Hercules Unbound* to fit into a post-apocalyptic scenario that Kirby was penning for DC Comics (*Kamandi*): in *Hercules Unbound* 1, Hercules had been imprisoned by Ares for centuries and awoke only after World War III and the nuclear devastation of Earth. Hercules immediately rescues a young man, Kevin, who will become his traveling companion for the remainder of his adventures; a busty blonde female model named Jennifer also joins their troupe in the second issue. It is evident that Kevin, the young man, skinny and wearing jeans, sneakers, and a UCLA t-shirt, is meant to stand for the typical (or perhaps ideal) reader of *Hercules Unbound;* like most comics of this era, every issue contained multiple advertisements for products that promised to increase the reader's height and muscularity, as well as expertise in martial arts. Kevin, just like Ulysses in *Hercules Unchained,* is positioned between the blonde beauty, who is both a mother figure and an object of desire, and Hercules, who is both a father figure and an object of desire that cannot be acknowledged as such. The marker of this fetishistic disavowal is that in *Hercules Unbound,* Kevin is blind but can "see" all the same: he shows both an unusual prescience and an actual visual perception that cognitive scientists today call "blindsight." To recall Benjamin's "optical unconscious" from chapter 1, what I called the "unseen seen," Kevin sees without knowing that he sees, and without conscious knowledge of his vision. In short, Kevin is the ideal spectator of the peplum's muscular male bodies since he looks at them, indeed, perceives them with an understanding and a depth that others cannot possess, but can simultaneously disavow his own gaze. The time of understanding his desire is perpetually deferred even as the time that he inhabits is defined by its posterity, its coming after the End.

Before the fracturing of mythical time and the emergence of historical time, and after the Apocalypse—both are revealed as the same impossible time in which "the real man" can appear. For the most part, barbarian peplums take an adolescent joy in the idea of an unfettered masculinity; most prefer to imagine their musclebound heroes living in lands populated primarily by fetching and willing women in chain-mail bikinis (the *Ator* films; *Gunan, King of the Barbarians; Ironmaster; The Sword of the Barbarians* [*Sangraal, la spada di fuoco,* 1983]). Others dispense with the necessity for the women to be willing. The *Gor* films are based on the John Norman novels that inspired an entire subculture in the real world based on sexual domination (by men) and submission (by women). Doubling the pleasure of this scenario, the hero of the Gor films is Tarl Cabot, a milquetoast professor who cannot work up the nerve to ask his pretty graduate student teaching assistant out for a date until he is magically transported to the world of Gor, where he learns how things are done in the "natural" world, free of civilized constraints.[15] Other films still are quite direct about the viewer's putative enjoyment of sequences of rape and sexual torture of women (the *Deathstalker* films, the two *Barbarian Queen* movies). These are decidedly adult films and depict men who live exaggerated and hyperbolic sexual lives.[16] Despite their apparent gratification of straight male fantasies (and we should remember Žižek's admonition that these fantasies actually stage the impossible divide between the putatively male viewer and his supposed fantasies), however, these films had little or no influence on the next four decades of peplum cinema.

After: More Birds

The film that did have a major influence was *Conan the Barbarian*. Although *Conan* is as sexually graphic as most of the other barbarian peplums of the 1980s, Conan's sexuality is handled quite differently. His origin as a subject is explicitly tied to a childhood trauma, the murder of his parents. Although the loss of his father is brutal (his father is axed in the back and then mauled by Rottweilers), it is also figured as an object of spectatorial desire. Conan and his mother, holding each other, watch these scenes unfold voyeuristically from hiding. The mother's death, however, is represented as essentially traumatic, as an event that one knows took place but cannot exactly recall (yet another unseen seen). We do not witness her being killed. The evil Thulsa Doom swings his sword, and the camera cuts to young Conan, holding his mother's hand. In a blur, her head tumbles past, and then her now headless body topples away in slow motion. Throughout, Conan simply stares uncomprehendingly at what is taking place and, most particularly, at the absence where his mother used to be, at the emptiness of his cupped hand (figure 2.3).[17] The moment of death, the actual decapitation, remains unseen.

For much of the film's first half, Conan is essentially treated as an animal. He is chained to a giant wheel (whose purpose is never clarified) along with other prisoners. In a variation of the training-montage sequence in numerous action films, we watch Conan transform into a youth, a young man, and finally the imposing, muscled bulk of Arnold Schwarzenegger (and we watch the other, weaker prisoners slowly disappear). One day, he is led away, completely ignorant and docile, and exhibited for money fighting against other musclemen in the pit. These sequences replicate the opposition I detailed earlier: the natural barbarian is understood in opposition to an artificial, sexually degenerate, S&M-inclined (and

Figure 2.3. The loss of the mother. *Conan the Barbarian*, 1982.

often racially other) horde, such as Conan's first opponent, who features the requisite face mask, dog collar, and leather straps, plus optional sharpened teeth.

Conan himself is treated as little more than a performing animal; he is kept nearby, on display, brought out from time to time to show how clever or strong he is. This public exploitation of the male body for a spectator's pleasure (and inevitably, we are those spectators) even becomes, according to the film's narrator, fully internalized, giving the developing Conan a "sense of worth." Conan exults in his victories and in the applause of the spectators and, by extension, the viewers of the film, who also wish to see Schwarzenegger's body and physical prowess on display. At the same time, the idea that the display of his body gives Conan a sense of worth suggests that he did not have one before, that it marks him as psychically wounded or deficient; indeed, this desire for approval must be seen as a compensation for Conan's traumatic loss of his mother. Does Conan represent an exemplary masculine subject or an exceptional one? Does his exceptional status lie more in his extraordinary physique or in his wounded interior, yearning for approval?

In *On the Genealogy of Morals*, Friedrich Nietzsche (1989) locates a moment in the evolution of morality in which the human, for the first time, becomes "an interesting animal" (33), and it is the moment in which the priestly caste becomes attached to the idea of nothingness. Abstinence, loss, fasting, a self-obliterating union with the divine—all these are the creative ways in which the members of the priestly caste, physically weak, were able to transform their proximity to death and illness into a positive value, something that one should strive for (the meek shall inherit the earth). More generally, this transformation of values is a manifestation of *ressentiment*, the creative turn away from great and heroic deeds (the natural response of the strong) and toward an imaginary revenge. The soul of the strong man of deeds, Nietzsche argues, is flat, simple, unreflective, and even boring. One might consider here the Hercules, Goliath, or Maciste of the midcentury peplum whose interior life is identical to his exterior life: grinning and flexing, fundamentally stupid. For Nietzsche, this existence has its attractions—strength, health, and vitality—but is essentially a dead end. In order to develop, the soul of the strongman needs to acquire depth by meeting some kind of frustrating blockage that is insurmountable and provokes *ressentiment*. Before Freud, Nietzsche imagines the psyche in a pneumatic sense, as a balloon that needs to be inflated in order to make the necessary space for that imaginary revenge. (*Conan*, in fact, opens with a citation from Nietzsche, a paraphrase of the famous "What does not kill me makes me stronger" from *Twilight of the Idols* [2003, 33].)

One immediately senses a contradiction here. How can one argue that Conan, especially as played by Arnold Schwarzenegger, is a man of *ressentiment* and not of epic and great deeds? Isn't he precisely the Teutonic "blond beast," the image that Nietzsche used to exemplify the unreflective "bird of prey" who inspired the priest's impotent, imaginary revenge in the first place? Yet *ressentiment* is indeed the emotional core of *Conan* and of the most successful later action films set in the mythological and classical worlds (*300, Spartacus: Blood and Sand, Gladiator*). For most of the film, Conan is essentially an unreflective child; he lives in the moment, and all his daring exploits are done simply in order to see what rules he can get away with breaking. This is true, however, only up to the moment at which Thulsa Doom kills his true love, Valeria, a clear traumatic repetition of the original loss of his mother. It is here, essentially, that Conan becomes Conan, becomes an interesting animal. He can and does avenge her death, beheading Thulsa Doom just as Doom once beheaded Conan's mother, but he cannot bring Valeria or his mother back to life. What was a loss has become a structural feature of Conan's identity, a process that LaCapra calls the conversion of loss into lack, "a felt need or deficiency, something that ought to be there but is missing" (1999, 703). Crucially for my argument here, LaCapra also correlates the two categories with temporality: "As loss is to the past, so lack is to the present and future" (703). This is what gives lack, unlike loss, its apparently permanent and structural character. No deed will ever recuperate Conan's plenitude of life with Valeria, and so it is here that Conan begins his endless wars of conquest and empire building, leading to the solitary, miserable figure we see on the throne at the end of the film. This more interesting animal is the essence of the strongman in later peplums, particularly those of the contemporary period. Conan is always positioned belatedly, after his mother, after the loss of Valeria, a man who may achieve anything and everything, but always melodramatically "too late." His emotional, sexual, and psychic lives appear to be forever after, determined entirely by the objects that were lost in the past. In this regard, of course, he is simply the essence of the psychoanalytic subject. The temporalizing of the strongman's life is visible at the most superficial level: unlike virtually all previous peplum heroes (Maciste, Hercules, Samson), Conan has a childhood, a backstory.

This development of a real psychic life of the peplum once again finds a direct parallel in one of the other fields that this book examines, namely, the haptic. Critics like Laura Marks and Jennifer Barker have emphasized the importance of the register of touch in cinema, the surfaces of people, objects, and even the film itself. Barker and Marks both attend specifically to the notion of skin, and in chapter 3, I discuss the immense importance of skin in the peplum. There, too, we find a significant shift in how the strongman's skin is handled beginning in the 1980s. In the midcentury peplum, the protagonist's perfectly tanned, hairless, and oiled skin may be scratched, but it is never pierced; he is, in short, invulnerable in its etymological sense "impossible to wound." From the perspective of Nietzschean psychology, this makes perfect sense. The psyche is without depth, volume, or interiority; there is no "inside" that one could get to, because the hero is all surface, all skin. Beginning in the 1980s, the strongman becomes vulnerable and, indeed, more and more so as time goes on; his skin is still hairless, tanned, and healthy, but it is also certain to be cut, penetrated, stabbed, or tortured. All these external wounds are a way to show on the surface what is happening on the inside, the gradual buildup of an internal pressure from the unavenged wrongs of the past, a pressure that inflates and creates the pneumatic Freudian psyche.

Beginning with Conan, the peplum hero is likely to be the last of his kind: the last Cimmerian (*Conan*), the last Akkadian (*The Scorpion King*), the last of his tribe (the television series *BeastMaster*). Unavenged and foundational traumas that the subject can never recover from proliferate. In some modern peplums (*Conan, Immortals*), the parent is murdered in front of the child; the 2001 *Amazons and Gladiators* offers a gender-switched version of Conan but also steals verbatim the "big reveal" of Sergio Leone's *Once upon a Time in the West* (1968), the traumatic memory of the death of the parent. In others, the traumatic, irrecuperable loss is the murder of the protagonist's wife or child, or both, either directly in front of him (*Spartacus: Blood and Sand, Hercules: The Legendary Journeys*) or at some remove (*Gladiator*). These unavenged wrongs provoke the strongman to action, but the deaths of his wife and family, along with the loss of his people and his clan, remove any prospect of meaningful futurity from his actions. He might, of course, fight to "save the people," as peplum heroes have done since the silent period, or even save the world. This is true of Theseus in *Immortals* and Mathayus in *The Scorpion King*. It is even more true of King Leonidas in *300*, who fights to save not only an abstract Western world of freedom and a more concrete home city of Sparta but also a wife and a son and heir. How is this not safeguarding a futurity, albeit not a personal one? Although it is certainly clear that the hero of the contemporary peplum is focused along an essentially suicidal dimension, his self-sacrifice represents not merely his own personal end but also, whether he saves them or not, the end of an era, an epoch, a people—antiquity as such, with its freedom for masculinity to flourish outside civilized constraints. There is a future for the weak, for the women and children, but no future for the true men of the peplum world.

With few exceptions, then, the modern peplum hero is located as much after sexuality as his predecessor was located before it. Characters such as Spartacus (*Spartacus: Blood and Sand*) and Hercules (*The Legendary Journeys*) are typical of the Conan model: their masculine greatness is predicated on the loss of their beloved women and their families and their concomitant solitary suffering. In *The Legendary Journeys*, Hercules wanders from location to location; in each, he saves a beautiful maiden who is filled with gratitude and love, and she offers herself to him. In each case, he smiles kindly and perhaps a bit regretfully and politely declines. But the series does offer a crucial break with the older peplum: Hercules does not avoid the woman because he does not know what to do with her, or even because he is uninterested—he avoids her because he is past that now.

The series begins with the cruel killing of Hercules's wife and children. In later peplums, this will be exploited to give the protagonist a monstrous and endless well of grief and resentment that will direct him on his suicidal quest to oppose the cruel authority figure responsible for taking away what is his. But in *Hercules: The Legendary Journeys*, it only briefly troubles our hero's emotional equanimity. More important, it maintains him as heterosexual while placing him after sexuality. Hercules, in a sense, is immunized against sexuality. This metaphor is not simply a casual way for me to work in Esposito's biopolitical theory but is quite purposeful: the show repeats the gesture of inoculation halfway through its run. In a series of three episodes in the middle of the third season, Hercules meets a beautiful young maiden, falls in love, and marries her (the actress, Sam Jenkins, would in fact become Kevin Sorbo's real-life wife). They enjoy approximately twenty minutes of wedded bliss together before the god Strife murders her in her sleep, providing a kind of booster shot of post-sexual immunity to Hercules, who then resumes wandering through ancient myth, saving grateful maidens, whom he refuses. In the series' final episode ("Full Circle"), he briefly debates retirement and settling down but concludes that only endless wandering with his male companion, Iolaus, befits him. They gradually disappear from view as they wander off into a desert that is as literal as it is metaphorical.

BeastMaster was the last of the television peplums, running from 1999 to 2002, and it exaggerated and exacerbated the same tensions already visible in *Hercules: The Legendary Journeys*. Of all the television peplums, *BeastMaster* features the most explicitly eroticized male object in Dar, played by Daniel Goddard, a former Calvin Klein underwear model (the body) and Dolce and Gabbana sunglasses model (the face). Dar rarely wears more than a loincloth and a leather strap or two, making sure that his body is always displayed to maximum effect. As in *Legendary Journeys,* Dar travels from place to place, saving oppressed peoples (and animals) and rescuing grateful damsels in distress. Throughout the first season, however, he remains faithful to his kidnapped beloved, Kyra, who eventually dies to save him. In the show's remaining two seasons, Dar remains generally aloof, forestalling romantic and sexual interests in favor of saving his animal friends or human companions and, in particular, continuing his long-term quest to defeat Balcifer, the Dark One, and free at long last his remaining family from the Crystal Ark. Like Hercules, he generally smiles wistfully and regretfully before turning his sculpted body away from the latest lady to lose her heart to him (see, for instance, the aptly titled episode "Mate for Life," originally aired on February 17, 2001). The series concludes with Balcifer's defeat and the liberation of Dar's family, but this does not free Dar to return to any of those former possible love interests: his mystical destiny lies in what is clearly the afterworld, a heavenly city devoid of any visible human presence. Dar bids his companions farewell and leaves the world of earthly desire behind, accompanied only by his animals.

Theseus in the 2011 peplum *Immortals* may fall in love, have sex, and even father a child, but his essential worth will emerge only in his eternal afterlife. His masculine value, in other words, is tantamount to his self-sacrifice; his life becomes meaningful (heroic, truly manly) only in the moment in which he regretfully concludes that he cannot give in to the temptation of staying with his beautiful lover. The heroic story, in other words, is what happens after they have sex and he leaves her and all other women behind. King Leonidas, too, must likewise regretfully set aside his love for his wife and son to embrace an obviously suicidal task. In his case, the battle against the god-emperor Xerxes is guaranteed not only to kill him but also to fail. Theseus manages to kill Hyperion at the cost of his own life, but Leonidas holds no such hope. He aims only to delay. Such films appear to fall into a fairly familiar discourse about the sacrifice of the soldier who stays behind to hold the bridge, but *Immortals* and *300* are actually rather different. Usually in war films, it is the soldier with no future who elects to stay behind, frequently whichever member of the team has appeared cowardly until the moment of redeeming sacrifice. In a telling sequence in the military sci-fi film *Aliens* (1986), it is the inexperienced, incompetent, and elitist Lieutenant Gorman and the butch Private Vasquez who remain behind in an air duct and blow themselves up with a hand grenade in order to briefly delay the relentless alien advance.[18] As the aliens close in on them, Gorman wraps his arms around the injured Vasquez, and they hold hands atop the primed grenade just before it goes off—an embrace without a future in every possible way. Gorman's self-sacrifice, in particular, is typical of the war film; he has been officious, incompetent, and cowardly, but his sacrifice is all the more noble for that. On the contrary, what is curious about the contemporary peplum is that it is the truest, most courageous, most tested, least troublesome exemplar of masculinity who must sacrifice himself, the man with a family and a burgeoning future.

I am specifically suggesting that there is something queer in the psychic temporality of the contemporary peplum, particularly in its deliberate withdrawal from futurity. In *No Future*, Lee Edelman (2004) provocatively argues against reproductive futurism, which he claims has been the grounding notion for virtually all political and ethical thinking until now—we must preserve the world for our children (the words "we" and "our" including, whether they like it or not, all those who do not have children). Edelman's book became a contested site within queer studies (Muñoz's *Cruising Utopia* [2009], for example, argued for a future-oriented, utopian conception of "queer"), but even without entering into that debate, we must still acknowledge that there is something quite odd about the embrace of the death drive that characterizes a character like Spartacus in *Blood and Sand*. He lives only in order to kill and, ultimately, to die, and, more important, it is precisely this exclusive focus on death that marks him for the viewer as an exemplary masculine subject. Even when we find a comparably gentle character like Dar, in *BeastMaster*, who refuses to kill and is dedicated to preserving all life, both animal and human, there is something strange about his blank refusal to pursue a life of his own and his endless pursuit of his quest, even when it leads him out of this life forever.

Edelman argues, using Lacanian terminology, that "queerness is a matter of *embodying* a remainder of the Real" and that "one name for this unnameable remainder is jouissance" (2004, 25). The Lacanian Real is a complex idea, but essentially it is what one cannot speak in language, what remains outside symbolization. It therefore contains not only the mute facticity of the world (the lowercase real) but also things like terrible traumatic events, the traumatic and "unspeakable" dimension of sexuality, and, of course, everything in the unconscious (the uppercase Real). That would include the death drive, which Freud had postulated ran unconsciously alongside the drive to live: subjects wanted to live, but they also wanted to die, even if they would not normally admit it, and that desire manifested itself in compulsive and repetitive stagings of traumatic events. For several generations, Lacanian critics connected the Real to *jouissance*, the painful pleasure of sexual climax, as a kind of marker of the way the Real transcended the ability to speak about it, in Burke's (1998) sense of the sublime: what provokes a speechless, terrified awe in the subject, not only when it confronts the divine, but also when it confronts its own self-destructive impulses, the void within. One of the most significant contributions of Slavoj Žižek, however, was to insist on translating the word *jouissance* in the most banal way possible: enjoyment. When Žižek was attacked by other Lacanians who derided this word because it appeared in commercial slogans like "Enjoy Coke!," he insisted that this was precisely how *jouissance* and the Real should be understood (2001, vii). For Žižek, the "enjoyment" of

Coca-Cola also had something repetitive and self-destructive about it, and capitalism in general could be understood as subjects repeatedly circulating around empty signifiers that gave no satisfaction; there was, in our consumption of empty products and our attachment to empty popular culture, something pathological, compulsive, and self-destructive. Žižek's second surprising move, however, was to suggest that the most effective strategy to combat this transaction was to fully embrace our enjoyment in its radical dimension. In his own work, this often consisted of analyzing popular culture so as to render visible its traumatic, even suicidal, dimension.[19]

For Edelman, too, an analysis of popular culture shows that it is at its most seductive when it embraces its death drive, when it orients us toward a queerly traumatic absence of a future. His account of Hitchcock's *The Birds* (1963) indicates the way in which the film resists a clear sense or meaning: *The Birds*, Edelman argues, is "a threat . . . to the narrative teleology of the subject" (2004, 133)— the implicit promise that our present existence is directed toward a meaningful future. Edelman's brilliant reading, working through almost every avian figure of speech in the English language, connects the birds of *The Birds* to homosexuality in all kinds of ways (their unpredictable emergence from San Francisco, their apparent targeting of children, the film's concern with Mitch's sexuality) but ultimately concludes that "it is not . . . that the birds themselves *mean* homosexuality, but that homosexuality inflects how they figure the radical refusal of meaning. Whatever voids the promissory note, the guarantee, of futurity . . . must be tarred, and in this case, feathered, by the brush that will always color it queer in a culture that places on queerness the negativizing burden of sexuality" (149). In short, because our culture has until recently made the homosexual "bear the burden of lack" (no marriage, no family, no future), every intimation that the future might be void, every suggestion that the present does not necessarily imply a future, is essentially queer insofar as it (potentially) opts out of reproductive futurism.

Does this happen in the contemporary peplum? Certain features that are typical of the genre suggest that it does. In the clearest case, *Blood and Sand*, Spartacus loses his wife and the promise of a possible future with her and loses a lover and the possibility of a future with her. He fathers a child with a woman whom he loathes, Ilithyia, but we eventually watch the deranged Lucretia, who was perpetually denied the possibility of reproduction, seize Spartacus's newly born son from its mother, clutch it to her breast, and topple in slow motion (see chapter 1 on slow time in the peplum as another expression of the death drive) backward over a cliff. Even when the protagonist reproduces (*300*, *Immortals*), the future that he may have secured for his child appears enfeebled, enervated, and even castrated.

It is really the peplum's ruptured and melodramatic temporality, before or after the Event, that marks its essentially queer aspect: the time of true men is already over, or, if it is in the future, it will be paradoxically after the End. Even in those peplums in which the hero's self-sacrifice is explicitly performed in the name of reproductive futurism, such as *Immortals* or *300,* the time of true masculinity can be found only after the renunciation of women and heterosexual reproduction. In the television series *BeastMaster,* Dar, from the first episode, is always accompanied by certain animal companions, particularly Sharak, a trusty falcon. Their rapport is so close, in fact, that Dar can see through Sharak's eyes, which provide him an aerial view. Eventually, however, the viewer and Dar both discover that Sharak was once a man; he reassumes his human form and explains that he became an animal and Dar's companion as the only way to recover from the loss of his beloved. "She was my life. Without you and Tao [Dar's human sidekick], I could not endure her fate." Once again, we find the male heroes located after a loss, indeed, after a renunciation. Dar and Sharak's companionship and partnership are founded on their shared "posterity," the fact that they come after heterosexual desire (Dar, as always, rebuffs the overtures that the two female characters in the episode make to him). Their lack of future, as Edelman would say, does not "*mean* homosexuality," but it is informed by it. Can it be an accident— Edelman would say it could not—that this all takes place in an episode titled "Birds" that is explicitly modeled on Hitchcock's film? (Or that this chapter begins with homing pigeons who need help to find the proper erotic object for their affection and closes with Dar's avian friend who finds solace only in their mutual muscular adventures?)

BeastMaster was obsessed with the future—the intrusion of technology into the natural world, climate change, loss of habitat and biodiversity—precisely because there was no future for its characters: no family left, no new family to be formed, no children. The show was (unwittingly) a melodramatic tragedy since the future of this world of "nature and magic" is never in doubt for the modern viewer: species will die out, the world will be technologized, and nature will be contaminated with pollutants. Insofar as Dar's world has no future, it is, as Edelman argues, already queer. Even in the most hopeful contemporary peplums, one must doubt the future. In *Wrath of the Titans* (2012), we learn that the happy heterosexual romance that concluded the previous film actually ended tragically with the death of Perseus's wife. *Wrath* ends with yet another elegy to the time of the greats, now over: Perseus hands his sword to the next generation, and the dying Zeus laments to him, echoing Conan's "There will be no spring for us," that "there will be no more sacrifices, no more gods." All these worlds are worlds without a future.

In the silent period of Maciste and in the midcentury peplum, the time of true masculinity was an innocent period before the recognition of sexual difference, and even some later peplums are set in this undifferentiated psychic universe. Men and women alike wear much the same costumes and have big chests and shapely legs, and the films aim to defer any definitive sexual orientation until their ending with their perfunctory and essentially sexless final kiss. The suggestion in almost all midcentury peplums, like the silent Maciste films, is that the next film will find our hero still single, still a de-sexualized man-boy, and still grinning and flexing his muscles—an impression intensified in the peplum television series, with their episodic, always-the-same serial narratives. Starting with *Conan*, the peplum film becomes sexually explicit but almost immediately locates the protagonist in a time after sexuality; indeed, this temporality is increasingly the slow motion and still time of death, strangely (queerly) identified as the true time of masculinity. His future is barren, meaningless (*Conan*), or explicitly located along a suicidal dimension (*Spartacus: Blood and Sand, 300, Immortals*). Although the people and the world may be saved, the hero consumes not only himself in his sacrifice but also the last true masculinity—everyone after him will be a lesser man. This is what gives these films and series not only their melancholy but also their melodramatic note. The viewer has arrived, in Linda Williams's (1991) memorable formulation about melodrama, "too late" for real heroism.

In both instances, the temporal rupture between the psychic time of the viewer and the time of the film insulates the viewer against the central problem with which this chapter opened: how to look at the exposed, muscular male body. Clearly, this provides a certain quantum of pleasure for both male and female spectators, regardless of sexual orientation (or lack thereof). These are bodies that have been carefully cultivated to provoke wonder, admiration, and amazement in the viewer, in any viewer, whether it is the spectacular definition and bulk of Arnold Schwarzenegger as Conan or the perfectly toned and idealized six-pack abdominal muscles of Daniel Goddard as Dar in *BeastMaster*. As Mulvey suggested in "Visual Pleasure" (1987), the problem is how to maintain the visual pleasure of looking at idealized, athletic male bodies without provoking concomitant anxieties in the largely male audience of the peplum—for example, the anxiety about men being placed, however temporarily, in the passive position of those meant to be looked at.

Figure 2.4, from *BeastMaster* ("The Demon Curupira," 1999), shows one attempt to assuage this incipient anxiety, although one that has the potential to create at least as much anxiety as it relieves. A surrogate female viewer within the diegesis displaces the (putatively male) viewer's admiring gaze while providing eye candy that can deflect any concerns about what the straight male viewer is looking at. "I didn't want to look at Daniel Goddard's amazing abs; I just watch it for the hot girls." But everything about the composition of the shot makes it impossible to look at anything but Goddard's body. The dominant codes of who looks and who gets looked at have changed remarkably little since Mulvey (1987) discussed the notion of a "male gaze": the scenario of looking at the girl who is

Figure 2.4. Dar as spectacle, arousing admiration in the spectator. *BeastMaster,* 1999.

looking at the guy still leaves behind a queer remainder when all the gazes have been subtracted. Indeed, the contemporary peplum has embraced that queer residue as a site of productive tension. *Spartacus: Blood and Sand* in particular showcases its muscular heroes as objects of everyone's gaze within the diegesis: the gladiators are gazed at by leering men and leering women, straight, gay, and bisexual. At a word from their *lanista* (owner and trainer), they might have to fight to the death to gratify an adolescent boy's whim or drop their loincloths to allow their genitals to be inspected by curious Romans, women and men both.

It is clear in the midcentury peplum that the viewer's pleasure is protected by a fundamentally fetishistic scenario: "I know very well that I came to the theater to look at Steve Reeves's magnificent body, but all the same, I will explicitly claim that I came here because I identify with him." I do not, of course, mean to assert that all viewers thought this way or had this particular psychic relationship to what they saw on screen, but rather that the midcentury peplum is characterized by formal structures that facilitate precisely this kind of fetishistic disavowal, particularly its depiction of a universe that is both intensely eroticized and presented as pre-sexual. What protects the putatively male viewer from a similar anxiety in the contemporary peplum, with its much more explicit content that can even include same-sex love affairs, is precisely the same temporal disjunction, but now in the opposite direction. It does not matter who is looking at Dar or at Spartacus. They are past the question of sexuality. Instead, their whole being is turned toward their inner wound, their tragic loss, the woman they will never have again. The peplum universe is steeped in a surface eroticism (leather loincloths and bikinis, codpieces and capes, and the oiled and hairless skin that is the topic of chapter 3), but rather than Linda Williams's temporality of pornography ("right on time"), we find a melodramatic masculinity that is always too late for love.

Notes

1. I ordinarily use the *Standard Edition*'s translations of Freud's works throughout (although I occasionally note the German original), but this is my translation: the *Standard Edition* "corrects" Freud's dreamy style, which leaves out some verbs in the original ("a hill, something on top") and places the rest in the present tense.

2. I recognize that there is a certain quantum of self-aware irony in both gestures. In the case of Austen, the irony is situational. Today's modern young woman may or may not feel a longing for a lost world of chivalry and clear gender codes (particularly as embodied by the wealthy and assertive Mr. Darcy) but takes a certain satisfaction in being like Lizzy Bennet in character, but not in occupying the same constrained social position she occupies. In the case of *Spartacus*, much the same situational irony may apply: I may not live in an age when men were real men, but I am also not a slave forced to fight to the death. Straight men watching *Spartacus* may also be showing a kind of ironic bravado in the face of the constant display of the male body in homoerotic scenarios, not unlike locker-room hazing. Not coincidentally, viewings of *Spartacus* are also frequently used as the occasion for drinking games to foster social bonding.

3. In the section that follows, I discuss principally midcentury peplum films in which the sidekick is an adolescent or young man; several midcentury peplums included young boys, children, who accompanied the strongman, gazing at him with love and admiration. This is relatively rare, however, probably because of the peplum's unspoken erotic content. That quantum of eros was generally defused by presenting the child as the strongman's younger brother (as in *The Vengeance of Ursus*) or related through marriage (*Goliath and the Vampires*).

4. The 1956 Winter Games in Cortina d'Ampezzo were the first Olympic Games widely televised outside the host country, and the 1960 Summer Games were held in Rome.

5. Indeed, peplum material was sometimes recycled as gay erotica, one of the many ways in which classicism was used to legitimate homoerotic imagery. Wyke (1997a) notes that classicism was widely invoked in gay subculture magazines as an alibi for homoerotic images such as "Spartan warriors at the baths." She gives numerous clear examples of how peplum films were recycled in specifically gay contexts, as when a 1959 issue of *American Apollo* included photos of Steve Reeves as Hercules, or a peplum film (Ducio Tessari's 1962 *My Son, the Hero* [*Arrivano i titani*]) was included in one of the earliest gay film festivals in the United States (66–67).

6. For a more detailed version of this argument, see Rushing (2008).

7. The film's reference to the Homeric epic ("Your destiny will be decided by an arrow") is an example of the oversaturation of the peplum film with classical culture and mythology that is typical of even such lowbrow Italian productions. The reference to *The Odyssey* is never explained to the viewer, who is expected to recognize this glancing allusion, and Ulysses shoots no such arrow in the film because he remains a young man, not yet the mature hero of *The Odyssey*. These references would have been obvious even to Italian high school audiences in the

1950s, although a teen and pre-teen US audience might have found them more obscure. Peplum films are not at all concerned with fidelity to their classical sources (see Solomon 2001), but they often show a great deal of erudition and familiarity with these sources. Carlo Ludovico Bragaglia directed the ludicrous and campy *Hercules vs. the Hydra* (*Gli amori di Ercole*, 1960, also known in English as *The Loves of Hercules*) with Jayne Mansfield and her bodybuilder husband, Mickey Hargitay (1960), which shows almost no literary fidelity, but Bragaglia came from a wealthy noble family, had a rigorous classical education, and knew quite well the myths he was mangling. This is still true today: *Spartacus: Blood and Sand,* for example, displays a painstaking attention to detail and history (the inclusion of the historical figure Oenomaus, for example), which is then warped almost beyond recognition (now Numidian, not Gaul, and an instructor at the *ludus* [gladiatorial school]).

8. If ever a subject was worthy of a long footnote, it is surely Freud, who turned the long footnote into something of an art form. Essentially, I am suggesting that we read Freud in a strictly Freudian fashion, attending to the excess of his rhetoric as a defensive strategy. Particularly important in this account is his "at once" (*sofort*) in "what at once occurred to me in the analysis" (1953–1974c, 5:469), a demand for immediacy that is a testament to the mediation of the unconscious, just as his excessive rhetorical insistence that the Oedipus complex is absolutely fated to pass away indicates that it might remain (see the discussion later in this chapter). If one examines the entire dream and analysis (5:468–471), one finds an abundance of overlooked libidinal content, including the "true exciting cause of the dream" (5:469): an adoring male student who followed Freud from his lecture, "begged leave to sit by me" in a café, and "began to flatter me" (5:470), a flattery that included a comparison of Freud to Hercules. Freud experiences disgust at this scene, precisely the affect that is surprisingly missing from his dream (both times it is the same word, *Ekel*); he leaves in order "to escape from" the student (5:470) and goes home to read Conrad Ferdinand Meyer's "Die Leiden eines Knaben," the story of a beautiful but mildly retarded young man known as "le bel idiot" (the beautiful idiot). Freud's hostility toward his student (*le bel idiot*) and disgust at these scenes of homoerotic desire can be disavowed by a simple affirmation of Herculean identity rather than Herculean desire: "Dieser Herkules bin ich" (I am this Hercules). Hercules is clearly the figure that allows for a surreptitious identification of homoerotic desire (he is beautiful), as well as its denial (I was disgusted, I had to escape). For a quite different but compelling reading of the dream as connected to Oedipal conflict between fathers and sons, see Weineck 2014, 24–26.

9. In this discussion, I rely on the dialogue of the Italian version of *Hercules Unchained,* which contains some scenes that are omitted from the English-language version.

10. This entire sequence may also be understood as class discipline: a warning to the working class that indolence and laziness are unmanly.

11. D'Amelio (2014, 266–267) very smartly applies Buchanan's (2008) account of "paternalistic" depictions of Italians in American films of the 1940s to the peplum in which the American bodybuilder appears as a massive and imposing father figure to the small, moody sidekick, who is generally played by an Italian (this might also explain why Italian bodybuilders in the peplum generally adopted American pseudonyms, such as "Alan Steel" for Sergio Ciani). D'Amelio's larger point is that the peplum hero's muscled body was also a "transatlantic" body in an already globalized form of transnational cinema.

12. In fact, such films are still being made in Italy today, such as the 2014 film *2047—Sights of Death* (Capone), whose title directly recalls those 1980s post-apocalyptic films by Castellari and others.

13. There was at least one midcentury peplum set in the Stone Age, the unimaginably dreadful *Fire Monsters against the Son of Hercules* (1962).

14. Already in 1963, Vittorio Spinazzola understood the midcentury peplum as a "sort of backwards [à rebours] Italian science-fiction" (98) that can be earlier or later but never now.

15. The author of the Gor novels, John Lange, who writes under the pen name John Norman, is still on the faculty of the philosophy department at Queens College, City University of New York.

16. As we will see, there are a few exceptions here: *The Barbarians* (1987) maintains a very midcentury "queer chasteness," for instance, and Lucio Fulci's *Conquest* (1984) features a young protagonist who apparently dies a virgin (the film is replete with graphic sexuality, however, and the film's strongman has no trouble making sexual conquests).

17. Although I disagree with much of what she says, see Falkof on *Conan* as an essentially post-Oedipal narrative (2013, 131–133) that uses an ostensible concern with avenging the father to mask the vastly more important loss of the mother. To my mind, Falkof, like Ipsen (2012), hugely overvalues the subversive potential of Valeria as a "strong female character," but Falkof's article is much more nuanced, and her suggestions about race—"I am not suggesting that Conan is somehow not white. Rather, within the *mise-en-scène* of *Conan the Barbarian*, no one is white" (139)—are quite interesting.

18. Although it is never stated in the film, virtually every commentator on the film has assumed that Vasquez is a "butch" lesbian (see Schubart 2007, 179–180, or Berenstein 1990, 62, where she refers to Vasquez's "stereotypical lesbian construction") or in some other way "sterile" (see Jeffords's Greimasian diagram, 1987, 76).

19. To be sure, Edelman also distinguishes these two "flavors" of *jouissance* (2004, 25). On the one hand, there is the fetishistic attachment to a particular repetitive thing that provides identity but not satisfaction (what Žižek calls enjoyment), which can range from the trivial (reading detective novels) to the graver (smoking, anorexia or bulimia, cutting). On the other, there is the radical and sublime self-destructive impulse that such fetishistic attachments can reveal, one that tends to disrupt any purported identity or grounding they might give the subject (what other Lacanians call *jouissance*). Both Žižek and Edelman are interested in the radical political gesture of embracing enjoyment/*jouissance*, but the two different flavors of it would appear to also generate rather different radical politics; Edelman's would certainly appear to be the more radical, and it is this form of radicalness that I want to suggest is at work in the contemporary peplum.

3 SKIN FLICKS
The Haptic Peplum

Increscunt animi, virescit vulnere virtus.
[The spirits swell, manliness flourishes through a wound.]
—Nietzsche's motto (attributed to Furius Antias)

The Haptic

The term "haptic" means "related to the sense of touch"; etymologically, it means "graspable" or "palpable," but in recent years it has acquired a specialized meaning, first in art history and then in cinema studies. This specialized use refers to the ability of visual art to produce a tactile response in the viewer or, more generally, the ability of visual imagery to activate senses other than sight. Film often uses slow, lingering pans across surfaces to reveal their tactile quality, from rumpled silk sheets after an erotic tryst to the hot, viscous goo dripping down the walls in the movies of the *Alien* franchise. If such images evoke a kind of tactile curiosity in the viewer, other images provoke an actual impression: we can readily (sometimes all too readily) imagine the tactile sensations produced, from the hypodermic needle in the chest in *Pulp Fiction* (1994) to the infamous razor blade slicing the surface of an eye in *Un chien andalou* (1929). In works such as Laura Marks's *The Skin of the Film* (2000) and Jennifer Barker's *The Tactile Eye* (2009), an attention to film's tactile capacity has also been part of a phenomenological analysis that stresses the proximity and intimacy of the viewer and the film and the breakdown of separate and separable positions as subject and object—ultimately, we are not just touched by movies in an exclusively emotional sense, but we also touch them and are touched by them in a more corporeal way (if not through actual physical contact).[1] For Marks and Barker, the haptic evokes a wide variety of different but interrelated phenomena.

Marks is particularly attentive to a quite different kind of haptic image: the film itself has a surface, and that surface may also call attention to itself, deliberately or inadvertently.[2] A decade ago, I attended a screening of Hitchcock's *Rear Window* (1954) at one of the art theaters in Champaign and was dismayed to see that the copy was worn, with numerous visible defects and scratches on the print.

After the digital revolution, however, I understood that surface deterioration as a sign of authenticity: I was watching actual celluloid, an old copy. I was perceiving the film, precisely as Marks suggests, as a skin, a surface whose texture was producing feelings in me (disappointment first, then a kind of auratic pleasure). In a theater in Paris a few years later, by contrast, the perfect, unblemished image of De Sica's *Miracolo a Milano* (1951) made me happy until I realized that I was seeing the faint pixelation of a digital projection from DVD (a discovery that led to other feelings about being cheated by the theater, the death of analog cinema, and wondering why I was in a theater rather than at home, watching the DVD). The screen always has a texture, and Marks is particularly interested in films that deliberately incorporate texture into their material medium, such as film grain, scratches on the negative or print, age and wear, and discoloration. The effect is to prompt the viewer's reflection on the film as a surface, a skin that has been touched by human hands and in turn touches us.

Barker extends the analysis of the haptic to include two additional dimensions. It is not enough to attend to the "skin of the film" and the viewer's "skin" (both skins are best understood as surfaces capable of being touched and capable of touching). After all, skin derives its expressive and receptive capacities (showing feeling and perceiving feelings) from what lies underneath it. "In its more general sense, the haptic includes tactile, kinaesthetic, and proprioceptive modes of touch" (37), writes Barker, linking these three modes of touch to the body's skin, the musculature just below the skin, and the viscera below that.[3] The "body" in question, however, is not just the body of the viewer, although that body is indeed touched by film in all these ways; it is affected by the film's tactile imagery, moved in its musculature by the movements, energetic or languid, of the film, and affected at a visceral level by cinema's internal mechanisms. Barker is particularly interested in film's regulation of time and how that regulation affects us at a gut level, so to speak.

From a phenomenological point of view, the sense of touch that cinema can evoke is not radically different from other senses. All our senses work because there is an unbroken and continuous medium between the subject and the object, an unbroken field of relations not only between them but also connecting them. Merleau-Ponty (1968) memorably describes this continuous medium that is in between the surfaces of things as "the flesh," a "connective tissue of exterior and interior horizons" (131n1). Tactility is privileged in this analysis primarily because the sense of touch requires direct contact, an immediacy that other senses (especially hearing and vision) actually share, but that is less evident in them. Implicit in this argument is the idea that phenomenology encourages a more ethical understanding of our relationship to the world, one that stresses our mutual constitution with the objects that we study, our connection to and implication in the world, and our embodiment in feeling bodies rather than as a pure observing eye.

"The skin is a meeting place for exchange and traversal because it connects the inside with the outside, the self with the other" (27), writes Barker (2009), who ultimately argues that "this notion of viewers' and films' bodies as surfaces in contact also problematizes the strict division between subject and object in the cinematic experience, suggesting a more mutual experience of engagement" (34).

Marks is equally clear about the ethical, political, and strategic implications of the haptic in cinema: "The haptic [is] a visual strategy that can be used to describe alternative visual traditions, including women's and feminist practices" (2000, 170). Indeed, Marks would like to link the haptic (or, at least, the strategic deployment of the haptic) to diasporic, post-colonial, migratory, and intercultural cinema. Barker, on the other hand, sees the haptic as a more generalized register present in all film (although she, too, would like to tie the haptic to certain ideologies, if not as tightly as Marks). Clearly, part of the appeal of a mainstream film franchise such as *Transformers* (which does not invest much of its energy in contesting sexual, racial, and cultural norms) lies precisely in its viewers' experience of a wide variety of surfaces and textures, from the endless rearticulations of smooth metal and glass car parts to Megan Fox's skin and hair. Indeed, Barker argues that one of the principal ways in which *Toy Story* (1995) appealed to its audiences (particularly to nostalgic parents who had grown up with many of the toys depicted in the film) was through the evocation of the shiny, smooth plastic textures depicted so successfully by computer animation.

Both Marks and Barker want to move beyond the surface. Barker's analysis in this respect is more complex and potentially more dynamic. We are quite used to thinking that the exterior world affects us from the outside going in. It begins at the level of the surface and slowly works its way inside us, as does warmth when we are really cold. In this sense, skin is a barrier that prevents or slows the penetration of the body. Skin not only conceals the interior states of the body, however, but also reveals them. Skin reveals the movement and tension of the muscles beneath it, what Barker calls the kinaesthetic register (which is also a cinematic register), signaling the stance and intention of a body. Skin reveals emotional states (fear, arousal), more general states (goose bumps from the cold, sweating from exercise), and the overall condition of the body (healthy, sickly). Even the body's deepest and most intimate states (the viscera, for Barker) can be displayed on the surface: a cold sweat and greenish pallor signal a deep, internal disturbance, blue-tinged lips and fingernails a body that cannot breathe. The interiority to be revealed can be even more intimate; sexual desire, embarrassment, anxiety, restrained anger, and the like all have their visible markers in the body's muscularity and skin.

Ultimately, this chapter aims to show the way in which the peplum generously rewards attention to the haptic dimension; more specifically, Barker's analysis, which establishes a phenomenological continuity between interior and exterior, is particularly well suited to the peplum, even if it does not always lead in the direction she might have wished. In what follows, I argue that an analysis of the haptic dimension of peplums is essential for understanding how the films conceptualize and construct masculinity. Skin in particular, far more than musculature, is absolutely essential for the peplum's conceptualization of masculinity, a conceptualization that has also changed over the past hundred years of peplum history. If the voluminous musculature of the midcentury peplum hero was his sign of masculinity, it was no indication of interiority; this ideal man was flat, unreflective, invulnerable. By contrast, the contemporary peplum looks for masculinity in the hero's interiority. As the hero's muscular bulk has decreased over the years, his muscular definition has increased; in other words, the fundamentally melodramatic soul of contemporary masculinity (oh, how I suffer inside) has become increasingly visible from the outside. Finally, this chapter argues that the haptic elements that Barker uses to establish the positive or ideologically open character of the films she discusses—in particular, a reciprocity between the filmic body (its surfaces, its movements, its rhythms) and the body of the spectator— are used to great effect in peplum films, often for racist and xenophobic ends. In short, the haptic is not just the way we reach out to touch and explore films but also a crucial way in which films grasp (*haptein*) us, seize us, and captivate our fantasies.

Peplum Skin

Let us begin with the skin of the peplum film, then, in precisely the most superficial sense. There is a lot of skin in peplum films, especially male skin. The classic midcentury peplum hero typically is dressed in little more than a loincloth and displays a massive body sheathed in skin that is hairless, tanned some variety of golden brown, and often oiled. One cannot ignore the muscles of the bodybuilder in discussing his skin, however, mostly because the massive increase in the muscular volume of the body also increases the expanse of skin and determines its character: at all times it is taut and stretched around the internal volume of musculature, and at moments of muscular excess, as when the hero strains to lift a heavy object, the impression is that of an elastic fabric strained nearly to the point of splitting or rupturing. The peplum hero never wears armor—indeed, he hardly wears clothes—because his skin is his armor. His skin attains its impermeability precisely through its perfect consistency. The tan is absolutely even, the muscle tone is the same everywhere, the skin is totally unmarked and undifferentiated by hair (except for the head and an optional beard), and the thin coating of oil over the hero's body provides a sheen that suggests a plasticine or vitreous armor (on the bodybuilder's shiny skin as armor, see Connor 2004, 53–58, particularly his observation that male bodybuilders cultivate a greater shininess than female bodybuilders). As Richard Dyer argues in *White* (1997), the peplum hero's skin suggests a certain proximity to nature, the source of his virile strength. It is tanned from exposure to the sun, and numerous peplums, both midcentury and contemporary, begin with the hero engaged in manual labor that places him in direct contact with nature (see, for instance, the 1961 *Goliath and the Vampires* and 2011's *Immortals*), plowing fields or chopping wood. At the same time, the skin's hairlessness and its muscular amplitude suggest cultivation (as do his nature-shaping activities, such as plowing and chopping), the technological development of this natural, pre-modern body.

The bodybuilder's skin is often threatened with penetration: he must hold off spikes driven with enormous pressure that threaten to pierce him (*Hercules against the Moon Men* [1964]), lie strapped to a table while spears fall on him from above (*Goliath and the Sins of Babylon* [1963]), or lie sleeping, drugged, while an assassin creeps up on his massive, muscular back with a knife drawn (*Colossus of the Arena* [1962]). Such attacks never succeed, however; as a rule, the peplum hero is never wounded. (Steven Connor notes that the inviolability of the body for the ancient Greeks was guaranteed by "smooth and immaculate skin" [2004, 10]). The hero can be scratched—indeed, the "shoulder scratch," usually inflicted by the claws of a wild animal, is something of a peplum cliché—but these scratches actually serve more to emphasize the impenetrability of his skin, not its vulnerability. The quality is that of a nonorganic material like metal or even stone—scratchable but not penetrable. Barker would quite rightly point out that this quality reinforces the peplum's "untouchability," its failure to really touch the viewer. The emphasis is entirely on skin as concealment and protection, and not at all on how it communicates with the interior. The suggestion is precisely that of a solid body entirely made of one undifferentiated substance, a body that is reflected both in critiques of the peplum hero's "wooden" acting and in appellations such as "slab of beef" to describe him. The hero is an impenetrable monad, very much the opposite of what Barker would like to find in cinema. Just as no one can touch the strongman, he fails to touch us, the audience. In figure 3.1 from *The Vengeance of Ursus,* for example, we see the young Dario touching his older brother's shoulder, but there is no sense of inner contact, a lack reinforced by the awkward pose of both brothers. There is no reciprocity in the touch; they are not in sync, not even looking in the same direction (we should contrast this image with the image from *300* later in this chapter, which does show a sense of meaningful inner connection). The hero's dermal imperviousness is matched by his psychic and cognitive density—he is entirely active in the Nietzschean sense. He has no psyche inside, just the joyous smashing of enemies or heaving of rocks.

The hero's skin as impenetrable armature was symbolized in Greek mythology by Hercules's donning of a second, tougher skin, that of the Nemean lion, but the governing logic of visibility in the peplum precludes the hero's skin being obscured by an animal pelt. His skin instead acquires its aura of perfection primarily

Figure 3.1. The strongman's perfect skin, expansive and swollen with muscles. *The Vengeance of Ursus*, 1961.

by contrast to other kinds of skin in the peplum. To begin with, his sidekick generally has a quite different appearance. He is also mostly unclothed and is healthy looking, if paler, but he is smaller and much slighter: there is no internal volume giving him a pneumatic, swollen look. The sidekick's skin is also hairless, but unlike that of the peplum hero, it is not invulnerable. In numerous peplums, the sidekick is wounded—an arrow or a spear leaves him incapacitated and dependent on the hero. This difference also extends to the sidekick's psychic skin: he is often suffering in love that cannot be requited, filled with resentment of the hero, or both. More sharply in contrast to the hero's skin, however, is the skin of his opponents: scarred (*Goliath and the Dragon* [1960]), cracked and pasty (*Giant of Metropolis* [1961]), mutated (*Hercules and the Captive Women* [1961]), black (*Maciste in King Solomon's Mines* [1964]), snow white (*Mole Men against the Son of Hercules* [1961]), or monstrous and hairy (*Goliath and the Vampires* [see the discussion of this film in chapter 4]; *Hercules, Prisoner of Evil* [*Ursus, il terrore dei Kirghisi*, 1964]).

Female skin in the peplum is equally hairless, is generally very fair, and also bears a relationship to the question of internal volume. This is not muscle, of course, but the impression of an undifferentiated zaftig flesh, at times impressively voluminous and pneumatic. Both male and female bodies in the peplum can give the impression of swollen balloons of skin, ready to burst with an overflowing internal vitality. Male and female bodies focus on the chest as the principal locale of impressive volume, and both Jayne Mansfield (*Hercules vs. the Hydra*, 1960) and Bella Cortez (*Vulcan, Son of Jupiter* [*Vulcano, figlio di Giove*, 1962]) have a volume that rivals that of Steve Reeves or Reg Park. Female peplum characters are more clothed than their male counterparts, generally in sensuous fabrics (thin and shiny silks or gauzy and translucent garments). Even so, the overall impression is not dissimilar to that of the male body: undifferentiated volume with no interiority and a corresponding impression of impenetrability. Both men and women in the peplum give off the curiously anesthetic impression of pneumatically inflated dolls or balloons whose surfaces are made out of a shiny plastic fabric (on the infantile image of the skin as an inflated balloon, see Connor 2004, 51). Art historian Margaret Walters has claimed that "the bodybuilder's exaggerated breast development . . . can make him look unexpectedly, surreally feminine" (quoted in Dutton 2013, 155), but Dutton suggests a haptic reading instead. The massive chest of the bodybuilder has "more to do with the modeling of the skin surface and the tactile quality of body-texture than with outline of the body" (157). Dutton's point is that while the outline of the bodybuilder's body is classically masculine even in some of its more extreme forms, its tactile quality is always erotic, fetishistic, and feminine (157–158). It is meant to be looked at, but it offers the viewer a specifically tactile invitation. This has been true throughout the history of the sport; in his biography of Eugen Sandow, the first professional bodybuilder, Chapman (2006) quotes an enraptured spectator in the early 1890s who described Sandow's skin as "velvety and most extraordinary . . . a transparent white without blemish. He shaved the hair, and the skin reflected the light with a glow" (64). Sandow also offered five criteria for judging bodybuilding competitions, including the condition of the skin (Chapman 2006, 131). Little has changed in the intervening century: the contemporary peplum features gauzy feminine fabrics and expansive surfaces of male skin—taut, smooth, defined, hairless (figure 3.2).

The goal of depilation for the bodybuilder is to make the underlying muscles more visible and more sharply defined—body hair blurs muscular definition and also detracts from the bodybuilder's uniform tan. A properly haptic reading of the peplum hero's skin would note that body hair is one of the principal ways in which the skin communicates with the exterior world. It is part of the continuum between inside and outside, the literal fuzz that renders the zone between inside and outside metaphorically fuzzy. It communicates touches that do not quite make contact but simply graze the surface of the skin—the movement of a breeze, for example. At the same time, it is one of the ways in which a person's interior state

Figure 3.2. Male skin and feminine fabrics in *Spartacus: Blood and Sand,* 2010.

is communicated to the outside world, for example, hairs standing on end with fright. Again, this changes skin from a two-way instrument of phenomenological communication into a thin shell of untouchable armor.[4] As Steven Connor notes in *The Book of Skin,* "Hair is immensely important as a way of focusing and amplifying skin sensation" (2004, 32), an observation that comes with the concomitant suggestion that while hairless skin may represent a haptic invitation, it simultaneously represents a libidinal deadening, a waning of receptiveness to touch.

This understanding of the bodybuilder's skin finds a significant resonance in the psychosexual and biopolitical readings of the peplum I elaborate elsewhere in this book. The removal of visible hair may enhance the definition of manly muscles, but it also removes one of the markers of sexual difference, a difference that in the peplum is consistently presented as a psychic threat to be avoided if possible. The peplum, in psychoanalytic terms, consistently reinforces what Didier Anzieu in *The Skin Ego* (1989) isolates as the first four functions of the skin as reflected internally in the ego, namely, supporting, containing, shielding, and individuating, while avoiding those functions that are directed at connection and sexuality (98–108). In part, the identity of male and female skin facilitates this kind of partial misrecognition, what Freud would call a fetish: I know very well that men and women are different, but all the same . . . At the same time, depilation creates a different sort of protection; skin becomes absolutely smooth and unbroken, highlighting its health and apparent invulnerability (if it were marred, diseased, or cut, we would see that). The body's overflowing health is thus made visible and guaranteed. It appears "immune" in the Italian philosopher Roberto Esposito's sense, who calls Hercules "the hero of political *immunitas*" (2011b 52). This extraordinary body no longer belongs to the ordinary community of vulnerable bodies (and thus guarantees a body politic that can be protected against foreign bodies). In all three cases—haptic, psychoanalytic, and biopolitical—what we see is the hairless, muscular body as a defense against an exterior threat such as the threat of sexual difference or even sexuality *tout court*. The strongman will shelter the body politic from its vulnerability.

Hairlessness has generally been the rule in the peplum: Maciste is essentially hairless in his original appearance in the 1914 *Cabiria,* and there is hardly a wisp of body hair to be found in the midcentury peplum. The 1980s barbarian peplums cultivated a distinctive "hair-metal" look, but this simply meant that hairless and tanned bodies were coupled with long shaggy manes (arguably even more androgynous) for men and women. A few actors, such as Peter McCoy (really Pietro Torrisi, who starred in a number of 1980s Italian peplums), cultivated a discreet scattering of chest hair, but never enough to obscure their musculature. This look generally persisted in the television peplums of the 1990s, where shows like *Hercules: The Legendary Journeys* and *BeastMaster* kept moderately long hair on their male protagonists, with body hair ranging from the same light scattering across the chest (Kevin Sorbo) to totally absent (Daniel Goddard). Contemporary peplums like *Spartacus: Blood and Sand* and the remade and rebooted *Clash of the Titans* prefer a military shave of the head for their protagonists but usually keep the body free of hair, again in order to best display the hero's musculature (one might contrast this to Russell Crowe's hirsute and largely armored body in *Gladiator*). Female bodies, of course, remain free of visible body hair throughout. Thanks to the explicit sequences in *Spartacus: Blood and Sand,* we no longer have to wonder about pubic hair in the peplum, which we now know was kept highly trimmed or entirely waxed on both men and women.[5]

Still, along the way, certain things change. In the midcentury peplum, it was not just the hero's skin that was perfect, unchanging, and invulnerable—it was his body as a whole. But already in *Conan the Barbarian,* the film that relaunched the peplum in the 1980s, this is no longer the case. The opening voice-over tells us that although this movie tells of his younger years, one day Conan will rule the kingdom of Aquilonia, with a crown on his "troubled brow." And the film quite famously closes with an image of Schwarzenegger seated on that throne, now an older man, bent with trouble and care, a graying beard covering much of his face. This image gestures both backward and forward, but in both directions we find a body that is no longer in its youthful prime. The image of Conan on his throne is a deliberate evocation of a scene much earlier in the film, when the young Conan first escapes from slavery and comes across an ancient king's underground barrow. Conan gazes raptly and reverently at the king's skeleton, and swelling extradiegetic music informs the viewer that something of emotional significance is happening. When Conan takes the dead king's sword, we understand that Conan is destined to become a king just like this one—great and splendid, yes, but also one day old, infirm, dead. Indeed, the image of the gray-bearded Conan on the throne also points to the future, in particular the upcoming sequel (currently titled *Legend of Conan*), which will star the appropriately aged Schwarzenegger. Producer Chris Morgan imagines a "warrior whose joints have started to fuse together, who has to crack the cartilage so he can pick up a sword again" (Lee 2012). And equally unlike the midcentury strongman, Conan may be (and is) beaten, wounded, pierced, starved, and tortured, most notably when he is crucified on the Tree of Woe. But Conan's vulnerability is not simply at the level of his skin, although we certainly see it cut and torn; more important, skin in *Conan* really does function as a means of communication, inside to outside. Conan is also wounded on the inside by two profound losses, both of women he loves: the first, his mother; the second, Valeria, his true love.[6]

Valeria's body is also penetrated, first by Conan when the two become lovers. As the viewer will learn, however, this penetration goes both ways. Although Conan has certainly had sex with other women, his affair with Valeria changes him—he is letting her in as much as she is letting him in. This becomes apparent after her death (she is penetrated again, this time by an enchanted snake arrow that Thulsa Doom fires into her back). The film strongly suggests that afterward, Conan is no longer (and never again will be) a whole man—he is vulnerable in precisely the etymological sense of the word: able to be wounded. The peplum hero is no longer sealed off from the external world, a slab of oblivious beefcake— or cheesecake. Both men and women in the peplum are now vulnerable, penetrable by the outside world. Indeed, some of the worst 1980s peplums were little more than complicated exercises in the piercing of the skin. The Argentine-US peplum *Barbarian Queen* (1985) was essentially a sexploitation/torture/rape revenge film set in a generic barbarian peplum universe: women are raped, are stretched on racks, and have their breasts pierced with spikes; men and boys have their throats cut and their noses cut off. (Its hunky male star, Frank Zagarino, remains unscathed throughout, however.)

Lucio Fulci's bizarre peplum *Conquest* (1984) is something of a visual testament to the vulnerable body, articulated through the well-known tropes of horror film's defining castration anxiety in the light of sexual difference (see Clover 1992 and Linda Williams 1991). A naked barbarian woman is torn in half by spreading her legs until her torso splits—complete with footage of skin stretching and tearing to reveal red tissues and intestines beneath—before she is then decapitated. The topless evil queen Ohkren then cracks open the woman's skull with a knife before feasting on the contents. The putative hero of the film, Ilius, is later seduced by a shy barbarian maiden, but before he can touch her proffered bare breasts, he realizes that her head has been split open by an as-yet-unseen assailant.[7] But women's bodies are not the only ones opened up by the film; indeed, Ilius's body turns out to be the principal target of Fulci's interest. First his skin is pierced by a poisoned arrow, whose poison makes his skin suppurate and form boils and blisters that ooze and then burst with fluid. A previous generation of peplum films had been virtually defined by their loving, slow pans across perfectly smooth and tanned pectorals; now Fulci's camera provides the same loving treatment for the body's disintegration, lingering again and again on pustules that swell, then burst. Something like six minutes of screen time are devoted to Ilius's suppurating blisters and sores and the ants that eventually crawl over them. Although his traveling companion, the strongman Mace, will manage to cure the poison, Fulci is not done with Ilius's body. Later in the film, Mace finds Ilius's body decapitated and hung upside down. He builds his friend a funeral pyre, but what we see is more like a roast being prepared: sizzling flesh, dripping fat, crisping skin (all accompanied by the sounds of roasting meat). Once Ilius is reduced to ash, Mace smears the residue all over his own skin, his arms, his palms, and, in a final close-up, his face. The gritty texture of the ashes against the bodybuilder's skin is palpable, all the more so since those ashes are what used to be skin. For all of the film's terrible production values, nearly incoherent plot, and gratuitous exploitation of female nudity, my students found these sequences viscerally troubling, repulsive, and uncanny. They were, to use Barker's and Marks's terminology, touched by these haptic images. Indeed, the funeral pyre in some ways deconstructs both body and film in Barker's exact terms: it reveals the body one layer at a time, moving from skin to musculature to viscera, rendering each layer visible in turn. "Render" means both to represent something in art and to process the body of an animal; Fulci does both at the same time. (For an extended biopolitical reading of precisely this play between the two meanings of rendering, see Shukin (2009), especially her chapter on "Automobility" (87–130), in which she addresses the literal rendering of animal bodies necessary to make the gelatin emulsion in film stock, placing slaughterhouses, cinema, and the nascent automobile industry in a productive dialogue, one that—in a moment that suggests a potential dialogue with haptic theory—she calls a "visceral point of connection" (88); the notion of the visceral will be explored in depth later in this chapter, discussing Barker's theory of the haptic.)

Fulci's film follows the usual midcentury peplum outline: an evil and illegitimate queen oppresses the people and must be destroyed. She represents both an exaggeration and an inversion of proper gender norms; indeed, Ohkren appears at all times with a snake that she caresses sexually, and she is terrorized by repeated visions of a faceless man who shoots an arrow into her receptive body. The film's gender ideology is not subtle. The slight and rather adolescent Ilius will prove to be not man enough for the task, and it will be the bodybuilding he-man

Mace who slays the evil queen and sets the world to rights. What attention to the haptic register indicates, however, is that there is something else going on. Ohkren's snake is as laughable as Mace's muscle-bound body—these images do not touch us. But Ilius's skin, burned to ash and smeared over Mace's face, remains troubling; it sticks out in precisely a tactile and haptic sense, breaking up the smooth consistency of the screen. While most peplums use the haptic register to reinforce their conventional messages, Fulci indicates that there is a source of pleasure—for him, at least, if not for most viewers—in the elaborate staging of the vulnerability of Ilius's skin. This rendering of the male body is repeated at even greater length in an episode of the television peplum *BeastMaster*. In "The Demon Curupira" (1999), we are treated to an even longer dream sequence in which the exquisite skin of Dar's body is assaulted by fire ants, roaches, worms, rats, and more before he is literally torn to pieces by a crocodile, but, quite unlike what happens in *Conquest,* Dar's manly stoicism throughout is enough to convince the demon Curupira to reassemble his body and bring him back to life. Manliness flourishes through a wound.[8]

In *Men, Women, and Chain Saws,* Carol Clover (1992) notes that the horror genre was largely about negotiating castration anxiety (and more generally, anxieties about masculinity); in particular, she reports that male horror fans cheered on the monster while he was decapitating and killing his victims, male and female, and then happily turned and cheered on the "final girl" as she hunted down and killed the monster. For them, and for the ideal viewer of *Conquest,* there is pleasure on both sides of the equation, not only in the destruction of the menacing, castrating monster but also in the spectacle of the male body with holes in it. We should notice that these two pleasures of the horror film are not equal in quantity or in kind. In the case of Fulci, the destruction of the castrating monster-woman is a narrative pleasure, while the male body with holes in its skin is an image—a haptic image. Let us assume for a moment that Fulci's primary interest is not in the conventional restoration of phallic power to the exaggerated masculine hero (which is arguably what happens in the case of *BeastMaster*'s Dar), but rather in the exploration of haptic imagery as a way of rendering—making visible and breaking down—the peplum's reliance on unbroken skin as a defense of masculine power, a defense against alterity.

This hypothesis finds some confirmation in a curious place: the literal skin of this film. In her study of the haptic, Marks is particularly attentive to actual, material surfaces in film, such as the condition of the print or the screen. A scratched and faded print projected on a dull screen covered with holes indicates a certain material status—or lack thereof—in the world of cultural circulation. This is so obviously part of the study of silent film, where each copy is of widely varying quality and missing different portions, that Usai (1986) and others have argued that, effectively, each copy of a given title is not a copy but a unique film of its own. A silent-era Maciste film may be visible only in a grainy VHS copy with Dutch intertitles (the copy of *Maciste della gabbia dei leoni* at the Bologna Cineteca) or in a pristine version with Russian titles—and, sadly, missing the final reel (*Maciste und der Tochter des Silberkönigs* in Moscow's Gosfilmofond). *Cabiria*, despite its fame and influence, exists in several versions of several different lengths, but the fullest and most restored version is shown only at festivals, and no high-definition or full-length version is available outside archives.

Many midcentury peplums, however, also bear testimony to their lack of status right on their surface; in many instances, the only surviving copies are terribly fuzzy, panned-and-scanned, 4:3 prints that were shown on American television in the 1960s and 1970s. The pan-and-scan process that turned widescreen films into the 4:3 aspect ratio suitable for television is effectively also an enlargement and hence makes the image even fuzzier. Not only have these prints lost a third of the image because of their reduction to 4:3, but they have also often been recut, sometimes for content, sometimes for length, sometimes in ways that are purely arbitrary. The American print of *Ulysses against the Son of Hercules* (*Ulisse contro Ercole*, 1962), for instance, not only removes some scenes but also inexplicably moves later portions of the original to the beginning. Some prints, such as those of *Samson in King Solomon's Mines*, have almost no remaining trace of color. Some scenes are almost incomprehensible because the surviving print is a copy of a copy of a copy, and color information that would help the eye discern outlines and textures is gone.

This is true even of some 1980s peplums. In the United States, the only available copies of *Gunan, King of the Barbarians* (1982), the first of many Italian *Conan* knock-offs, are homemade DVDs sold on eBay that use a pan-and-scan transfer from a VHS tape (the distinctive distortion lines of VHS transfers run throughout the film at the bottom of the frame, a visible mark on the skin of the film). Pirated copies on the internet of 1983's *Ironmaster* show a different dermal vulnerability: the only copy I could find had fairly pristine visuals, but the US audio track and burned-in (the language is already that of a wound) Swedish subtitles. Like my downloaded copy, the hero of *Ironmaster* carries a wound throughout the film, too. Encoded on the surface of the digital film, on its skin, audio and subtitles can be almost effortlessly swapped, removed, or altered. I found very high-quality copies of the midcentury peplums *Colossus of the Arena* and *Goliath and the Sins of Babylon*, both with Italian audio, but the English subtitle files included had been supplied by a fan who had a tenuous grasp of both Italian and English. Like that of a real body, the skin of film is vulnerable. With no artistic prestige to protect it, the skin of the peplum inadvertently reveals that the strongman's impervious skin is just a fantasy. And this is where we find a suggestion that Fulci's interest in broken skin extends to the phenomenological level. The oddest thing about *Conquest*—and it is a very odd film on many accounts—is that cinematographer Alejandro Ulloa shot the entire film through fog and soft-focus filters. It is not clear whether the intention was to give the film a "mythical" look, to hide the film's (many) visual flaws, or simply to carry out a formal experiment. The look is certainly consistent (Ulloa often shoots characters directly in front of, or just next to, sources of bright light, turning them into wavering, unclear figures), but the overall effect is that of a print that was damaged or incorrectly developed. Or, one might hazard in a haptic key, it is as if this were another moment for Fulci to revel in the pleasures of damaged and broken skin—this time the surface of the film itself.

Conquest is pretty clearly exceptional, but more in degree than in kind; from *Conan* on, the peplum hero has exemplary skin in its consistency, hairlessness, and muscular definition, but a vulnerable skin that reveals a vulnerable psyche. Indeed, as a rule, peplum heroes after Conan who have invulnerable, unblemished skin are also emotional throwbacks to the Nietzschean "man of action" that typified the midcentury hero. This is true, for instance, of almost all the television peplums of the 1990s, which make token moves toward giving their heroes a traumatic back-story that is mostly ignored afterward. Hercules in *Hercules: The Legendary Journeys* is upset when his family is killed at the start of the series, but he quickly recovers his equanimity and in subsequent episodes is as unscarred as his skin, always wise, benign, patient, and strong. Dar in *BeastMaster* is much the same, with skin and psyche a harmonious, smooth whole. Even in a film like *The Scorpion King* (2002), Mathayus is supposed to be seeking revenge for the genocide of his people, but mostly he grins, grabs the girl, wisecracks, and flexes his muscles. By contrast, most peplum heroes who emerged in the early years of the twenty-first century have bodies subjected to massive abuse and trauma, a trauma that is merely the exterior sign of an interior wound. Their skin, in Barker's language, "connects the inside with the outside, the self with the other" (2009, 27). Although their newly penetrable skin connects them to the world, it does so in an essentially regretful way, reinforcing—with the possible exception of *Conquest*—the standard "crisis of masculinity" narrative.[9] The time of true men is over and cannot be regained; this is the wound that they must carry forevermore, and the exterior wound is simply a sign of this inner trauma.[10] This is how, in Dominick LaCapra's (1999) terms, an absence (men do not have the freedom to kill and rape) gets converted into a loss (the time of unrestrained masculinity is over) and eventually into a traumatic lack; *ressentiment* is essentially the surplus ideological value that results from this operation.

This narrative, well established already in the 1980s, has become increasingly fraught and melodramatic in the twenty-first century, since the influential success of Ridley Scott's *Gladiator*. That film tells the story of yet another "last real man," a simple man (and amazing warrior) who wishes only to raise his crops and son with his loving wife, but who is surrounded by a corrupt and decadent society that turns its back on him. *Gladiator* was directly tied to previous Hollywood historical epics (such as Stanley Kubrick's *Spartacus* [1960]) and had virtually no debts to peplum films of the past, other than a kind of general awareness of the long tradition of classical films (see Solomon's [2001] definitive work on the subject). Many of the peplum films that followed *Gladiator,* however, relied strongly on its melancholy and resentful affect while drawing visually on mid-century and 1980s peplums, as well as video games, comics, and graphic novels.

If *Conan* presented Valeria's death as a trauma that ruined Conan's future emotional life, Zach Snyder's *300* is careful to present the trauma of the male subject at both ends of his life. The opening montage presents scenes from the early life of the film's hero, King Leonidas. We see him first as an infant, then as a boy, and then as a young man, and in every case, what we see is the suffering of the body, the marks left on its skin. Indeed, the film begins with an examination of the skin: the baby Leonidas is held aloft by an elder over a pit filled with skulls, and the narrator ominously informs us, "When the boy was born, he was *inspected.*" If he were misshapen or blemished, "he would be discarded," the voice continues, as the camera cuts back to the bottom of the pit, and the viewer realizes that these are the skulls of babies, previously discarded. The next cut takes us to the age of nine or ten; the boy, shaven headed, looks up at his opponent, and we see immediately abrasions and bruises, a cut over one eye. That opponent, a fully grown man (indeed, the boy's father), disarms the boy and then backhands him in the mouth. The boy wipes away blood and then returns to the fight undaunted, a true Spartan warrior. We then cut to the boy Leonidas sitting next to his father on the steps in an evident moment of father-son bonding, caressing his father's shield with one hand (figure 3.3; a shift in color temperature from de-saturated and cool blues and grays in the combat sequence to a warm golden light alerts the viewer to the affectionate nature of the scene). A close-up of the boy's bruised face and hand on the shield mark the moment as particularly important emotionally, and what follows cements the idea of a connection that is both emotional and sensorial. The father (in slow motion, as is the case with virtually every shot in the film) reaches down and raps slowly twice on the shield, making it ring like a bell (the sound throughout is muted and distant, as if it is heard only dimly through the intervening decades). In slow motion, the boy looks up at his father and then nods twice in the same slow rhythm. Something has been communicated and understood; moreover, it has been communicated without words—through sounds, through textures. It has been understood, in other words, haptically.

What is it that has been communicated? In their earlier combat, the two fought with swords, but it is the shield that distinguishes the Spartan warrior (indeed, later in the film, this will be the primary reason that Ephialtes the hunchback cannot be part of the Spartan army: although his spear thrust is excellent,

Figure 3.3. A touching moment in *300*, 2007.

he cannot hold his shield properly). The Spartans in the film, it is safe to say, are obsessed with their shields and not at all concerned with their weapons. It is the shield makes the boy into the man, not the sword or the spear. The bell-like ring as the father raps his knuckles against it shows its literal soundness, a wholeness that is amplified all the more by cementing the auditory and the visual together. Yet the boy's fingers cannot help but notice that it is not a smooth and impenetrable expanse. Except for its edges and the raised chevron that crosses it, its surface is textured like pebbled leather. Moreover, the boy must *feel* what the viewer sees: the shield is covered with scars, punctured everywhere with holes. The mark of the man is in the scars of his skin, not its impervious and uniform perfection. This is not to say that the ideal male subject being presented here is open in any way to the outside world, penetrable or permeable. Quite the opposite. Skin can be either Marks's and Barker's raw surface, not only open to the outside world but also part of that world, or the first line of defense against that world; the Spartan warrior understands that that line of defense must be augmented, amplified.

Again, this doubled layer or skin simply reflects a doubled layer of an interior psyche. The male psyche is withdrawn, buffered, insulated from the hostile outside world.[11] Herein lies the key to *300*'s success as a male melodrama. This doubled psychic skin means not only that the man may put on the proper appearance of stoic resolve, but also, and equally, that his true interior is all the more raw, exposed, and throbbing with pain and sorrow. As the rest of the sequence progresses, we see the development of precisely this psychic armature: the boy is taken away from his parents altogether; he is forced to beat other children (on occasion, it is implied, to death) in order to obtain food; and he is beaten with a cane for some minor infraction, "taught to show no pain," before being turned loose, nearly naked, in the snowy wilderness, entirely alone. This incredibly nationalistic, misogynistic, militaristic, and homophobic film uses its haptic imagery throughout to underscore this interior tragedy of the contemporary man, whose interior suffering can be measured precisely by his stoic resistance to the agonies that the outside world brings him. This is particularly true of a sequence that effectively bookends the film. Early on, as the young Leonidas tries to survive in the snow, he encounters a monstrous wolf. The narrator explains as Leonidas prepares to kill the wolf, "It is not fear that grips him, only a heightened sense of things: the cold air in his lungs [cut to the boy's feet in the snow], windswept pines moving against the coming night . . . his hands are steady, his form—perfect." These lines reappear in an altered form at the end of the film as Leonidas confronts his final enemy, the emperor Xerxes, face to face. Leonidas reminisces about the wolf, recalling his bare feet in the snow as he hunted. "It's been more than thirty years since the wolf and the winter cold and now, as then, it's not fear that grips him, only restlessness, a heightened sense of things: the seaborne breeze coolly kissing the sweat at his chest and neck, gulls cawing [cut to an extreme close-up, a bead of sweat tricking down his neck] . . . his steady breathing."

These moments in *300* are not simply haptic but intensely so. I can barely look at the feet in the snow without becoming conscious of my own feet, comfortably indoors and in slippers; the image of the bead of sweat trickling down Leonidas's neck is almost unbearable to watch—my hand yearns to wipe the neck (whether his or mine does not matter) or the screen to get rid of it. (In both cases, the peplum's penchant for slow and dilated time intensifies this haptic reaction.) The voice-over calls out the haptic register explicitly: "a heightened sense of things." *300* is perhaps most famous for its completely and deliberately artificial sprays of computer-generated blood, intended to look like Frank Miller's graphic novel, but they in fact detract from these vastly more intense (and more ideologically effective) haptic images that so successfully communicate not the phenomenological union of self and other but the yawning gulf that separates man's experience of his true inner self (nostalgic, intensely emotional, the boy's love for his father) and his exterior self (stoic, impervious to the snows of winter and the heat of battle, the boy able to touch only the shield, not his father). Man is loss.

Not surprisingly, this coupling of an ideologically charged affective stance (no one knows how much we men suffer inside!) with the haptic attention to touch and skin was carried over into the television series *Spartacus: Blood and Sand*, which copied as much as it could from *300*. Spartacus initially looks like an impenetrable midcentury peplum hero; note, for example, the clichéd "shoulder scratch" in figure 3.2, already present in Steve Reeves's Hercules. But the show delights in the many ways in which skin can be broken and bodies can be penetrated. In any given episode, the viewer is likely to see men being impaled or beheaded, limbs amputated, teeth knocked out, bones broken, or skin branded. These injuries are constantly coupled with psychic humiliations: Spartacus must subject himself to verbal abuse, to physical inspections, and to being used as a sex toy by wealthy Roman women. And this is true not just for Spartacus; for other gladiators (particularly Crixus, initially Spartacus's rival and later his friend and ally), stoic resistance to agonizing bodily torment always runs hand in hand with a heightened sense of regret for their lost lives, for what they long for and cannot have. In two episodes in particular, the breaking of the peplum hero's skin gives particular insight into the male psyche, normally so carefully hidden away.

In "The Thing in the Pit" (2010), Spartacus has lost everything: his wife, his name (the series never reveals his real name; Spartacus is the name given to him by his owner and master, Batiatus), his pride, and even his newfound minimal status as a gladiator. He is demoted to "the pits of the underworld," a sort of ultra-*lumpenproletariat* version of the arena. As the name suggests, this is as far as one can fall—the episode might easily have been called "Spartacus in Hell." In the first fight, a burly giant in a mask dispatches one of Spartacus's former companions with repeated blows of a giant hammer to the head. Then he surgically removes his victim's face with a knife, and we realize that his mask is nothing more than the skin of the faces of the men he has previously defeated. Although this sequence is just a prelude to the truly graphic (and psychically important) violence that follows, in a very real sense, this is the skin of the film—the male subject is constituted by the armor with which he defends himself against the exterior world, and this armor, if we are to see the inner, true self, must be stripped away. I will not belabor the endless abuse to which Spartacus's body, and especially his skin, is subjected (e.g., fists, knees, needles, hooks, spikes), but the ultimate message that emerges through the episode's long exploration of the haptic register is precisely the depth of that skin. Masculinity lies in the distance between the interior self and the exterior of the world, not in the absence of feelings, sensitivity, and dependence but in how well they are kept hidden. Fundamentally, the contemporary peplum's masculine melodrama is produced by how far we have to go to get under the male subject's skin and find that interior space. *Spartacus* makes it clear that the measure of a man is to be found in his psychic depth, not his phallic length, and thus it is that when Spartacus has had all this exterior stripped away, he can be proclaimed a man (at least in its most minimal form, the gladiator) once again.

The second episode that revolves around male skin and directly champions skin, rather than the phallus, as the real mark of masculinity is "Mark of the Brotherhood" (2010). Batiatus, the owner of a *ludus,* or gladiatorial training school, shops for slaves to turn into new warriors. The slave seller cries his wares in terms that underscore how the haptic can be used expressly to create a masculine distance from the world: "Let us begin with a Celtic Gaul of imposing virtues. I give you Segovax. Skin—his armor. Hands—his steel." One might wonder, given this skin as armor, how one can mark it; what is the "mark of the brotherhood"? A previous episode showcases the gladiators bragging about the brand in the shape of the letter B that ostensibly marks them as the property of Batiatus, and indeed, for them, the mark on their arms really proves their status as part of an elite brotherhood—those worthy of fighting in the arena. But, as this episode's title indicates, the "mark of the brotherhood" has not yet been revealed. Perhaps this mark lies elsewhere on the skin. When the rich, spoiled Roman woman Ilithyia arrives at the *ludus,* Batiatus offers to let her pick one of the new recruits as her own. To help her, Batiatus orders the men to disrobe and display their *virtus,* their male organs. In one of the program's many full-frontal male nudity shots, it is Segovax whose phallus is the most impressive.[12] Perhaps it is this extension of skin that is the mark of the brotherhood of true men? We will see.

The other man (besides Spartacus) who plays a prominent role in the episode is Crixus, the Gaul, whose genitalia have been displayed to prominent effect in previous episodes. Crixus, however, has been terribly wounded, and a massive gash is visible throughout across his chest. Moreover, as my students have noted, Crixus begins the series as the ultimate stoic, trash-talking warrior, but by this point, he can hardly talk of anything but his weepy love for the slave girl Naevia. The now stoic and imperturbable Spartacus repeatedly humiliates Crixus in front of all the other gladiators, demanding that he take a subordinate role in the *ludus,* and Crixus is even insulted by the handicapped former gladiator Ashur, who doubts aloud whether Crixus's wound "will ever heal." This wound would appear to be the opposite of Segovax's prominent manliness. One still might wonder, however, which is the mark of the brotherhood: phallus or wound? Here we can return to the epigraph from Nietzsche that opens this chapter, which equates *virtus* with *vulnera,* phallus with wounding. The wound is necessary for masculinity; it is what allows manliness to flourish (or in an obscene reading absolutely implied in the original Latin, the wound is what allows the penis to grow).

Ilithyia has a long-standing hatred of Spartacus and engages Segovax to kill him. The assassination attempt fails when Crixus, despite his hatred of Spartacus, intervenes as Segovax attempts to throttle the hero in one of the series' most homoerotic violent confrontations. Crixus explains that he "saved a brother who shares the mark," but does he refer to their shared brand or to their unspoken personal melodramas? As it turns out, the show's most powerful mark on the male body is yet to come. Segovax's phallic power is revealed as a literal nothing in the episode's final sequence: for his transgression against Spartacus, Batiatus punishes him with crucifixion and *emasculatio* (the removal of the penis, rather than *castratio*, the removal of the testicles). The viewer is spared nothing here: the shot begins with Spartacus in the foreground and Segovax's figure lying limp against the wall, with a shallow depth of focus permitting only a clear view of Spartacus before the camera racks the focus onto Segovax, revealing a conspicuous absence. A high-angle shot shows us Segovax's body being hoisted into the air, and the camera pushes in on the site of his wounding, showing his testicles surmounted by nothing but a hole spurting blood. This is the mark of the brotherhood, the only mark that Spartacus, Crixus, and Segovax all share, at least on a metaphorical level. Again, the skin—the skin of these films—that conceals this wound is nothing but the distance that separates inside and outside. Spartacus's exterior certitude and stoicism simply conceal what Crixus and Segovax cannot hide. In all three cases, in fact, it is Žižek's (1994) form of courtly love that produces this distance: an incomprehensible dedication to an impossible woman. In Spartacus's case, this is for his wife, Sura, now dead and forever beyond him; for Crixus, it is the stereotypical forbidden love between himself and Naevia, slave to the lady of the house, a love in which Crixus invariably assumes a position of powerlessness and helplessness, in stark contrast to his aggressive blustering early in the series; and for Segovax, it is his inexplicable devotion to the patrician Ilithyia, whom he refuses to name as the one who hired him to kill Spartacus, even under threat of emasculation. In short, woman is the hole in the skin of man; what marks the man is how well he conceals this hole in his skin, ranging along a continuum from Segovax's literal castration to Crixus's weepy melodramatic effusions of love and to Spartacus's grim determination to follow Sura into death.

Peplum Muscles

In moving beyond skin in her analysis of the haptic in film, Barker (2009) also moved beyond the surface in a different way: tactile readings were no longer just about a variety of literal surfaces. Barker's next level of analysis was less on the surface not only because it attended to the musculature that lies beneath the skin, but also because that musculature is more metaphorical. Musculature is what allows the film to move: dolly shots, pans, tilts, Steadicam technology, Skycams, and the like. Barker is particularly good at noting the various ways in which the movements of film—such as chase sequences—not only make use of the film's musculature but also activate the viewer's "virtual musculature," allowing us to experience haptically, and not merely observe, sensations of chase, leaping, or flying. The "trench run" sequence of the original *Star Wars* (1977) provides a clear example. The shot is an exertion of the body of the film, specifically its musculature, and that muscular effort produces a concomitant mirrored state in the viewer, who ideally feels the giddy sensation of masterfully flying through a narrow space at incredible speeds. The haptic is not simply texture but movement as well.

Part of Barker's larger point is that this mirroring is essentially empathetic, a feeling of exhilaration that is shared by both the body of the viewer and that of the film. Ultimately, for Barker, this amounts to a demonstration of a congruence and a reciprocity between the film's body and the spectator's body, what she calls "muscular empathy" (73)—that they can work well together and feel each other. It is no accident that Barker turns principally to cinematic actions that require reciprocity, both willing (the handshake) and unwilling (the chase). To meaningfully render these reciprocal actions calls not only for human bodies to be in sync with each other, but also for the cinematic musculature (camera movement, editing) to be in sync with fundamentally human movements. "When the film swivels suddenly with a whip pan, or moves slowly with a long take or a tracking shot, or stretches itself out in widescreen to take in a vast landscape, we feel those movements in our muscles because our bodies have made similar movements: we have whipped our heads from side to side, moved slowly and stealthily, and stretched out our bodies in ways that are distinctly human" (75). Key terms include "mimicry" (70, 73–82, 94), "empathy" (73–83, 91–94, 108–110), "mirroring" (69–72), "reciprocity" (15, 27–28, 93–94), and an intriguingly orthopedic metaphor that Barker uses throughout the chapter: we "hitch" our bodies to the film's body for the duration of the screening—we are, if the film works, along for the ride. As is the case more generally with phenomenological readings of film, all this comes with a certain set of values: the more reciprocity, empathy, mirroring, and hitching together of bodies, the better. As a result, a handshake is, in some sense, a better gesture than a chase, which involves a kind of trickery, where we are playing a game, "follow the leader," in which we are "enticed to follow . . . [but] can't possibly keep up" (107). It must be said that Barker's argument does not hold together perfectly here: chase sequences are bad because they emphasize the discrepancy between the filmic musculature and our own; cartoons are good for exactly the same reason. Barker's lament that action films are "more antagonistic . . . than poignant" (106) indicates that she does not always appreciate that hostile feelings can do the work of ideology as well as, or better than, nicer feelings do. In fact, if we take Barker's argument seriously (and I do), then any film that works on its audience works precisely because our feelings *for* the film emerge from our ability to feel *with* the film (92)—including all sorts of films that Barker might not want to like.[13] What would she think of the peplum?

The peplum presents at least two immediate problems for Barker. The first is that although it privileges musculature perhaps more than any other film genre, its muscles appear to have very little to do with movement. Indeed, they seem decidedly opposed to it. It was almost impossible for viewers or critics to miss the midcentury bodybuilder's stiff and awkward walking and often comically poor choreography in sword-fighting sequences; at times, even for the bodybuilder to turn his head seemed to require a massive effort, as if the dense and inflated musculature was there to hinder the body's movements. Even in the silent period, Maciste was often paired with another character who could provide movements that were acrobatic to give a sense of brio and sprezzatura to the filmic body. Maciste, by contrast, was heavy; at his best, he was an immovable obstacle, a piece of machinery. Indeed, part of the success of the character was in seeing him perform the actions of large and immobile machines: he could be a jack (lifting up the front end of a car) or a crane (lifting an entire car into the air). Where an acrobatic character might nimbly scale a wall, Maciste bends an entire tree down to lift himself over the top in *Maciste contro lo sceicco* (1926). In the midcentury peplums, the strongman typically stands in one place, poses, hefts, hurls, or resists the horses pulling at his body with ropes, always replicating the various postures of bodybuilding competitions. These postures generally aim at creating a static tension rather than a productive movement. The bodybuilder strains for what seems like hours to lift a boulder, topple a tree, or crush the monster; his movements must be an agonizingly slowly developed tension since this is what best showcases his muscles. The central terms of value in bodybuilding—mass, volume, definition—all seem to be opposed to cinematic body, which is in its very name a body in movement. As the Italian peplum/exploitation director Joe d'Amato (actually Aristide Massaccesi) said of his bodybuilding star Miles O'Keefe in the 1980s, "Like everyone who comes from the world of bodybuilding, he moved and walked like a paralytic" (Giordano 1998, 142).

There is a larger issue for Barker in the peplum (and in other cinematic forms), however, and that is the question of reciprocity. The strongman's muscular actions are generally not reciprocal but solo in character. Dyer noted in *White* (1997) that the peplum bodybuilder was usually kept off to one side, out of the main action of the battle against the evil queen's forces (166–167), performing singular actions. In some films, of course, this action is antagonistically reciprocal, such as combat, but in plenty of films, the strongman must simply strain his muscles in some extraordinary way: he must ring a giant bell in *Samson and the Seven Miracles of the World*, destroy a magic rock in *Hercules and the Captive Women*, throw boulders at zombies in *Hercules in the Haunted World*, turn a huge wheel in *Mole Men*, knock over a statue in *Moon Men*, push over a boulder in *Hercules, Prisoner of Evil*, and the like. In some sense, of course, every action is reciprocal ("For every action, there is an equal and opposite reaction"), but for Barker, it is clear that the reciprocity she is interested in is human. The handshake is her model—it is a muscular act that brings skin into contact with skin; it must be

simultaneous and reciprocal; it denotes, at least in theory, a mutuality of recognition and respect. Even certain antagonisms, however, are truly reciprocal: the
chase, the duel, and the shootout, for example, all require two people to play their
mutual and interlocking roles (indeed, the Western shootout often implies a mutuality of respect). But the knocking down of a rock, the ringing of a bell, or the
turning of a wheel do not imply any mutuality.[14] In particular, these sequences
are isolated. They take place in spaces without any other human presence, with
the protagonist separated from all the other characters. Even in sequences in which
other characters are present, the strongman's muscles seem to function more
like a pneumatic, inflatable body armor than the empathy machine of mirrored
mutuality that Barker envisions.

This is equally true for the body of the peplum camera. Until the peplum
films of the 1980s (and really, not until the peplums of the twenty-first century),
camera movement was standard, formulaic, and predictable—the films were
made as quickly and as cheaply as possible, so there was little attempt on the part
of the filmmakers to hitch the viewer's body to the cinematic body. By and large,
the camera in these films aimed simply to show rather than to make the viewer
feel. Already in the Maciste films of the silent period, the preferred shot was a
static medium shot that could best show the action. In the midcentury peplum,
nothing changed: the aim was to make the action clear. Even in fight sequences, the
camera's only interest was in making sure we could see—not feel—the protagonist's beefy physique.

One must stop here and wonder: Is this then the feeling of movement in the
midcentury peplum: nothing? A dense mass of muscles or mammary tissue that
keeps the world separate, cushioned, raw feelings tempered to a novocaine-induced
faint buzzing? We might couple this nonfeeling with the earlier suggestion about
the muscular movement of the peplum, or the lack thereof: it is virtually defined by
its lack of movement, by the frozen poses of the bodybuilder (see the discussion of
statues and slow time in chapter 1). Perhaps we might understand the peplum as
a kind of haptic vaccine, a cinematic injection intended to reduce our tactile and
muscular sensitivity in properly manly and stoic fashion. Before we understand
the peplum as a totally anti-haptic genre of the anesthetized paralytic, however,
we need to note that there are sequences that are clearly aimed at making the
audience feel something, and that adopt the appropriate cinematic musculature
to do so. In film after film, we are treated to spectacles of muscular strain as the
protagonist attempts to lift a massive object that threatens to crush him, to bend
bars that block his way, or to remove the boulder in front of the cave where the
princess is trapped. In the silent Maciste films and particularly in the midcentury peplum, these sequences are surprisingly long (four minutes of nothing but
a man trying to lift something heavy is an eternity in film time) and often astonishingly boring, since there is, quite literally, nothing to show except the hero's

muscles. The strongman strains to lift, the queen stares at him, he strains to lift, his sidekick stares at him in desperation, the strongman strains to lift, the princess bites her knuckle in worry, the strongman strains to lift, and on and on. Mirroring the strongman's strain against an apparently immovable object, the camera is similarly stuck, apart from the occasional close-up pan across bulging biceps strained to their limit. The movement lies in the editing, which generally alternates between the strongman and some other perspective, slowly moving closer to show an increasing psychological intensity.

As easy as these sequences are to mock, however, at times I find my muscles involuntarily straining along with the strongman because, at least at this moment, I find that my body is successfully hitched to the body of the bodybuilder in a muscular mutuality. Who is not familiar with the experience of straining to move something heavy, certain that with just a little more effort or a slightly different angle of attack, it will give way? Even an experience as banal as trying to open a stuck lid on a jar of jam is reflected in heroically magnified form in the peplum, along with the feeling—and it is a feeling—of muscular satisfaction when the lid finally gives way. The muscular release that occurs when the boulder topples or the ropes give way in the peplum is replicated by the release of the camera: as soon as the boulder is toppled, the camera returns to its normal (if rather uninspired) movement. Within the diegesis, as well, the properly empathetic reaction is modeled for us by those who anxiously watch the strongman struggle to keep the massive spike-covered rock from crushing his sidekick; the good princess writhes in anxiety, biting her knuckles or covering her eyes, while the evil queen pants in erotic anticipation at the satisfaction of her sadistic desires (destined, alas, to be disappointed).

An entirely different analysis of musculature becomes necessary after the midcentury period. Already by the 1980s, the strongman was slimming down, losing much of his immobilizing and anesthetizing bulk. Schwarzenegger shed thirty pounds for *Conan the Barbarian,* and the bodybuilders in other 1980s peplums are conspicuously less massive than their 1950s and 1960s counterparts (indeed, they are increasingly not bodybuilders at all, since competitive bodybuilding has simply continued to add mass with each passing decade). Sequences of pure muscular effort disappear almost entirely; instead, the hero's muscles take on a more symbolic function, a visible guarantee of his prowess as a warrior or even of his special destiny as the last of the great heroes, the last real man. He now wears his muscles more like a badge of honor and less like a suit of armor. The same sequences of torture occur in virtually every film, but there is no epic struggle against the ropes that bind the hero to a makeshift crucifix (see, e.g., *Conan the Barbarian, Conquest, The Sword of the Barbarians* [1982], and *The Throne of Fire* [1983]). The crucifixion positions the male musculature so that the viewer can see it unimpeded. As I suggested earlier in regard to skin, starting in the

1980s, the hero is vulnerable both psychically and physically. The hero's musculature is decidedly not armor and serves, if anything, as a measure of how even the
most intensely and visibly masculine subjects suffer as the world turns against
them. The slow pan across the hero's muscles as he stands tied to the cross would
have meant something different in the midcentury peplum: the unstoppable
power of the superman. Now it emphasizes his helplessness. Starting with Conan,
the musclebound protagonist can no longer lift absurdly massive objects (the
horse-drawn cart that Hercules hefts and hurls in *Hercules in the Haunted World*)
or topple massive buildings just by pushing on them (*Samson and the Seven Miracles of the World*). If his muscular bulk averages 20 percent less than that of his
midcentury peers, his strength is diminished not correspondingly but categori-
cally. The feats of strength that formed the principal staple of the Maciste films
and the midcentury peplum begin to disappear. Conan does not perform any
such feat; even the quite massive Paul twins (Peter and David) who star in *The
Barbarians* (1987) limit their feats of strength to winning an arm-wrestling match
and lifting their smaller opponents into the air. More typical of the era is the lanky
and comparatively less brawny protagonist of the *Gor* films, Urbano Barberini,
or Rick Hill, star of *Deathstalker*—big and muscled, but hardly competitive bodybuilder material.

　　In a certain sense, the cinematic body took another generation to slim down
(or rather, the technical advances that allowed big-budget films to develop a more
mobile camera would have to wait a generation to become cheap enough to be
used in peplum films). But by the time of *300*, the camera had found ways to express a certain empathy and mirroring between the movement of the protagonist's musculature and the movement of the camera. In a memorable sequence, a
Persian emissary arrives to see that the Spartans are building a wall made of equal
parts heavy boulders that they have lifted into place and the bodies of the enemies
they have slain. Outraged at this barbaric treatment of the dead, the emissary
prepares to whip the Spartans as he whips the slaves who carry his palanquin. As
his arm swings back the whip in slow motion, the camera tracks Stelios (Michael
Fassbender), who draws his sword and charges (all in slow motion, as usual). The
camera tracks Stelios as he runs and then leaps off a boulder into the air across an
impossible distance, where he neatly amputates the emissary's arm. The initial
shots (close medium) emphasize not only his musculature as such but also
the pleasure of his spontaneous and acrobatic movement, just as the cut to a
long medium shot allows the viewer to appreciate his soaring through the air
(figure 3.4).

　　Part of the pleasure in all this lies in the muscular effect produced by slow
motion. As I noted earlier, Barker (2009) seems to have a strange notion of the
function of slow motion in the action film, linking it to muscular paralysis and
fear (110) when it instead often signifies a kind of muscular ecstasy, a hallucinatory

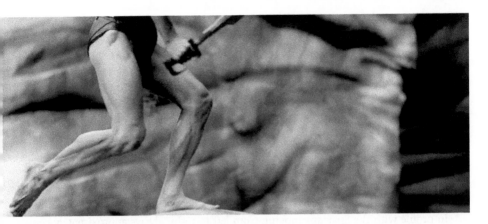

Figure 3.4. The muscular ecstasy of slow motion. *300*, 2007.

extension of speed and strength. Already in a campy 1970s television show like *The Six Million Dollar Man* (1973–1978), it was sufficient to show the cybernetically enhanced protagonist, Steve Austin, in slow motion to convey to the audience that he was using his bionic super strength and speed. Throughout *300*'s fight sequences, the film uses slow motion to convey the speed, strength, and superhuman precision of the Spartan warriors. But this is not all that takes place here. In Stelios's run-up and leap, the viewer is almost returned to Muybridge's original photo sequences of athletic, nearly naked men leaping and fighting; one can see the body's movements in moments of muscular exertion with a clarity and an intensity that never appear in real life.[15] I not only admire Fassbender's leg muscles but also see how they move—or better, as Barker or Marks might say, *I feel* how they move. My seeing becomes precisely a way of feeling, of feeling the muscles coil, tense, and spring into life, of seeing and feeling their bounce as foot lands on rock, as tensed muscles go slack. When Barker suggests that chase sequences "trick" the viewer because they "move in such a way that we can't possibly keep up" (107), it seems to me that she has misunderstood the muscularity of action films in general. The pleasure—not only for me but also for many other viewers I have spoken to—in watching a chase sequence, a duel, or Stelios's leap lies precisely in my experience of a vicarious musculature that is like my own but beyond my own. The contemporary peplum's conspicuous staging of masculine musculature, reveling in it through slow motion, allows the viewer to experience that muscular perfection and to have the haptic pleasure of muscularity hitched to the visibility of the male body that the peplum excels in.

In a different and quite influential sequence (one repeated identically in the 2011 peplum *Immortals*), King Leonidas leads his soldiers in a charge against the

Persians. It is one of the sequences that most clearly showcases the film's reliance on video games, specifically side-scrolling "beat-'em-ups"; such games generally feature massively muscled protagonists, and some, such as *Golden Axe*, are set in peplum universes (*Golden Axe*, a creation of the 1980s, made extensive use of Conan-inspired elements).[16] They are still popular today: *God of Blades* is a contemporary example, for instance. The side scroller is a perfectly familiar muscular action, if not perhaps in the way Barker would like. Not only have so many of the young men who watch *300* played such games before, often extensively, but it is also familiar to anyone who has ever looked out the window of a moving bus, automobile, or airplane: the landscape, sites of interest, and people all scroll by for my visual pleasure without any sense of connection, reciprocity, or mutual recognition. This battle sequence in *300* is, in side-scroller fashion, shot entirely in profile with the Spartans moving from left to right, always approximately centered on King Leonidas (side scrollers almost invariably move from left to right, although in *300* this is probably also linked to a general sense of Western progress). The camera exhibits multiple forms of movement as Leonidas presses forward, not only scrolling from left to right to keep him centered but also often zooming in to catch some movement of particular importance, such as a death or a wounding, and continually varying film speed to create a sort of rhythmic ramping (see chapter 1 on peplum time for a further discussion of this technique).[17] Together these effects create a spectacle of muscular violence that once again generates a maximum visibility that is perfectly linked to a muscular hapticity. (Reliance on the conventions of video games also helps implicitly suggest that the viewer's body in some sense controls the muscles seen on screen, that they are "hitched," in Barker's language.) The sequence concludes, as does the one in *Immortals*, with a tracking shot that follows a spear thrown by the protagonist into his last enemy, a final left-to-right muscular impulse that again provides the sensation of a muscular action perfectly executed: speed, force, and precision.

All this feeling is produced, of course, with a concomitant numbness, an anesthesia; there is no feeling whatsoever for the skin, the musculature, or the viscera of one's opponents. The Persian emissary in *300* is quite right to call the Spartans' treatment of enemy soldiers "barbarism," and the same might be said of the contemporary peplum's treatment of the enemy in general. *300*, like any number of side-scrolling beat-'em-ups, produces huge numbers of corpses along the way that literally disappear from the frame, forgotten by the camera's musculature (its left-to-right forward scrolling) just as our musculature and Leonidas's prepare for the next enemy. Bodies, sprays of blood, and amputated limbs tumble repeatedly out of the frame in this film; the only feeling that might be produced is a sense that clutter is being cleared from the screen, never more so than when the Spartans drive a cohort of Persian soldiers off a high cliff overlooking the sea. The larger theoretical point here is that this lack of fellow feeling, mutuality, and reciprocity does not make the film's use of the haptic any less successful (or, for that matter, any less haptic). As much as we feel the muscular exertion of Stelios's charge and leap, we do not feel anything for the emissary's amputated limb, which spins free of its original body without any muscular control and without any haptic element at all (indeed, the actual moment of amputation happens offscreen).

I suggested that the feeling produced by bodies disappearing from the frame because the camera moves beyond them (the forward scroll of the video game) produces in turn the sensation of the screen being cleaned of rubble, debris, or detritus. In the case of *300*, as many critics have noted, this is an ethnic cleansing—that is, the human detritus that is being cleaned up here is all dark skinned, exotic, ethnic, and all too frequently disabled (see Chemers 2007). In fact, the Spartans spend much of their down time in the film cleaning the field of battle, arranging the bodies of the dead into piles or a wall, and going around to make sure that each Persian is really dead. Here we must link this muscular pleasure at making things clean, clearing the field, and its concomitant ethnic cleansing to the biopolitical, specifically to Agamben's (1998) concept of "bare life" or *zōē*. For Agamben, there is a crucial split in our conceptualization of life that goes back at least as far as the ancient Greeks, the split between *zōē*, or individual animal life, and *bios*, elevated and dignified human cultural life, life within the community. Although this division makes it possible for us to conceive of human life as possessed of a special inherent dignity, it also allows us to imagine (and in exile, the asylum, the concentration camp, and other such spaces, put into practice) the human being deprived of *bios* and reduced to the state of bare, or animal, life. In both its treatment of skin and cinematic and human musculature, the haptic elements of a peplum like *300* do precisely this: they selectively target and amplify our sense of feeling so that we feel keenly the tragedy of the honorable and muscular white man whose historical supremacy appears to be coming to an end, but experience a simultaneous anesthesia for the fate of his opponents. In other words, although the haptic may produce a sense of empathic feeling, mutuality, and recognition, there is no reason that this feeling (or feeling in general) should be generalized, and no reason that it should be particularly ethical.

One might broaden this issue a little further and suggest that there is a general critical desire to find a particular formal technique or device (e.g., deep focus, haptic imagery, the long take) that would have a sort of built-in ideological content that would automatically produce a particular ethical or political result in the viewer. I have yet to see any reason to think that things work this way, however. I am reasonably sure that one could take all the hallmarks of Italian neorealism (natural lighting, nonprofessional actors, use of documentary and documentary-like footage, a focus on the poor and downtrodden, a view of history from below) and make a right-wing, nationalist film using those techniques, not least because Alessandro Blasetti did precisely that in 1934 when he made *1860* under Mussolini and in explicit support of the Fascist regime.[18] *300* may very well be the most haptic peplum film, but it certainly does not produce a sense of ethical recognition or empathy in its viewers; indeed, its success would seem to depend precisely on the repression of such responses, a repression achieved largely through haptic means.

Peplum Viscera

I have already addressed the question of interiority in the peplum in reflecting on the bodybuilder's skin and muscles, but it is important to recognize that this is not what Barker (2009) means by her final level of haptic analysis, viscera. Instead, she has in mind all those elements of the cinematic body that are autonomic, that work in the background without conscious attention, much as our liver, stomach, or kidneys do not require our conscious control—normally, we do not really think much about our insides at all. For the filmic body, she mentions as viscera examples such as "the movement of celluloid through sprocket holes in a certain rhythm . . . the power source, light source . . . projector's gate, and other parts of the mechanism" (127). One might even talk about the screen, the theater, the seats, the camera operator, the theater chain, the distribution and advertising network, the audience as a collective, and a good deal else that could be put in this category of cinematic viscera, including the entire structure of capitalism. (For Merleau-Ponty [1968], even a single color, such as a red dress [see 131–133] is always part of the total "fabric of the visible," a punctuation mark in "the field of red things" [132] that extends throughout all time and space, what he ultimately calls once again "the flesh.") Barker's attention, however, is primarily devoted to the question of "the secretive rhythms of the body" (2009, 123), both cinematic and biological, and, as one might expect after her treatment of skin and musculature, how those rhythms are compatible and harmonious with each other, generating an "embodied experience of film" (123) for the viewer, an "affinity . . . that gives us a feel for our own deep rhythms, reminding us what we're made of" (129). The match of cinematic rhythms to our own inner rhythms can be literally breathtaking, as Barker argues about a film like *Run Lola Run* (*Lola rennt*, 1998).

I will return to several points here shortly (what are our inner rhythms, since it seems unlikely that they are the rhythms of the secretions of the spleen?), but I begin by pointing out that the peplum as a whole would pose an interesting case for Barker's understanding of cinematic rhythm. I have already talked extensively about the peplum's love of slow time in chapter 1, but here one would have to attend to a different kind of slow or stopped time in the peplum: boredom. Whenever I have taught a midcentury peplum to my students, they have noted the extraordinary amount of agonizing dead time. When the strongman mounts a horse and rides off, the film never simply cuts to him arriving at his destination; we must watch the horse ride off down the entire length of the beach until he disappears from sight. Establishing shots are often double their normal length. Many films set in exotic locales include extensive footage (sometimes documentary) of the landscape, the animals, the trees, or the long grass of the savannah, all included as pure filler. Other films of both the midcentury period and the 1980s (e.g., *Atlas in the Land of the Cyclops* [*Maciste nella terra dei ciclopi*, 1961], *The Witch's Curse* [1962], *Gunan, King of the Barbarians*, most of the *Deathstalker* movies, and the *Ator* series) include copious amounts of footage taken from other films, especially from films the viewer is likely to have already seen, or footage so generic that one has already seen it before having seen it. *Deathstalker IV: Match of Titans* (1991) is practically a clip show of the previous three films; the 1985 *Adventures of Hercules* spends some eight minutes of opening credits (out of a running time of less than ninety minutes) replaying expensive special-effects sequences from the 1983 *Hercules*. More generally, the narrative structure of peplum films is wandering and vague, often embodied by long, pointless sequences in which nothing of import happens at all: the gold standard is still the thirteen-minute sandstorm sequence of *Hercules against the Moon Men*, in which characters do nothing but stagger through a sandstorm, lost, for almost a quarter of an hour. All this might mean something greater in an Antonioni film, but here the problem is more literally palpable and material: peplum films are often based on approximately thirty-five minutes of narrative material that is stretched out to the bare minimum necessary to qualify as a feature-length film. The effect is, as Barker might predict, a radical mismatch of cinematic rhythm to the inner rhythms of the spectator.

Just what are these inner rhythms, and where do they come from? Barker seems to have in mind the natural ebb and flow of attention and interest, the alternation of moments of intense engagement and excitement with lulls that are more contemplative in nature. In her reading of *Run Lola Run*, for instance, she is interested in how the film plays with the conventional time of the action film, often bringing moments of high speed (a chase, for instance) to a crawl without losing a sense of an overall breathtaking narrative pace. But we might consider the possibility that even for Barker, the spectator's bodily rhythm does not actually come naturally from the body but rather from the conventions of the typical Hollywood action film. When I go to see a new action film, my internal rhythmic sense is not based on my heartbeat but on my previous viewings of previous *Die Hard* films and other action films. That is, the spectator's "secretive rhythms of the body" are not immediate and natural (nor terribly secret) but rather are mediated and implanted there by a lifetime of media experience. In this vein, then, we might ask what else has been implanted in the viewer's body, what else enables "its conscious activities, but [is] not, except in extraordinary circumstances, under its direct control" (127). What else is there in me that is brought there by mass media that allows me to go on with my life without being properly aware of it? One might suggest, looking back at chapter 2, the unconscious; one might just as easily suggest, looking forward to chapter 4, ideology.

Barker is principally interested in the cinematic viscera insofar as they are an element of the cinematic body that is normally left unseen, of which we are normally unaware, but that the films she examines do call attention to. There is, of course, a long-standing tradition in film criticism of valuing films that do not appear simply self-referential but perform a Brechtian or Godardian de-mystification of the cinematic apparatus (McGowan 2007, 9–10).[19] Barker (2009) extols *Run Lola Run* for not flaunting the cinematic fantasies that are typical of action films but rather copping to them, reminding us that "action-film speed is an illusion, an effect of narration, editing, camera movement" (120), just as she shows how an art film like *Street of Crocodiles* (1986) makes the connections between the surface image on the screen and the inner workings of the cinematic apparatus "palpable" (130). The viscera are interesting insofar as they might be made visible to the viewer—or palpable, to use more haptic language. Here, the haptic is pressed into service as a de-mystification machine, but, as my earlier reading of *300* shows, it is just as likely (indeed, rather more so) to be used as a mystification machine, one that produces ideology, or, in other words, conceals the relations between the outer appearance and the inner workings, precisely through its most visceral appeals. Indeed, *300* does this ideological trickery most precisely at those moments in which the insides of bodies appear on that glowing surface of the theater screen, in decapitations, dismemberments, amputations, gorings, sprays of blood, and the like. The viewer does not realize here that those bodily invasions of the viscera are occurring at the same time as a different invasion of the viewer's insides, which are becoming accustomed precisely to the secretive rhythms of death—the death of the other. What conceals that foreign body entering the viewer's viscera is precisely the breathlessness of King Leonidas's unstoppable muscular charge forward and the viewer's fascination with his (as yet) unbroken skin, not to mention the spectacle of his enemies' insides spraying into the outside.

This is true, however, only up to a point. *Spartacus: Blood and Sand* suggests that even in the peplum, a particular formal technique does not always have the same value. In the episode "Shadow Games," Crixus, the unbeaten gladiator, Spartacus's rival and later friend, suffers defeat in the arena while battling a superhuman adversary. Spartacus, on the other hand, survives and manages to slay the man-monster. As Crixus lies, terribly wounded, on the sand, we see him look down at his own battered body, and we notice that a loop of his intestines has pushed its way out of his abdominal cavity through one of his wounds. He pushes his viscera back inside his body, arching his back with agony as he does so. What is one to make of this moment? Is it haptic (making us feel), anesthetic (making us numb), or perhaps both at the same time?

Part of the point of phenomenological analysis is that the longer we look at an object, the more it changes and continues to change, part of the ongoing process of establishing and defining a relation between subject and object, of establishing that subject and object are effectively both parts of one continuous revealing of the world. Let us return to the image of Crixus pushing his viscera back inside his body and suggest that here, too, repeated or continued viewing might suggest that we see it in a different way, not simply as an example of the show's love for extreme forms of violence and brutality. If we are initially left numb by this excess, perhaps we can dwell on it, palpate the numb area, and see what feeling it produces. As I suggested earlier, the penetrability of the peplum hero after 1980 becomes a way of measuring the depth one must go to in order to arrive at his secret kernel of anguish, the psychic trauma, usually lost romantic love, that drives him and makes him miserable in a cold, cruel world. In the case of Crixus, of course, he is less of a man than Spartacus; his wound, his insides, and his secret misery (his impossible love for Naevia) are always closer to the surface, and it would appear that so are his viscera. In that sense, the image really is haptic: it is an image of a tactile, muscular, and visceral experience (the intestines are normally held in place by the abdominal muscles, as well as the skin), and it is one that is supposed to make the viewer feel for him. We are not supposed to feel what he is feeling on the surface (which is no doubt a fairly intense pain in his abdomen) but rather to viscerally connect to his humiliation at being beaten by a hated rival. This image in its larger context evokes not only a physical response but also an emotional one that produces a shared sense of mutuality, an empathic recognition on the part of the viewer. "I've been there before," thinks the viewer in sympathy, even though we have (probably) never been lying on the sand watching a loop of our own intestines protrude through our abdominal walls. Excess may be excess at first, then become camp, then become uncanny, and finally elicit a rather more complicated and nuanced haptic reaction on the part of the viewer. *Spartacus*, after all, reveals a surprisingly de-centered vision of masculinity, especially in comparison to *300*, to which it owes so much—the viscera of *Spartacus*, for example, must learn to digest not only violence but also racial difference and differences of sexual orientation, differences to which the cinematic viscera of *300* are intensely allergic. One would never call the show sensitive, but it is surprisingly nuanced in its depiction of masculinity. Perhaps this more nuanced portrayal will become part of the tacit underpinnings of the next generation of peplum films, the next generation of skin, muscles, and viscera. "The thickness of flesh . . . is not an obstacle between them [the viewer and the thing seen], it is their means of communication," writes Merleau-Ponty (1968), before continuing, "The thickness of the body, far from rivaling that of the world, is on the contrary the sole means I have to go unto the heart of the things, by making myself a world and by making them flesh" (135).[20]

Nietzsche suggests in this chapter's epigraph that true virility and manliness are to be found through a wound, and the contemporary peplum offers a remarkable confirmation of this idea; the formerly impenetrable armor of the hero's skin—indeed, the depths of his being, his viscera—now must be perforated by a wound that is simultaneously psychic and physical. In each of the chapters so far, we have seen a similar logic: the peplum hero is led into a surprising intimacy with death, from the shadowy stopped time of cinema gone dead to a queer sexuality that comes after all desire is extinguished and the protagonist takes on a suicidal mission of revenge and then to a haptic logic of masculinity that measures a man by how deeply his skin has been breached. In each case, this fatal intimacy is also a central point of fascination for the spectator: the contemplation of the still body, an infantile refusal of sexual difference, or the pleasures of skin, muscles, and viscera on screen. In chapter 4, I argue that this fascination with vital pleasure and death provides a kind of phantasmatic support for what Roberto Esposito (2011b) has called in biopolitical theory "the immunitary paradigm," in which the pleasures of immunity invariably turn toward an impulse toward self-destruction. The peplum itself, I argue, is a biopolitical intervention, depicting the concentrationary spaces of bare life and obsessing over the link between masculinity and the vital health of the nation within the action of the films themselves, which, in turn, have proven a surprising platform for the muscular actors who star in them to make their own biopolitical interventions in the real world.

Notes

1. Vivian Sobchack's 1992 *The Address of the Eye* is one of the earliest works of phenomenologically oriented haptic film criticism. Other works outside cinema studies in the past decade or so have investigated the sense of touch as deeper and more important than previously thought, such as Steven Connor's *The Book of Skin* (2004), Mark Paterson's *The Senses of Touch: Haptics, Affects and Technologies* (2007), and Constance Classen's *The Deepest Sense* (2012); some of these, such as Paterson's, explicitly position themselves against a perceived "ocularcentrism" in Western culture, as described by Martin Jay in *Downcast Eyes* (1993).

2. The words "skin" and "film" are both terms for thin surfaces, of course. The word for "film" in Romance languages is some variation on *pellicula*, the Latin diminutive for "skin" or "hide," and the English word "film" comes from Germanic roots with exactly the same meanings. In Merleau-Ponty's *The Visible and the Invisible* (an important interlocutor for haptic theories of film, especially Sobchack's), one finds frequent references to "la pellicule superficielle du visible" (the superficial pellicle of the visible); for Merleau-Ponty, as for Marks, the apparently superficial quality of the visible conceals a "depth beneath the surface" (1968, 138). In general, one of the most appealing aspects of Merleau-Ponty is his repeated insistence that it is a mistake to identify the "message" or "content" as somehow riding on top of a surface, perceivable to our disembodied mental eyes: "There is no vision without the screen: the ideas we are speaking of would not be better known to us if we had no body and no sensibility; it is then

that they would be inaccessible to us" (150). The surface, like the air in between, like our eyes and our bodies and ourselves, and eventually, the whole world, is what we see the image with.

3. The tactile mode is relatively clear, referring to contact with the skin. The kinaesthetic in Barker refers to the body's sensation and awareness of movement, while the proprioceptive refers to the body's awareness of its own internal workings. These terms come from medical discourse but are not always used in precisely the same way: proprioception in neurology usually refers to awareness of one's own bodily position and movement, for example (my awareness that my legs are crossed, of where my hand is in space, and so on).

4. Dutton presents an excellent discussion of the complex codes invoked by the bodybuilder's hairlessness (2013, 159–161). He concludes that the bodybuilder's hairlessness gestures primarily at neoteny, the childlike body, as a way of deflecting social concerns about the bodybuilder's hyper-masculinity. He does not connect this understanding, however, to his earlier observation about the tactile invitation present in the bodybuilder's skin: the bodybuilder (and peplum hero) is presented as both an adult sexual object and an object that is pre-sexual at the same time. In both the reading I offer here and in Dutton's, however, the bodybuilder's hairlessness functions paradoxically as a defense.

5. Bernard Rudofsky (quoted in Dutton 2013, 159), claims that in fact, Greek athletes did remove their pubic hair before appearing naked in the arena.

6. On the vulnerability of the 1980s "hard-bodied" hero, see Jeffords 1994, 49–52. My reading is quite different from Jeffords's, however. We agree that the hard-bodied hero's vulnerability generally works to reinforce the dominant ideology, but in quite different ways. For Jeffords, the hero's wounding is an unfortunate but necessary sign of weakness that emphasizes the need for continued strength and ever-harder bodies; in my view, it is a sign of strength, and indeed, a necessary one. The wounded hero is stronger and more manly than a hero who remains unscratched. I must also say that my experience of audience reaction to the wounded male body in film is quite different than hers. Jeffords states that the male audiences of *Rambo III* she observed squirmed in discomfort and disgust when he treated his wounds with burning gunpowder; my audience laughed, apparently perceiving the scene as hyperbolic and comic in its exaggeration of his masculine stoicism.

7. I say "putative hero" because the film begins with Ilius as a young man, and we do not meet his companion, Mace, until a good fifteen minutes of screen time have elapsed. For most of the film, the camera privileges Ilius as well. As soon as we see the film as a peplum, however, we recognize that the huge, muscle-bound Mace (whose skin is never broken over the course of the film) is the peplum strongman, here relegated to the role of mentor and protector for much of the film before eventually emerging as the protagonist. There were several midcentury peplums that treated the strongman in the same way, however, including several Mark Forest peplums in which he is part of a fairly large ensemble cast, such as *Goliath and the Sins of Babylon* or *Colossus of the Arena*. Other peplums of the 1980s also put the strongman to the side, including peplums that starred women as the central character (*Red Sonja* [1985], *Barbarian Queen*, *The Throne of Fire* [Il trono di fuoco, 1983]).

8. The name "Curupira," a demon in Brazilian mythology, means "covered in blisters" in the Tupi language it emerges from.

9. Since the 1990s, many critics (Neale 1993, Savran 1998, and others) have argued that as social and economic forces have gradually eroded traditional gender norms and male privilege, some mainstream films have responded by depicting exaggerated and hyperbolic visions of masculinity and male privilege, depicting a violent and competitive world in which traditional masculinity can excel. The *Rambo* films serve as a convenient touchstone for this "crisis of masculinity" narrative in which masculinity is threatened and then reaffirmed in an exaggerated or even hysterical fashion.

10. This is true, of course, only of the men. Several barbarian peplums of the 1980s have sword-wielding women as their principal characters (*Red Sonja, Barbarian Queen, Barbarian Queen 2: The Empress Strikes Back* [1989], *The Throne of Fire*), and all experience bodily trauma, usually rape. Even so, there is no sense that bodily trauma is a sign of a complex soul, let alone the melancholy nostalgia that characterizes a Conan or a latter-day Spartacus. Rape in the 1980s peplum film is a trivial, forgettable experience that leaves no lasting issues—it is something to be shrugged off, even with a laugh. Virtually all the female characters in *Barbarian Queen* are raped, but although they take vengeance on the perpetrators, there is never any sense of a permanent *ressentiment*, a nostalgia for a spring that will never come again. The closest we see to something like a female equivalent is in *Red Sonja*, where Sonja is vaguely haunted, not so much by her rape or even the death of her family as by her life without a man. In other words, rape is not figured as a loss in LaCapra's sense. Ultimately, *ressentiment* is not permitted to woman, who are seen as structurally lacking rather than having once had something that is now lost.

11. In an article about Tom Ford's *A Single Man* (2009), Kyle Stevens (2013) notes that the film makes extensive use of de-saturated colors to reflect its protagonist's "bleak worldview" (115). Although one should not discount the fact that color manipulation, especially of temperature and saturation, is particularly fashionable at the moment, Stevens's argument carries weight precisely because of how saturation changes in the film. In a technique he calls "flushing" (115–117), the world fills back with saturated color when George sees a desirable body. Stevens does not cite haptic theory, but he is very much in line with Barker here: like a blushing face or an organ that engorges with blood, the filmic body also fills with color. The two kinds of bodies speak to each other, are in sympathy. In the contemporary peplum, de-saturated color palettes are absolutely de rigueur, and *300* and *Spartacus: Blood and Sand* share the same kind of flush: spectacular sprays of blood whose red is the only saturated color the viewer will get to see. At times, these sheets of blood fill almost the entire frame. What if this "flush" has the same sense that Stevens argues for in Ford's film? That is, is this the only moment in which the destitute and solitary male psyche comes back to life for a brief moment?

12. The fact that his penis is also visibly (if just barely) a prosthesis adds an interesting wrinkle to the question of how self-evident masculinity is; its prosthetic nature will be key later in the episode.

13. Barker's lack of love for genres, such as action films, that are based on antagonism is revealed as unfamiliarity when she calls the X-wings of *Star Wars* (1977) "fighter planes" (2009, 113) and refers to the use of slow motion in action sequences as reflecting the body's fear of paralysis (110) when it is almost always used to highlight the viewer's pleasure in high-speed action (see the discussion later in this chapter, as well as chapter 1). This is not meant as a critique, but simply to point out that she does not *feel* these movies in the same way in which she does others.

14. One could make a much more substantial phenomenological argument here about the hero's interaction with inanimate objects, about the difference, in Heideggerian terms, between objects that are present-at-hand and those that are ready-to-hand, and particularly the obtrusive unready-to-hand, for all those objects that Maciste and Hercules must smash, push, and lift. One could talk about how reciprocity might emerge also in our relationships with inanimate objects, but even so, it is quite clear that the point of these scenes in the peplum is to emphasize their nonreciprocity. The pleasure of the spectator lies in Maciste bending the unwilling material of the world to his will.

15. At times, the peplum seems like nothing more than an extended elaboration of Muybridge's initial photo sequences: men leaping and fighting, horses galloping, or women dancing.

16. For an excellent essay on the classical world in video games, see Dunstan Lowe's "Playing with Antiquity" (2009), which delineates the transformations and meanings of the ancient world in an impressive number of video games; the essay focuses primarily on the reworking of the classical heritage but also notes the unusually tight "affinity" (73) between video games and classicist films today, particularly in *300*. The same issue is treated for *Spartacus: Blood and Sand* in Simmons (2011).

17. The "zooms" are computer generated; Snyder's director of photography, Larry Fong, filmed these sequences with essentially three lenses and focuses at the same time; zooms were actually high-speed digital morphs from a medium shot to a close-up (see D. Williams 2007).

18. It is worth keeping in mind that the original propagandistic ending of the film, which explicitly connected the historical moment of the Risorgimento to Fascism, and did so in glowing terms, has not been widely seen since the film was re-edited in 1951 for a rerelease. As much as *1860* was trying to rewrite national history for propagandistic ends, the history of Italian cinema is often rewritten to "purify" neorealism (such as the often overlooked fact that Roberto Rossellini made a trilogy of Fascist military propaganda films shortly before making the neorealist trilogy of *Open City*, *Paisan*, and *Germany Year Zero*), including the position of *1860* as a precursor to neorealism.

19. One might go back to André Bazin (1967–1971)—or, for that matter, to Plato's allegory of the cave in *The Republic*—to find the perennial desire that cinema, an art form based on a host of optical illusions, could be somehow honest and direct with us, rather than illusory and deceptive. But this desire is strangely self-deceptive, since it is the illusion itself that we enjoy.

20. Elsewhere, Merleau-Ponty describes the viewer using his or her body to look at the "superficial pellicle of the visible," only to discover that "the depth beneath this surface contains my body and hence contains my vision. My body as a visible thing is contained within the full spectacle" (1968, 138).

4 IMMUNE SYSTEMS
The Peplum as Biopolitical Genre

Hercules is the hero of political *immunitas*.
—Roberto Esposito, *Immunitas*

The Peplum between "Bio" and "Politics"

The term "biopolitics" is used in a number of different but interrelated ways, all referring to the state's interest in the regulation and management of life as a source of power. One usage is essentially (although not exclusively) metaphorical and applies to attempts to think about the nation as a body, a recasting of the state in biological terms, such as the body politic, the health of the nation, and the border patrol as a kind of immune system. The most extreme example of this metaphorical thinking was no doubt the Nazi conception of the Reich as an idealized and racially pure body in need of *Lebensraum,* uncontaminated space for (German) life, but menaced by internal foreign bodies (Jews, homosexuals, Gypsies) that were conceptualized in biomedical terms (parasites, disease, cancer, degeneracy, hygiene, immunology), and that deprived the Reich of an imagined vitality. This metaphorical conception still persists in extreme forms of nationalism today, where a phrase such as "ethnic cleansing" speaks directly to a conception of the nation as a healthy, clean body that has been contaminated and needs to be sterilized. Entwined with this metaphorical view is Foucault's (2003) recognition that the modern state has increasingly wished to regulate and manage the actual stuff of life as a form of power (biopower): the health of its citizens, their hygiene, their reproductive capacities and sexual lives, the care and feeding of children, and the like. For Foucault, this was part of a slow transition from a political order founded on punishment (in which disobedience is repaid by state-sponsored execution or other bodily punishment) to one founded on discipline: the constant, subtle application of power to manage the life, not the death, of the subject.

Biopolitics in the contemporary American context appears in a number of ways: California's $3 billion stem-cell initiative (endorsed, against his party's platform, by then Governor Arnold Schwarzenegger), regulation or banning of abortion providers, and a nationwide melodrama about Terri Schiavo's life-support apparatus are all clear moments in which we recognize state power attempting to manage the very stuff of life. But biopolitics also makes daily appearances in our ordinary lives, often in ways that we are not entirely conscious of. Reminders in public restrooms about washing hands, billboards telling people to buckle up, and flyers urging the elderly to get vaccinated against the seasonal flu or expectant mothers to take folic acid—all of these are voluntary, but they represent a subtle but continuous form of pressure on the subject to maximize his or her vitality. They often come with reminders that the wrong sorts of behaviors—those that do not maximize life—represent a cost to the nation. As these examples demonstrate, there is a certain ambiguity in this form of the biopolitical: it is without doubt a form of coercion, but it is a curious form that aims to maximize the subject's well-being (albeit with an eye toward increasing productivity and hence state power). This well-being can include even the subject's happiness (public service campaigns about depression) or a fulfilling sex life (attempts to de-stigmatize erectile dysfunction, for example).[1] Such campaigns may at times represent a collusion of state power and business interests, as with pharmaceutical companies that manufacture vitamin supplements, anti-depressants, and Viagra, but this is by no means always the case. The state may also attempt to limit consumption (of cigarettes, of time spent watching television, of alcohol, of junk food) in opposition to capitalist imperatives to maximize it, a sign of how important the actual well-being of the citizen is to the metaphorical health of the nation.

Exercise, fitness, and sports are also in the domain of the biopolitical. It can take forms that are quite obvious and directly coercive, such as New York's 2013 attempt to ban large containers of sugary drinks, a response to an increase in rates of obesity and diabetes (an increase that has been given a biomedical metaphor: the obesity epidemic). Other examples clearly fall under the "soft power" of Foucaultian discipline; for example, a 2012 public service announcement encouraging exercise reunited the cast of the popular American television series *The West Wing* (1999–2006). The series was famous for creator Aaron Sorkin's technique of pairing expository dialogue with rapid and complex choreography, typically as the characters hurried from one busy and hectic location to another. The technique became known as "walk and talk." In the public service announcement, the characters of *The West Wing* explain to the fictional President Bartlett that the American people could combat the obesity epidemic at no cost by simply "walking and talking" for some twenty minutes a day; they explain this, of course, during a classic Sorkin walk-and-talk sequence. I want to pay particular attention to this walk-and-talk ad because it combines in an unusually clear way three elements that are essential to biopolitical discipline: the biological concern with the nation's health, the role of the political in managing that health, and the appearance of mass media to mediate the two, particularly in the creation of fantasy worlds (such as *The West Wing*) that can provide a phantasmic support for the resulting biopolitical ideology. As much as Esposito is inspirational for the work I do in this chapter, I take issue with his assertion that "the biopolitical apparatus [*dispositivo*] tends to eliminate any mediation," reducing life "to a state of absolute immediacy" (2011b, 14); I argue instead that the political only appears to directly manipulate life, and that this impression of immediacy is produced precisely by the media. "Look at President Bartlett telling me to get more exercise," the viewer might think, inserted more or less unconsciously into a frequently naive fantasy about American politics, the soap-operatic delights of the characters' love lives, the fetishistic re-creation of the Oval Office, and the other elements of the show that viewers might find appealing or alluring.

To take an obvious example of such mediation, the Olympic Games have always been biopolitical in nature, a display of state power by means of the strong, healthy, athletic body. It was, however, equally evident to everyone during the Cold War that the Olympics represented the idealized forms of life of the two superpowers in direct competition, and that their vital capacities could be directly and quantitatively measured by medal count. In both instances, it was the mass media that made their biopolitical character literally and metaphorically visible (Hitler's 1936 Olympics were the first television broadcast on Earth), transforming the athlete's body from a synecdoche for the healthy, vigorous nation to a form of Foucaultian discipline. Today that discipline is more evident than ever; the entire ritual of the televised games is surrounded by massive advertising campaigns directed at getting the audience to purchase goods from Nike, but also to "just do it"—become active and involved in sports, a contributor to the vitality of the nation.

Let us continue with the Olympic Games, which already invoke a mythology about Greece and athleticism, and in particular, the athletic male body. The relatively banal midcentury peplum *The Minotaur, the Wild Beast of Crete* (*Teseo contro il Minotauro*, 1960) stars, like most peplums, an American. Typically, that role was played by a bodybuilder like Steve Reeves, but in this film we have Bob Mathias as the Greek hero Theseus. He is certainly extremely fit and tanned, but he has nothing even approaching the musculature of Steve Reeves, Reg Park, or Gordon Scott. Normally, films set in classical or mythological antiquity that did not stress the male protagonist's extraordinary body tended toward high epic drama, such as Stanley Kubrick's *Spartacus* (1960) or William Wyler's *Ben-Hur* (1959). But *Minotaur* follows every peplum convention (an exotic dance sequence, the sacking of a village by marauders, an evil queen with a good twin sister, and more). Moreover, the film references Steve Reeves's 1958 *Hercules*—there is a nearly identical training-camp sequence, and characters in the film make such comparisons explicitly by insisting that Mathias's character, Theseus, is "stronger than Hercules."

The film could make these comparisons because Mathias was a famous athlete, at least as well known as Reeves at the time: he had been the first back-to-back gold medalist in the decathlon, at the 1948 and 1952 Olympics (in the 1948 games, in London, he was the youngest gold medalist in track and field). He retired from sports immediately after the 1952 Olympics and parlayed his celebrity into relatively small-time appearances on television and in film. In 1960, when he made *The Minotaur,* he was precisely midway between two different careers: in 1952, he had been in the Olympics, and in 1967, he would be elected to the US House of Representatives as a Republican. I suggest that in some sense, this positioning—the peplum being located precisely in the space between athletics and politics—is not an accident. Every generation of the peplum has suggested a powerful link between the extraordinarily fit, athletic, and healthy body of its protagonist and the health and vitality of the nation. I use the word "vitality" advisedly because what is at stake is life itself as an object and source of political power.

President Gerald Ford asked Mathias to serve on the President's Council on Physical Fitness; in the early 1980s, President Ronald Reagan contacted him about creating a private-sector version of the council, the National Fitness Foundation, "an organization that would specialize in promoting physical fitness within the business community and show the public ways to keep active, healthy and fit" (Mathias and Mendes 2001, 197). Both the council and the foundation emerged from a political concern about the health and vitality of the nation. The President's Council on Physical Fitness and Sports was founded by President Dwight Eisenhower as part of a Cold War panic about the fitness of American youth, specifically in comparison to their European peers. Over the next several administrations, the council instituted a series of biopolitical interventions, such as public service advertising campaigns, a national testing program in schools, regional clinics, awards for high-performing children, boys' and girls' clubs, and employee fitness programs (hence expanding the scope of the council to the fitness of older Americans). Among the tools deployed to encourage the fitness of American youth were educational films, recognizing the power of the medium to influence the behavior of young people through identification, as well as specifically military exercises.

Bob Mathias in *Minotaur* was not the last intersection of the vital, muscled body, the peplum, and the world of politics. Arnold Schwarzenegger made a similar transition from the world of professional bodybuilding to the world of politics by way of the peplum. Schwarzenegger became a major bodybuilding star in the late 1960s, inspired by bodybuilders like Steve Reeves and Reg Park; he traces the origin of his first career to the moment when, as a fourteen-year-old, he saw a bodybuilding magazine whose cover featured Reg Park as Hercules in an Italian peplum and decided that he would emulate Park in all things (Leamer 2005, 20–21).[2] In 1970, after he had repeated Park's success in the world of bodybuilding, Schwarzenegger had his first starring role in a peplum parody under the pseudonym Arnold Strong. *Hercules in New York* (1969) is widely regarded as a terrible film and a commercial failure, but a decade later, Schwarzenegger returned to film in a blockbuster that not only inaugurated a new cycle of barbarian-themed peplums that would run throughout the 1980s but also made him a major star: *Conan the Barbarian* (1982).[3] He was interested in politics from very early on and lent his post-*Conan* celebrity to the Republican presidential campaign in 1988, accompanying then candidate George H. W. Bush at campaign rallies. Bush reciprocated by appointing Schwarzenegger, just like Bob Mathias, to serve on the President's Council on Physical Fitness and Sports. As Schwarzenegger's appointment to the council might indicate, there is most assuredly a place for the spectacularly muscled male body in the realm of the biopolitical. Erasing any doubts about the links among the peplum, the vitality of the male body, and the exercise of political power, Bush repeatedly referred to Schwarzenegger in speeches as "Conan the Republican."[4]

In today's neoliberal political world, the biopolitical task is best left to private enterprise and individual initiative, such as A World Fit for Kids!, a not-for-profit foundation started by Kevin Sorbo, star of the extremely successful television peplum *Hercules: The Legendary Journeys*. His foundation aims at childhood fitness and nutrition (the biopolitical imperative) as a pathway to academic success, personal fulfillment, and leadership, including political leadership. Sorbo also participates directly in politics by lending his celebrity to Republican causes, including advising the House Republican Conference on how to defend Mitt Romney from Democratic attacks during the 2012 presidential campaign. When Sorbo criticized Republicans in 2014 for being too weak and insufficiently conservative, allowing the United States to become ever more socialist, media outlets played up his identity not as Sorbo, but as Hercules: TMZ, for example, captioned the video of Sorbo's remarks with "Sorbo says the Republican Party better find a real-life Hercules before 2016" (although the actor had in fact made no such comparison); in 2012, the Huffington Post repeatedly referred to the actor, who had just spoken to Republican lawmakers, as Hercules, while "a House Republican leadership aide joked that [Paul] Ryan is in good company when he's stumping with demi-gods. Hercules is, after all, the son of Zeus" (Bendery). The implicit link between the peplum's mythically powerful men and right-wing politics (not without certain complexities and nuances, however) has been clear since Maciste first appeared in *Cabiria* in 1914, a film that was universally understood as arguing in favor of Italian colonialist intervention in North Africa, and it continues today.

The *homo sacer* and Immunity

Let us turn to two of the most important biopolitical thinkers, both Italian: Giorgio Agamben and Roberto Esposito. Agamben traces the emergence of certain negative features of the modern state that would appear to be aberrations or exceptions (e.g., the concentration camp, the "state of exception" in which laws are temporarily suspended because of a crisis, and ethnic cleansing) to an originary split in our thinking about life and politics. This is the split between *zōē* (animal life, also called "bare life," "naked life," or "mere life") and *bios* (human cultural and political life). It is apparent, however, that this cannot be a division between humans and animals, since humans have an animal life as well as a political life. The split is instead between two dimensions of life, my merely biological life and my life as a citizen. This split, while seemingly allowing for the elevation of human lived experience to something of transcendent value, simultaneously permitted a concomitant de-humanization of the subject. A given individual, an exception to the community, such as the criminal, the terrorist, or the pervert, could be categorized as "an animal" and hence not participating in the good life of *bios*. Agamben calls this figure, the human being stripped of *bios* and reduced to bare life, the *homo sacer*, a term from Roman law for one whose crime allowed anyone to kill him with impunity. Drawing on the German political theorist Carl Schmitt, Agamben describes a more generalized "state of exception," a space in which the law declares that the law does not apply, such as Nazi concentration camps or the American facilities at Guantánamo. In such spaces, the inmates do not have *bios*, but only *zōē*; they can be force fed or denied food, executed without a trial, or held forever. Agamben's argument (which he made before 9/11) was that the state of exception would tend to become permanent and spread.

For most of this chapter, I will be discussing Esposito and the "immunitary paradigm," but Agamben's concepts of bare life and the *homo sacer* are also recurrent themes in the peplum. "Vud has spilled the blood of our tribe. He is no longer one of us. From now on he can be hunted, like an animal," pronounces the musclebound, shaggy-maned hero of *Ironmaster* (1983). The film's borrowings from the myth of Cain and Abel are quite obvious: two "brothers," light and dark, who battle for supremacy and the right to lead the tribe, the loser to be expelled into the wild. This was not new material in the peplum universe; both *Duel of the Titans* (*Romolo e Remo*, 1961), recounting the struggle between Romulus and Remus, in the midcentury period, and *Gunan, King of the Barbarians* (1982) tell essentially the same story. What these films can help us understand is that Agamben and Esposito are also essentially recounting an alternate version of a myth about human origins, and like most origin myths, it recounts the story of a rupture and a fall. The story that biopolitical theories tell are not radically different in kind from other mythic origin narratives: there was once a community that was whole, and then something happened to it. For Agamben, this is the split between *bios* and *zōē*, which allows for the creation of the image of a people at the expense of the reduction of others to bare life, or, as God says to Cain, "When thou tillest the ground, it shall not henceforth yield unto thee her strength; a fugitive and a vagabond shalt thou be in the earth" (Genesis 4:12). Cain replies by describing himself as *homo sacer*: "I shall be a fugitive and a vagabond in the earth; and it shall come to pass, that every one that findeth me shall slay me" (4:14). Cain cannot be sacrificed, but can be killed with impunity.[5] While God does not accept this (he prefers Cain remain alive), Vud no longer possesses *bios* but has been reduced to "bare life" or animal life (*zōē*); he may "be hunted like an animal."

Roberto Esposito has made an especially valuable contribution to biopolitical thinking, what he calls the "immunitary paradigm" (see 2008, 45–77 and 2011b, 1–20). Biopolitical thinking at its most straightforward—the nation is a body that should be productive, healthy, and vital—would seem to aim toward essentially positive results. In order to maximize the health of the nation, however, it must protect itself against everything that might cause it harm, such as an obesity epidemic, a real disease (say, drug-resistant strains of tuberculosis) brought in by immigrants, or a computer virus released by hackers that threatens the nation's financial infrastructure. Esposito argues that biopolitical responses to these threats depend on immunitary thinking: "Someone or something penetrates a body—individual or collective—and alters it, transforms it, corrupts it" (2011b, 2). What is called for is an immune response to these foreign bodies. For Esposito, as for Agamben, the clearest and most extreme version of this immune response is that of the Nazis, but what Esposito adds to Agamben's analysis of the "state of exception" and the bare life of the camps is the recognition that there is something fundamentally contradictory within the very notion of immunity.

For example, Esposito notes that the Nazis initially made use of a series of "comprehensible" (by their standards) biopolitical immunities, such as the forced sterilization of homosexuals, the handicapped, the mentally retarded, and other "undesirable" categories that might, if allowed to reproduce, threaten to contaminate the healthy German body. The good body is now immunized against the bad foreign bodies around and in it. But immunitary logic never stops there: Esposito cites Fritz Lenz, the Nazi geneticist, speculating that up to a third of the German people would also have to be sterilized, including all women over the age of thirty-five (2008, 143). The immunitary paradigm could go further still, and did: Hitler's Telegram 71, sent from his bunker at the end of the war, concluded that Germans had proved themselves weak by losing the war, and so Hitler ordered the "destruction of the conditions of subsistence for the German people" (2008, 116). To save the German body, in other words, the whole German body must die. This is Esposito's immunitary paradigm: the community attempts to immunize itself against alterity and risk, but immunization always requires injecting that alterity and risk into the core of the community. Taken to its extreme, the logic is "auto-immunitary," or self-destructive.

Esposito finds this immunitary paradigm everywhere in modernity, however, and not simply in medical handbooks and Nazi geneticists; he also finds it in culture, the mediating terrain between the "bio" and the "politics" of biopolitics. He briefly but convincingly reads three nineteenth-century texts: *Dr. Jekyll and Mr. Hyde*, "The Picture of Dorian Gray," and *Dracula* (2008, 124–126). For

Esposito, these texts all attempt to think through the problem of immunizing oneself against biological degeneration—a return to the atavistic animal within, the gradual decline of age, the degenerate as such—and all conclude that destroying that degeneration, the other within or without, is tantamount to destroying oneself, a dynamic that is particularly clear in the case of Stevenson and Wilde. For Esposito, however, Dracula exemplifies the immunitary paradigm in that, in the case of the undead, what must be given to them in order to stop their contagion is precisely death itself; moreover, this ritualized gift of death is what one is by extension guaranteeing for the whole community. The undead put the body (and the body politic) at risk of never dying, and the immunitary response here, as it was in Nazi Germany, is to guarantee the death of the body as part of its determination to maximize life. Esposito's theory finds an astonishing confirmation in a 2013 film, since, in the most literal manner possible, this is the exact plot of *World War Z*, in which the hero discovers near the end of the film that the few people who have survived the zombie apocalypse can be immunized against zombies by injecting themselves with fatal diseases (for which they can later receive treatment). These moribund soldiers and citizens become invisible to zombies; death becomes the way to immunize the community.

The Peplum as Biopolitical

I hope that the biopolitical character of the peplum, centrally invested in the appearance of an exaggeratedly healthy male body, is at least somewhat apparent already. Certainly, the films are centrally concerned with bodies, particularly the spectacularly muscled bodies of their heroes. Those bodies are presented as images of absolute and uncontainable vitality. They are not simply strong but overflowing with health: they are tanned, waxed, and oiled, and their muscles bulge in a constant state of muscular tension and capacity. The heroes laugh and grin as they smash obstacle after obstacle, enemy after enemy, filled with overflowing good humor and well-being. These bodies must be placed in comparison to the other male bodies that populate the films. The hero's sidekick is slighter, paler, and often blond and is generally moody and melancholy and occasionally even given over to despair. Finally, there are degenerate bodies, such as the scarred and corpulent King Eurytus in *Goliath and the Dragon* (1960) or the many undead-like figures that populate the peplum, such as the monstrous and vampiric Kobrak in *Goliath and the Vampires* (1961), who also commands an army of faceless and mindless zombie-like soldiers, normal people who have been drained of life. At stake throughout all these bodies is the question of vitality, from Hercules, who has so much life that he can share it abundantly with those around him, to the villain, who is incapable of thriving on his or her own and must drain the life of others.

From the early Maciste films to the most recent sword-and-sandal extravaganzas, virtually every peplum turns on two plots, usually interrelated: while the subplot is romantic, the primary plot is invariably political. In the most typical midcentury peplum, an evil, corrupt, and degenerate ruler has taken control of the country as a usurper or, even more commonly, as someone who stands behind the throne (this structure is essentially unchanged in the contemporary peplum). That is, most often the state is subverted by a wicked adviser or a scheming seductress who manipulates the ruler by sex, magic, or both; occasionally this structure is even doubled or tripled. In *Goliath and the Vampires*, the proper ruler of the city of Salmanac should be the wise and virtuous Kubrik, but his throne has been usurped by the current sultan, Omar; Omar, passive and melancholy, is not man enough to perpetuate the cruel miseries we witness on his people but has been manipulated into doing so by the wicked and sensual Astra; Astra, however, is eventually revealed as the right-hand woman of the demonic monster, Kobrak, the real source of the film's villainy.

The peplum makes a repetitive and generic appeal to "the people" and their suffering caused by the illegitimate ruler in almost every film. This suffering is always literal and corporeal and almost always involves forced labor by populations in concentrationary spaces (underground spaces, such as mines, are particular favorites), coupled with arbitrary executions, ritual human sacrifice, and scenes of public torture. What is happening is quite clear: the degenerate body of the ruler requires a vampiric supplement for his or her own life and so drains the life of the people through magic, forced labor, or ritual sacrifice. In terms of biopolitical theory, the sovereign has declared a state of exception and has reduced a portion or the entirety of the people to "bare life." Indeed, the peplum often literalizes the symbolic demotion from *bios* to *zōē* that takes place in the space of exception: these drained subjects may become abject, but more often they become zombies, robots, mindless drones, faceless beings, identical clones, or simply lifeless statues.

Intervening in or mediating between the bare-life space of the biological and the sovereign space of the political is Maciste, Hercules, or Goliath, a muscular antibody who is ready to destroy the foreign body that has so severely reduced the vital powers of the people. I use the term "antibody" advisedly, since in what follows I want to highlight the immunitary thinking that Esposito indicates is typical of biopolitical thinking. As Dyer has noted (1997, 169–176), the peplum as a genre was aware of its proximity to Italian Fascism and generally presented right-wing and authoritarian "structures of feeling" coupled with an ostensible anti-fascism; as a result, the midcentury peplum almost never pursues its immunitary thinking all the way, but there are plenty of signs that immunitary logic does indeed characterize its workings.

The basic structure of the peplum's (bio)political plot (mysterious foreigner depletes the strength and vitality of the nation; strongman arrives in order to prevent it) has been present since the silent era. The film *Maciste medium* (1918) is lost, but the surviving title cards indicate that in it, the mad Argentinian scientist

José Olivares is intent on developing a serum that will bring his dead beloved, Carmencita, back to life, and that he must drain Maciste's vitality to do so. One of Maciste's competitors, Luciano Albertini, played Samson in the 1919 *Sansone e la ladra d'atleti* (*Samson and the Athlete Thief*, also lost), which tells the "story of a mysterious organization, headed by a woman, that has the curious objective of annihilating the Italian athletic heritage, and which, to that end, has decided to kidnap its most famous champions" (Farassino 1983, 36). Very little had changed forty years later, when Samson once again had to stop a mysterious woman from draining the vitality of the people. The Egyptian-themed midcentury peplum *Son of Samson* (1960) begins with an explanatory voice-over:

> More than 3,000 years ago, the Egyptian people eked a hard and miserable existence in the barren fields, while in the capital city of Tanis, their Pharaoh was permitted to live in luxury by the conquering Persians, who plundered the country's wealth and enslaved its people. To ensure the success of their unscrupulous mission, the Persian masters placed the beautiful but cruel Queen Smedes on the throne as the wife of the elderly Pharaoh. Threatened with the discovery of her unholy alliance with the Persians, and in the hope of practicing her evil more effectively on the Pharaoh's successor, his son Kenamun, Queen Smedes plotted to have the Pharaoh ruthlessly assassinated, while the Persian invaders continued to bring suffering and devastation upon the unprotected people of the Nile, who could not gather the strength to overpower their enemies and regain their liberty.

Virtually all the biopolitical tropes that are typical of the peplum appear here. The vitality of "the people" is drained in order to prop up a parasitic and degenerate body: the Pharaoh (who is also, as we will learn, under the queen's hypnotic power). His vitality ("[life] in luxury") is directly paid for by a corresponding lack of vitality, not only in the people (whom "a hard and miserable existence . . . enslaved") but also in the land, which has become "barren." As is often the case in the peplum, the adversarial relationship between authentic community (the Egyptian people) and the truly foreign body (the Persians) is mediated on multiple levels: the Pharaoh's inadequate and aged body, which cannot stand up to Queen Smedes, whose origin remains ambiguous (is she Persian or an opportunistic, gold-digging Egyptian?). Moreover, a direct relationship is posited between the misery and lifelessness of the people (suffering and devastation) and a missing immunity: the people are "unprotected." Finally, the name and nature of that immunity are made clear: the "strength" and "power" incarnated in the muscular body of the overpoweringly vital bodybuilder.

The usual tactic of the peplum is to split the enervation and degeneracy into two spaces, one collective, the other individual. Collectively, we see masses of "the people," segregated into camp-like spaces, suffering in body and soul as they are forced to work the mines, give up their children, or send their daughters off for another human sacrifice. Individually, a single person will be enervated, weakened, without spirit or mind. So it is with Deianira in *Hercules in the Haunted World* (1961): as the people suffer under an unjust and improper ruler, Lico, she has become listless, absent in mind and spirit (the viewer easily infers that Lico has taken possession of her mind). Her body reflects the body of the people, as one of the town elders explains to Hercules in directly immunitary terms: "It's not only in Deianira—it's in the people." Deianira is restored by Hercules, but Lico has new, vampiric plans for her: he will drain her blood and take it into his own body, thus becoming the immortal king of Ocalia.

We see this again in *Hercules against the Moon Men* (1964), in which Billis is turned into Selene, the queen of the Moon Men, again by having her blood drained in order to create the perfect form of the other. In *The Minotaur, the Wild Beast of Crete*, we see again the same split between a collective pestilence and an individual one: youths (although we see and hear about almost exclusively female victims) are sacrificed to the Minotaur, a degenerate beast who consumes them, while the evil Phaedra attempts to solidify her hold on Crete by having her good twin sister, Ariadne, killed. In every case, we see a fundamentally immunitarian paradigm exactly as Esposito describes it: it is precisely native blood that is the basis for the idealized form of foreign blood. That is, Esposito wants to show how the concept of immunity always carries its own destruction at its core, and over and over again, the peplum presents the degenerate and the healthy, the native and the foreign, as essentially identical.

If female blood is drained in order to create this idealized, superhuman subhuman, we should not infer that male vitality is not at risk. In stories with an evil female queen, the man's strength may be sapped directly through sexual enervation. In later peplums, this draining can become literalized, as in *Conan the Barbarian* when Conan copulates with a witch who transforms into a grasping, clawing vampire. In the midcentury peplum, the sexual draining is generally more metaphorical: in peplum after peplum, the evil queen arranges sadistic scenes of torture that test (and consume) the hero's strength. Almost invariably, these scenes feature the risk of penetration: a massive weight with an attached blade presses inexorably toward our hero's chest, or horses pull at him while he stands inside a cage filled with knives. The technique of filming these sequences is inevitably the same: shots of the hero's muscles straining and the spike approaching his magnificently taut pectorals are intercut with the evil queen's increasingly aroused face and body. As his energy is expended, her degenerate and perverse vitality is augmented.

Alternatively, the peplum hero may run the risk of being transformed into one of the undead, the de-vitalized, but the exceptional form of these faceless masses. In Esposito's immunitary logic, the robotic, undead alterity that Maciste or Hercules fights against finds its most perfect expression in his own body. In

Samson in King Solomon's Mines (also released as *Maciste in King Solomon's Mines*, 1964), the strongman is turned by magic into one of the suffering masses who are forced to work the mines, but unlike the rest of them, he works without complaint, without resistance, carrying ten times as much for twice as long. In *Goliath and the Vampires*, the evil Kobrak plans to turn Goliath with "his magnificent body" into the model for a new race of mindless, robotic slaves. Here, too, there is the same paradoxical immunitary logic at play, since with Goliath's body, Kobrak will be unstoppable, an ideal form of the degenerate body. The same is true in *Hercules and the Captive Women* (1961): if Hercules can be transformed, they can make a mindless clone army of Herculeses, making the evil Queen Antinea "unstoppable"—that is, the deficit of her deficient body (she is both sexually predatory and devoid of maternal feelings, offering up her own daughter as a human sacrifice) can be made up for, but atop the base of the super-healthy, vital body of the peplum muscleman. Dyer (1997) notes precisely this contradiction in political terms in his discussion of the film: when Queen Antinea "encounters Hercules she of course realises that here is the ultimate specimen of ideal manhood; Hercules is opposed to this fascist regime, but Reg Park's muscles embody its very ideals" (176). The idealized form of the male body is always the same as the idealized form of its alterity.

Biopolitical Vampires and Fascist Zombies

In this section, I will analyze in some detail two midcentury peplums that are particularly clear about the biopolitical character of the genre, but I will try to make clear in parenthetical notes along the way how many other peplums feature the same kind of thinking. It is not the case that the silent-era Maciste films were less biopolitical; Farassino (1983) cites, for example, a pamphlet from Albertini Film in the 1910s that already justified its production of strongman films in explicitly biopolitical terms. The company was "convinced that physical culture is the basis of the triumphant energy of a people" (46). Even so, the biopolitical element of the peplum is at its clearest beginning in the midcentury period. Both films I examine in detail are from 1961, approximately halfway through the midcentury peplum cycle, at a point when the norms of the genre were well established but before the worst excesses of the peplum's final years had arrived. Both are well regarded, at least by the rather low standards of the peplum. *Hercules and the Captive Women* (there is, in fact, only one captive woman) was directed by Vittorio Cottafavi and was the first of two Hercules films starring Reg Park. Already in 1963, Spinazzola called it "the best of the peplum films" and could say that it was certainly "the one that has most excited the critics' attention" (107), a claim that is probably still true today. *Goliath and the Vampires* (there is, of course, only one vampire) was directed by Giacomo Gentilomo and Sergio Corbucci, the highly regarded director of several significant spaghetti Westerns. Although both films are qualitatively better than the run-of-the-mill peplum, they are exceptional not for their biopolitical character (which is, as we have seen, typical of the peplum in general), but for the clarity of their biopolitical thinking.

Both films share one other characteristic: they are part of a subgroup of peplum films that also includes films like *Conqueror of Atlantis* (*Il conquistatore di Atlantide*, 1965) and *Giant of Metropolis* (1961). Karine Lannut's phrase "paleo-science-fiction" (1998, 74) for these peplums is quite apt, since these films have a fundamentally magical and atavistic relationship to science. Science certainly represents yet another form of modernity that Hercules must defend against or destroy, along with the industrial machines that he wrecks in more conventional peplums. Like those industrial machines (made out of primitive logs lashed together), we are presented with an ancient image of modernity, whose menace is more ambiguous. In a film like *Giant of Metropolis,* we see a royal throne hall that is as 1960s mod as anything in *Star Trek* (automatic, pneumatic, sliding circular doors appear throughout), but the dancers who perform for the king wear primitive loincloths and feathered headdresses, yet they dance to experimental, electronic music as part of some sort of futuristic mating ritual. In *Goliath and the Vampires,* we see Kurtik's laboratory, filled with glass retorts and tubes intermingled with primitive constructions. It is almost certainly no accident that these films are also the most direct about the peplum's interest in the threat that modernity poses to life itself, a threat that directly conjures up an immunitary response in the figure of the strongman's overflowing vitality. "He [the strongman] is endowed with a vitality above the ordinary," explains a scientist-priest in *Giant of Metropolis* before going on to locate that vitality in the usual place: "His blood is a rarity that should not be wasted." As always, the wicked king sees in the strongman a chance to create the ideal race that will be the fulfillment of his monstrous and degenerate dreams.

Goliath and the Vampires poses the question of the biopolitical directly. A monstrous vampiric figure named Kobrak oppresses his people with public impalements and literally drains the life from the surrounding regions by sending his soldiers to capture young women, on whose blood he feeds. At some level, of course, this is the plot of every peplum—an evil ruler oppresses the people, forces them into slave labor in the mines, and so forth—but many peplums make the vampiric consumption of life more literal through the figure of an evil ruler who demands human sacrifices. Such sacrifices may take the form of gladiatorial combat to the death (*My Son, the Hero* [1962], *Colossus of the Arena* [1962]) or sacrifices to the gods (*Goliath and the Sins of Babylon* [1963], *Hercules against the Sons of the Sun* [1964]); they may directly refer to the myth of the Minotaur (*The Minotaur* and many others), or the sacrifice may be to a monstrous equivalent of the Minotaur (as in *Conquest of Mycene* [*Ercole contro Moloch*, 1963], a sacrifice that is a direct reference, once again, to the 1914 *Cabiria*, whose most influential sequence is the sacrifice of small children in the Temple of Moloch).[6] Generally the victims are young women. In *Goliath and the Vampires*, the forms of vampiric draining multiply and acquire progressively more and more uncanny forms of vampiric parasitism. Young women are drained of blood; a slave merchant is offered only a single coin for all his slaves, but the coin is stained with blood, so he understands that he, too, is being drained by Kobrak; many men are drained by Kobrak as well, who become an army variously described as "living statues" and "robots" with masks in lieu of faces; Kobrak is uncannily duplicated in Kurtik, who commands an army of equally mask-like "blue men"; Kobrak changes shape to become Goliath's uncanny double; and on and on.

But let us attend to the actual vampire in this film and to the first, and really only, explicit scene of blood being drained. When Goliath's village is attacked, the menacing invaders kill everyone, including Goliath's mother, except for the young women, especially Goliath's fiancée, Guja. On board the attackers' ship, the chief pillager, Amahil (played by African American dancer and actor Vanoye Aikens, here billed as Van Aikens), inspects the women before choosing some to cut and drain of blood. When he comes to pale, blonde Guja, however, it is clear that there is an unspeakable bond between them, and her will and resistance fade away— she slowly offers her arm to him voluntarily, but he only caresses it before choosing her companion to bleed instead. When Amahil offers the goblet full of blood to his master, Kobrak, we see only an inhuman arm emerge through fog and mist from behind a red velvet curtain (figure 4.1). Is it covered in hair? Elephantine, wrinkled hide? Its exact nature remains unclear, but its contrast to the perfectly smooth and pale arm of Guja could not be clearer. Ultimately, however, it is Goliath's oiled and taut skin that forms the real counterpart to Kobrak's monstrosity. We need to pause for a moment and consider these contrasts in skin, black male and white female, on the one hand, and monstrous degeneracy and idealized perfection, on the other.

As chapter 3 on skin detailed, a good deal of work in film theory since the publication of Laura Marks's *The Skin of the Film* (2000) has looked at the haptic dimension of cinema. In that book, Marks made one of the best-known elaborations of the idea that cinema does not speak exclusively to the visual and (secondarily) to the audial. In fact, as a material medium, it is perhaps primarily concerned with surfaces (the surface of the screen, the celluloid substrate, and the photosensitive chemical film on its surface that eventually lent its name synecdochically to the entire art form). Marks argues that a number of alternative forms of visual culture engage a "haptic visuality," a notion she borrows from art historian Alöis Riegel, allowing one to "[touch] a film with one's eyes" (162). Marks, of course, is interested in images that evoke the tactile character of surfaces, such as the slow pan across an object to reveal its consistency or grain (e.g., variegated, rough, smooth, woven, or slippery) or filmic techniques that reveal the texture of the film

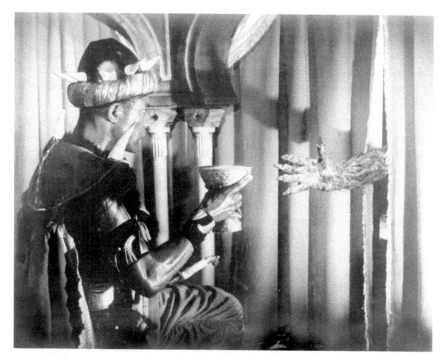

Figure 4.1. The monstrous hand of Kubrick, reaching for his goblet of blood. *Goliath and the Vampires*, 1961.

itself, its granularity, its varying exposure, scratches on the negative, and the like. The analytic idea that film can activate our sense of touch is extremely useful, but some readers have been more skeptical about Marks's endorsement of the haptic as somehow inherently tied to intercultural spaces or as a form of resistance to dominant (Western, patriarchal, white) cinematic norms. All cinema evokes the haptic to some degree. In the case of the peplum, however, there is perhaps something to be said for Marks's understanding of surface, particularly skin.

Skin in the peplum not only is tense, stretched across the bodybuilder's skin, but also produces tension. It is, as in most films, a site of the film's psychoanalytic tension, a source of visual pleasure for the audience, as well as a surface on which various desires can be projected. One of the most striking features of the peplum is just how much skin is exposed; at times, one has the curious impression of watching a pornographic film made by children, a combination of total innocence and overwhelming pleasure in bare skin.[7] This is part of the campiness that characterizes all real peplum films and that does not appear in, say, *Gladiator*. At the same time, the peplum prioritizes male skin for a male spectator. That skin is ideally in a state of readiness, swollen by the muscle beneath—in a state of maximal tension, but one that produces a kind of ideological tension in the normative spectator. Peplum skin confuses heterosexual identification and homoerotic desire; better still, it points out that these two axes are not separable in a facile or thoughtless way. There is a certain quantum of work that must go into maintaining their separation, work that is normally concealed but is revealed in the adulation of the idealized masculine body. In one of the most infamously bad peplum films, *Hercules against the Moon Men*, the evil Queen Samara places Hercules in a torture device that threatens to pierce his body with sharpened spikes; the viewer can then enjoy the sight of Hercules's straining muscles as he attempts to hold the spikes off. So far, this scene is pretty clearly aligned with normative ideas about heterosexual masculinity: the male body must not be penetrated. But as the sequence progresses, we are treated to more and more shot/countershot constructions that locate the place of our gaze in Queen Samara's eyes, and the shots become increasingly erotic, until nothing is left except close-up slow pans across his taut, muscled, tanned, oiled, hairless, massive pectorals. This is properly haptic: the cinematic gaze invites us to touch the surface, and when Hercules breaks free at last, the queen, breathless, can only command her guards, "Take him to my chambers." In short, the impenetrability of taut, vital male skin is explicitly eroticized, not only for the spectators within the diegesis but also for the spectators in the theater.

Finally, the haptic dimension of peplum skin also produces a biopolitical tension, one revealed in the contrast between Goliath's perfectly smooth, continuous, hairless, and white skin and the wrinkled, hairy monstrosity of Kobrak's skin. Skin is the body's first—and in many respects best—line of defense against the foreign bodies that might menace its health and vitality. Because the strongman represents an immunitary response that protects the community (the people), his skin represents a precious symbolic economy. The tension emerges insofar as the bodybuilder's skin must be maximally stretched over his massive muscles, taut, in a constant state of rigid tension that can signify his instant readiness to defend the body politic. His skin is like the skin of a balloon, however, threatened not only by the tiniest pinprick from the outside but also by the pressure from within. One sometimes has the impression that the bodybuilder's muscles might pop through, leaving behind what is in fact a kind of extreme ideal form of the built body: the flayed man. Indeed, some contemporary bodybuilders have come close to achieving a look that effectively makes the skin virtually disappear; what is left is muscle and blood. In her study of the skin of the film, Marks valorizes texture, scratch, and grain, as opposed to the smooth and glossy, as a kind of aperture and rupture of rigid ideology. Esposito does much the same, suggesting in *Immunitas* (2011b) that the immune response that resists the opening (including the perfectly unbroken skin) is what ultimately destroys a community. For both Esposito and Marks, for both the biopolitical and the haptic, what is needed is a rethinking based on the notion of aperture.

The skin of the film in *Goliath and the Vampires* should thus preserve the essential difference between the vital, healthy body and the corrupted and degenerate body that threatens to parasitically destroy the community. But immediately we notice the self-contradictory character of the immune response. As I have already noted, Kobrak is as enamored of Goliath's body as any of the women in the film (and the ideal male spectators of the film), but even characters within the film seem to be aware that the desire to possess Goliath's body is nonnormative. Kobrak explains to Astra, his servant, "I want him alive: his magnificent body can serve as a model for the army of slaves with which I shall conquer the earth—why are you looking at me like that?"[8] The opposition between the healthy and the degenerate body reveals a curious problem: Goliath represents the perfected form of both kinds of bodies. Moreover, Esposito's immunitary logic is characterized by two moments: a first moment (immune) in which the opposition between inside and outside is strenuously asserted so that the immune response can defend the body and keep the outside out, but also a second moment (autoimmune) in which the immune response discovers the essential alterity of the body itself and turns to attack what it was supposed to defend. We might begin to wonder here about the strange doublings of inside and outside, familiar and alien, that characterize the whole film. Opposing the evil Kobrak and his zombie-like living statues, his robot army, we find the rather ambiguous figure of Kurtik and his legions of equally uncanny telepathic blue men. We are told explicitly that Kurtik is one of the blue men, but the only one with white skin, but it will eventually turn out that Kurtik is the proper inheritor of the throne of Salmanac, the rightful sultan. That is, even after this film performs the political restitution that is at the heart of every midcentury peplum, it will turn out that a radical and uncanny other is at the heart of the inside, that the body of the self is foreign at its core.

Even Goliath, an agent of the immune system meant to protect the people, does not escape this alterity. Surrounded by the creepy blue men, he is served a highly symbolic meal: bread and wine, flesh and blood of the body. They are, of course, blue bread and blue wine, and Goliath partakes of them and pronounces them good. The alien other is now on the inside. As the immune response, Goliath literalizes the second movement of immunitary logic by turning against the body at the end of the film. Kobrak takes on the shape of Goliath, and so the final duel is indeed between the body and itself, one magnificent body against another, identical magnificent body. In their ensuing duel, their vital forces appear evenly matched until a decisive break—and it is precisely a break in the skin. One Goliath suffers a tear in the skin along his jawline, an open wound, and the true Goliath manages to grasp at this tear and pull the skin of his enemy's face off entirely. This reveals, at last, the monstrous face of Kobrak, a skull made of uneven paste, with vampire teeth.

Although this device allows the viewer to project the degenerate body into another space and destroy it, it remains literally true that the vampiric parasite is found precisely underneath Goliath's skin, behind his face (this duel of the strong-man against himself, with one eventually unmasked as a monstrous other, reappears in Lucio Fulci's 1984 peplum *Conquest*). In short, everyone is contaminated by alterity by the end of the film: Guja has been transformed into one of the uncanny living statues with their uncanny, paper-white skin and then turned back; Kurtik is the alien other, and it is precisely his skin that, rather than defending the community against this foreign body, allows him to pass as one of the people and, indeed, their rightful ruler; and Goliath has incorporated the substance of the blue men into his body (in a clear analogy to the transubstantiation in the Catholic Mass of bread and wine) and has found the foreign, degenerate body underneath his own skin. Although the peplum always goes in search of the ideal embodiment of the male body as a defense against what is other to that body, alterity does not just creep back in; it is always present, always alongside, always part of the self that swerved away from it.

In *Hercules and the Captive Women*, there is a political threat in the film that has to do precisely with the vitality of bodies. After the film's opening sequence (an exotic dance sequence that turns into a tavern brawl), Hercules and company are suddenly overwhelmed by a sandstorm that proves to be a vision on the road back to Thebes. The light turns red, the sun appears to shrink or recede, and a voice cries out, "It is bleeding, it is bleeding—our poor fatherland!" Once they are in Thebes, the prophet Tiresias reveals that there is a terrible menace coming from the west, from beyond the Straits of Gibraltar—known at that time as the Pillars of Hercules.[9] The Greek political response to this threat of a foreign body is feeble. The king of Thebes, Androcles, is willing to take the fight to the Atlanteans, but the other kings are too weak: two cowardly brothers reason their way out, another king is controlled by his mother, a third is willing only to stay behind and "defend" (i.e., take over) the others' kingdoms while they are gone, and the rest offer various other excuses. It becomes clear that the enemy is at least as much internal as it is external: the other kings cannot wait to consume the Kingdom of Thebes for themselves the moment the king leaves to defend their common community. The impulse of immunity becomes autoimmunity; to save the body politic, the body must be sacrificed.

   As always in the peplum, it is the strength of Hercules that keeps both external foreign bodies at a distance and internal degenerate elements under control. Speaking of the character in general in peplum film, Gregori (2009) notes that "Hercules is a sort of nobleman who becomes a paladin who protects the poor and oppressed. His ultimate aim, then, is social peace, even if we're left with the impression that this means, more than security from an external enemy, elimination of a threat or opposition that might rupture the order of the community from the inside" (228). Hercules resolves the political impasse with a purely symbolic gesture that is at the same time an expression of his overwhelming strength and vitality: he guarantees that no one else will sit on Androcles's throne by hefting the massive stone throne into the air and smashing it. Once Hercules arrives on the island of Atlantis, his formidable strength once again resolves the impossible immunitarian paradox. Upon landing, he discovers the Atlantic princess, Ismene, trapped within the rock of the island, slowly becoming one with the rock itself. Once Hercules defeats her guardian, Proteus, she reveals that she was sacrificed by her own people to Proteus in order that he might protect the island from outsiders with a dense veil of fog. The body, in other words, must be sacrificed in order to protect the body, but Hercules's strength shatters the autoimmune response once again as he frees Ismene and dispels the fog.

Esposito writes that "immunity is essentially a comparative concept: its semantic focus is more on the difference of condition from the others than on the notion of exemption . . . —so much so that the true antonym of *immunitas* may not be the absent *munus* [debt or obligation], but rather the *communitas* of those who support it by being its bearers" (2011b, 6). In other words, immunity would initially appear to be focused on exclusion of the thing that you are immune from; the opposite of immunity would be something like susceptibility. But no, says Esposito: your immunity is a privilege, something that sets you against all the others who are not immune. The opposite of immunity is the community that pays the price for your immunity. Unfortunately, we have classically constituted communities precisely through immunity: our shared immunity to risk is always produced by the shared susceptibility of others, while we are let off the hook (*dispensatio*).

Hercules and the Captive Women could not be clearer about how immunity always comes at the cost of someone else's susceptibility. Hercules learns that the children of Atlantis are rounded up and taken away in order to be exposed to the Stone of Uranus, a monstrous magic object that either transforms them into perfectly identical, black-shirted Aryan supermen or into a mass of miserable, deformed wretches. If they are immune, they become supermen; if they are susceptible (common, the opposite of *immune*), they acquire a kind of leprosy that manifests itself in lesions of the skin.[10] There is no immunitary impulse without a corresponding autoimmune impulse, so what makes some of the people immune poisons and destroys others. The peplum is absolutely obsessed with skin, of course, here as elsewhere, but it is perhaps no accident that susceptibility is marked on the surface. Here, too, one must note the paradoxical construction: the savior of these tormented souls is Hercules, and never was skin more taut and healthy, tanned by wealth and luxury, carefully cared for, waxed and shined, than the skin of the bodybuilder. For Esposito, the mythological figure of Hercules is skin, "a protective barrier . . . a boundary [*confine*] between inside and out" (2011b, 44). Indeed, the evil queen wishes to use him as the new model for her idealized supermen. Hercules, in short, is the ultimate immune subject—in perfect health.

Moreover, although we have little sense of the people of Atlantis in this film, there is a real community in Esposito's sense within the concentrationary space, the community of the lepers who were not immune to the queen's magic stone.[11] They are those who support (i.e., bear the burden of) the immunity represented by the heroic bodies of white perfection that the queen has made and the easy lifestyle of the Atlanteans.

The film is quite clear about its references to the camps, genocide, the Nazi obsession with the perfect Aryan (male) body (Della Casa says that the queen's vision is "no different from Hitler's" [2001, 312]), and even what is perhaps the ultimate expression of immunitarian logic that can destroy all life in the name of life: nuclear power. The lepers are, of course, segregated in a camp. They live in what appears to be an old quarry, with sheer walls over a hundred feet high. They are dressed in rags, covered in sores and scabs, and clearly emaciated. When Hercules asks why they are treated this way, why their own queen would wound their bodies, one of the inmates explains that it is "in order to create a new race." That new race, which the queen calls "a chosen race" (*una razza eletta*), is to be determined on a strictly biopolitical basis, specifically, the question of the body's strength. The queen intended to make use of Androcles, the king of Thebes, as her husband, but she declares that he is "too fragile for the weight that he was to bear" before ordering her uncanny, blond, black-shirted henchman to take him to the valley and let him die "like all of the weak." Already in 1963, Spinazzola noted the film's clear references to atomic power and Hitlerian supermen clones, although in a telling Freudian slip (108), he characterized their uniforms as brown shirts rather than black, missing the film's possible critique of Italian as well as German fascism (O'Brien deplores this "nazification" [2014, 68] of the villains by Italian scholars). In reviewing the film's parallels with Nazi Germany, Frank Burke (2011) very nicely notes that the queen even attempts to kill Hercules and Androcles in a gas chamber (41). The genocide that will be carried out in the film will not be carried out by the Queen and her minions, however.

The unnamed prisoner who informs Hercules that the queen is creating a new race also explains how: the Stone of Uranus can mutate men. As Shahabudin (2009) points out in a very perceptive essay on the film, the Stone of Uranus, a source of power that can also mutate men, is surely nothing other than uranium (211). Erich von Däniken famously claimed a few years after the release of *Hercules and the Captive Women*, in the 1969 *Chariots of the Gods*, that Atlantis possessed—and was destroyed by—nuclear power, a notion that has since become a commonplace in psychic, new age, and extraterrestrial revisionist histories.[12] *Hercules and the Captive Women* was clearly ahead of the curve, since the suggestion that the miraculous crystal that powers the island might also be nuclear and mutagenic is clearly part of the general concern about the body being degenerated by modernity and its radioactivity.[13] What is certain is that those who can resist the degenerating force of modernity are *fortissimi* (incredibly strong). It is the same source of energy, however, that generates both *forza* (strength) and *morte* (death). All good and evil comes from the stone, explains the prisoner, but the words that he uses, *bene* and *male*, also mean "healthy" and "ill" in Italian. In short, the peplum makes the connection again and again between Hercules's strength and an immunitary defense against modernity—specifically, modernity's corrupting, degenerating, mutating power. It is throughout the visibility of Hercules's strength that serves as the real guarantee of its efficacy. Health and strength are knowable and can be possessed only insofar as they are visible in the form of healthy bronzed skin stretched taut across bulging muscles. *Hercules and the Captive Women* finds its unusual immunitary clarity in two places. The first is the implicit contrast between the skin of Hercules, whose dermal perfection is maximized throughout (he is, of course, immune to the power of the Stone), and the unfortunate victims of the Stone, whose skin is marked by countless lesions, cracked, open sores that mark not only their susceptibility but also the burden of the state that they bear/support in common.

The second aspect of immunitary thinking that is unusually clear in this film is the capacity of the immune system to turn its purifying power against the very body it was supposed to protect in the first place; what we might call today "the nuclear option" that Esposito points out was already fully developed in Nazi policies that turned not only against foreign bodies but also against German bodies (2008, 143). In order to defend the world against the terrible threat posed by Queen Antinea and her army of immune supermen, Hercules subjects the Stone of Uranus to the light of the sun by tearing open a hole in the roof of the cave where the Stone is housed. In doing so, he is besting the power of nuclear fission (atomic power) with the power of nuclear fusion, the source of the sun's power, and, by extension of its Cold War allegory, the power of the atom bomb with that of the hydrogen bomb. Despite his earlier protestations that he would stop Antinea without destroying the island and all its inhabitants, he stops Antinea precisely through the destruction of the island and all its inhabitants. Stock footage of volcanoes erupting and tidal waves is intercut with ordinary Atlantic citizens perishing beneath falling rubble, crushed by massive statues or enormous boulders (some of the footage deliberately evokes well-known documentary footage of nuclear blasts—a flash of bright light and a wooden hut bursting into flames, for example). Virtually every peplum film ends with a dramatic architectural collapse, but *Hercules and the Captive Women* is unusual for midcentury peplum films in that the collapse is tantamount to genocide. Only Princess Ismene survives. Esposito argues that this excess of violence (as the immunitary impulse becomes undifferentiated) is inherent in the Hercules myth: "Heracles' violence is unleashed against the very people it was supposed to protect" (2011b, 43); Agamben makes much the same point, arguing that "the most ancient recorded formulation" of the principle of sovereign power and its relationship to law is to be found in Pindar 169, and that it is the "reference to Hercules" that makes it absolutely clear that the sovereignty of the law is "a justification of violence" (1998, 31).

My argument in this book, however, is not that the peplum is a simple allegory of biopolitics, but that it is a fantasy about biopolitics (and indeed, that biopolitics requires a phantasmatic support to mediate between political power and life), and fantasy cannot be understood without also addressing its sexual component. Indeed, Ismene's sob at the death of everyone she has ever known and the total destruction of her native land is silenced by the teenaged kiss she then shares with Hylas before the film cuts to a long shot of their vessel sailing untroubled and empty waters (no longer contaminated by the foreign body of Atlantis) at sunset (see figure 4.2). The final closure of the heterosexual kiss is neither an accident nor a mere convention in this film, however.

As Shahabudin very nicely argues (2009, 211), *Hercules and the Captive Women* offers a phantasmic repair of multiple but connected wrongs. The uncanny distortion of the natural world produced by radiation is provoked by the Stone of Uranus. The Stone was created when drops of Uranus's blood fell on the earth, but those drops of blood are from Uranus's mythic castration, an event never referred to directly in the film. Here we can see that the biopolitical reading of the peplum is persuasive but incomplete. It promises immunity not only from modernity and alterity but also from the originary threat to masculinity itself. In other words, the peplum is produced at the intersection of the biopolitical and the psychoanalytic, and this intersection allows us to understand something about biopolitical theory that it does not consciously understand about itself: the body politic that is constituted through immunity, as well as the immunitary paradigm in general, refers to a male body. Immunity is also, above all, immunity from a symbolic, social, and economic castration, a protective sheath of skin without any clefts or fissures. (By extension, following this rather essentialist logic, Esposito's ideal community, founded on openness to difference rather than closed immunity, would implicitly be a female body politic.) Hercules's destruction of Atlantis defends the Western world from its other, tradition from modernity, the body from disease and degeneracy, and masculinity from loss.

The Giant of Metropolis is another science-fiction peplum that exhibits the same essentially genocidal structure as *Hercules and the Captive Women*, positing a mad scientist-king who calculatingly breeds his people to "create a superior race" and dominate the earth, but whose entire people must be wiped out by the strongman, Obro, in order to prevent this genocidal plan. Here, too, we see the inherent logical contradiction of the immunitary paradigm in the peplum. The king drains some subjects of life (rendering their skin impossibly white and cracked) in order to enhance other subjects who will become a master race through calculated eugenics; but it is the strongman with his vitality who represents

Figure 4.2. Ismene weeps next to Hylas; Hercules and Timoteo the dwarf watch Atlantis sink. *Hercules and the Captive Women*, 1961.

the apotheosis of that master race.[14] We might paraphrase Dyer here and say that Obro is opposed to this fascist regime, but Gordon Mitchell's muscles embody its very ideals. This is played out at the most biological level possible, that of blood and race: "Destiny has brought to Metropolis a stranger of a race superior to ours," explains Queen Texen, and it will be this stranger of "a race superior" who will stop their plan to "create a superior race." *Giant of Metropolis* even reuses some of the footage of the collapse of Atlantis from *Captive Women*, but it also shares with that film the ideological use of a kiss in order to make the viewer forget that genocidal immunitary logic: "When the scientists attempted to probe the structure of death, nature rebelled . . . love alone triumphed . . . and remained the sole source of life," the introductory scroll-over informs the viewer. Indeed, the strongman will unite with one female survivor of Metropolis (this time in an embrace and kiss on the beach). As we will see, later peplum films would shed the midcentury reluctance about openly acknowledging the genocidal thinking that often animates their essentially immunitary logic—a logic, as Esposito notes, that is ultimately suicidal (2008, 45–77).

Nothing had changed by the time of the 1983 *Hercules*, directed by Luigi Cozzi (under the pseudonym Lewis Coates) and starring Lou Ferrigno. The film is a richly campy example of paleo-science-fiction, including Daedalus as a buxom babe in a *Flash Gordon*-style bathing suit, helmet, and cape, manufacturing Hercules-killing robots with lasers; chariots carrying Hercules through outer space; and what appears to be a fiery, rainbow-colored light-saber. The film again replays the Atlantic apocalypse through an energy source that combines a volcano, the mythical phoenix, and the "fusion" of a sacrificed virgin (Cassiopeia) with the volcano's magma that will produce "pure energy"—a fusion that Hercules disrupts, provoking the same stock footage of volcanoes erupting and cities collapsing that we have seen before. At the very end, after untold thousands have presumably died, Hercules and Cassiopeia share a chaste kiss on the beach at sunset.

We might finally note that *Goliath and the Vampires, Hercules and the Captive Women, The Giant of Metropolis*, and the 1983 *Hercules* (as well as many other peplum films) also all make reference to one of the most direct forms of biopolitical control: eugenics. In all of them, the evil ruler plans to use the strongman to breed or create a perfect race, an idea that once again can be found already in the silent period. According to Farassino, there is a 1919 film, titled *Le fatiche di Ercole* (The labors of Hercules), well before the 1958 *Hercules*, starring one of Maciste's competitors, Ausonia, in which we learn that "the Duke of Montpreaux, on the basis of certain of his theories about the regeneration of his stock, seeks a modern-day Hercules for his daughter" (1983, 36); I can find no record of such a film, but he may be thinking of the 1918 *L'ultima fatica di Ercole* (Hercules's last labor). Reflecting the Italian enthusiasm for eugenics that would run throughout the Fascist period and well beyond (see Cassata 2006 on the continuity of Italian eugenicist thinking up through the 1960s), the film endorses the match. By the time of the midcentury peplum, we see once again Dyer's formulation: the film is ostensibly anti-eugenicist, but the strongman's muscles embody its apotheosis. Indeed, if the midcentury peplums consistently reject the plan of creating a master race, it is largely because such a rejection would be futile: Hercules, Maciste, Samson, Goliath, Ursus, and the rest already constitute it. In the modern peplum, the eugenic fantasy continues, from the use of Conan as a stud to the disability-eliminating infanticide of the Spartans in *300* (viewed positively by the film) or the terrifying genetic monoculture proposed by King Hyperion in 2011's *Immortals*.[15]

Kill Them All

Starting already in the barbarian peplum films of the 1980s, revenge becomes the principal motivation for the muscular protagonist, and Nietzschean *ressentiment* becomes the dominant affect of many of the films. In both *Conan the Barbarian* and *Gunan, King of the Barbarians*, an Italian knock-off released the same year

(1982), the film begins with the massacre of the strongman's family and his people. Indeed, *Conan* opens with an epigraph that paraphrases Nietzsche ("That which does not kill us makes us stronger" in *Conan*'s version) before showing how Conan's strength is produced precisely by his masculine *ressentiment*—the desire to strike back at those who hurt him, but the inability to do so. As discussed in chapter 2, Nietzsche (1989) argues that *ressentiment*'s urge to strike violently outward, blocked by the strength of one's adversary and one's own weakness, instead turns inward. This inward turn makes man, for the first time, a subject divided against itself, a subject that can become cunning, deceptive, or reactive, a subject with interiority.

Conan becomes, however, not the reflective and cunning priest but an unthinking and impulsive warrior. Even so, his character is a strange mix of active and reactive; for his part, he is generally directionless and compliant, happy to perform for others (both acts of violence and sexual acts; we are told that "he was bred to finest stock" and see him in action), and he generally wanders until someone else (Subotai, Valeria) provides a direction for him. His only real source of internal motivation comes from the slaughter of his people, the Cimmerians, by Thulsa Doom and his followers. As is often the case in peplum films, there is a complicated and largely incoherent sense of race. At first, the marauders attacking Conan's village appear to be Mongols, but a second glance shows us warriors who look Nordic, and they are accompanied by Rottweilers who will eventually eat Conan's father. Ultimately, their leader arrives, Thulsa Doom, played by James Earl Jones with long, straight hair, lightened skin, and blue contact lenses. Although his men kill Conan's father, and he personally kills Conan's mother, Doom will insist throughout the film's final section that Conan is in some fashion his son. This curious affirmation ties Conan's genesis not to his race (whatever "Cimmerian" might mean) but to the birth of his *ressentiment*: "Look at the strength of your body. Look at the desire in your heart. I gave you this," Doom explains. Later, "Who gave you the will to live? I am the wellspring from which you flow." Although these sequences trade heavily on the shocking revelation in *The Empire Strikes Back* (1980) that Darth Vader (famously voiced by Jones) is Luke Skywalker's father, that film was about establishing a biological line of descent; in *Conan* it is an affective one. Conan's body and mind were shaped primarily by Doom: his great strength was produced by the many years Conan spent turning the giant Wheel of Pain, and the burning desire for revenge in his heart was produced by Doom's abrupt decapitation of Conan's mother and the later death of Conan's lover, Valeria. The many ways in which Conan is an interesting animal are all due to Doom. The upshot is that Conan's actions are all bound to the past: "For us, there is no spring," Conan muses regretfully after fondly recalling the springs of his childhood. In a fantasy of true, total genocide that denies any futurity, the narrator informs the viewer that the Cimmerians were destroyed so thoroughly that "no one would ever know that my lord's [Conan's] people had lived at all."

The peplum hero from this point forward (and in contrast to the heroes of the midcentury peplum) has a background and a history, a history that is always the same. In the film *The Scorpion King* (2002), the hero, Mathayus (played by Dwayne "the Rock" Johnson), is the last remaining Akkadian, and in the television series *BeastMaster* (1999–2002), the muscular Dar is the last of his tribe, as are his sidekicks; indeed, the *Wikipedia* article "BeastMaster (TV Series)" notes that "genocide appears to be common" in the world of the Beastmaster, which is "full of lost tribes." Even in the lightest peplum fare, such as *Hercules: The Legendary Journeys*, the series begins with the rather incongruous murder of Hercules's entire family. In *Spartacus: Blood and Sand* (2010), Spartacus witnesses the complete destruction of his village and eventually the death of his wife, the only other survivor. In many respects, it was *Gladiator* that definitively established this melancholy and melodramatic masculinity for our fantastic imaginations of the ancient past; it is always now "too late," in Linda Williams's (1991) formulation of melodrama for the male hero. The tacit understanding is always that this is a way of talking about the contemporary condition of (white) masculinity, whose time of hegemony is over (we should note that this "loss" may be a particularly Anglo-American obsession that began in the 1980s, which is why it appeared only when the peplum moved away from Italy at precisely that historical point).

From its beginning, however, the peplum has imagined a kind of phantasmic wrong done in the past that explains the end of white male hegemony and justifies the protagonist's immunitary action to defend it. Virtually every critic has understood that *Cabiria* was a way of justifying contemporary Italian colonial wars (specifically the recent acquisition of Libya and continuing struggles in Ethiopia), but the curious psychological character of this justification has not always been appreciated. Within the film's diegesis, not only has Africa in the form of the Carthaginian Empire threatened Italy, but also Hannibal has in fact successfully invaded the Italian peninsula. This provocation, of course, eventually led to Rome's total victory over the Carthaginians, a victory that decisively established Rome's supremacy in the Mediterranean. The film's emotional impact and consequent ideological pull on the audience, however, do not derive from this historical narrative, which retains the character of a backdrop. The historical narrative's protagonists (Sophonisba, Massinissa, Syphax, and Scipio) offer little traction for audience identification; they remain distant, their actions already decided over two thousand years earlier. Instead, the draw for the audience in 1914 was clearly Maciste, Fulvius Axilla (Maciste's master), and Cabiria, who begins the narrative as a little girl kidnapped by the Carthaginians and ends it as a young woman in love with Fulvius Axilla. It was Cabiria's abduction, in other words, that remained for the contemporary Italian viewer the "wrong that must be righted." We must invade North Africa in 1914 because they stole a little girl in 200 BC.

In the case of Maciste, the immunitary response is the military defeat of Carthage and the rescue of Cabiria; her union with Fulvius Axilla at the film's end—a union presided over by Maciste, the first of many matches that the strongman will watch over—marks not only her definitive restitution to the Romans but also her status as "uncontaminated" (*virgo intacta*) by her long Carthaginian sojourn. As I hope I have already shown, by the time of the midcentury peplum, the immunitary response to the threatening foreign body had grown potentially more vigorous, up to and including the total annihilation of the other people, a genocide that would be disavowed or left unacknowledged. Already in the 1980s barbarian peplum, this genocide could be made explicit. In *Gunan, King of the Barbarians*, the protagonist, Gunan (known as Zukahn in some dubbed versions), avenges the death of his mother and father at the hands of the Ungat tribe, and the universe will not be set to rights until they are all killed. "The Ungat have been annihilated," the queen of the Kuniat rejoices, "so finally we can live in peace."

No disavowal is necessary in the contemporary peplum, either. In *Spartacus: Blood and Sand*, an explicitly genocidal response bookends the first season. The series begins ("The Red Serpent," 2010) when the Roman legate Claudius Glaber comes to the warriors of Thrace in order to enlist them in a fight against the Getae, a neighboring tribe and traditional enemy. The hero listens to the legate's proposal but eventually interrupts his call to join Rome. "To what end?" he asks.

GLABER: [*indignant at the interruption, as if the answer were obvious*] Victory.

SPARTACUS: And how is it to be measured? The Getae have raided our villages in the past, raped our women, killed our children [*to a growing chorus of agreement from the crowd*]. Each time we have pushed them back, only to see them return. If we are to align with Rome, the purpose must be clear—the Getae, dead. All of them.

GLABER: [*After a long pause, he nods.*] Dead. All of them. [*The Thracians cheer.*]

But this sentiment acquires its real force slightly later in the episode. As Spartacus prepares to march, he has a final meeting with his wife, Sura, who has risen early, troubled by prophetic dreams that "great and unfortunate things" will happen to her husband. They discuss her dreams (which Spartacus dismisses), have some erotic banter, and kiss passionately. As they separate, Sura looks him directly in the eyes and says throatily, "Kill them all." This is an ideological powerful moment in the show: it is not simply violence that is fetishized and eroticized, but genocide directly. Spartacus's reply is clear: he offers her genocide as a romantic gesture. "For you," he replies, and she smiles gently and lovingly at him as he departs.

Glaber does not keep his promise to exterminate the Getae; he sees a better political opportunity in leading his troops against Mithridates in Asia Minor. This failure to commit genocide is experienced by the viewer through Spartacus's eyes as a betrayal, a disappointment, and a failure to maintain his masculine word (Glaber is in fact persuaded to turn away from the Getae by his wife, Ilithyia, who manages to be both vapid and scheming). As a result of Glaber's betrayal, the Getae will return to the village and destroy it, attacking and attempting to rape Sura as well, although Spartacus saves her. They are cartoonish villains, wearing furs and skull-like masks and even dragging Sura, cave-man-style, by her hair. But it is the Romans, of course, who represent the real villains. They capture and enslave Spartacus, selling him as a gladiator to a *ludus*, or gladiatorial training school, so that he may fight to the death. The Romans are degenerate, dishonest, manipulative, sybaritic, wealthy elites devoid of honor or integrity (the peplum, as ever, finds a comfortable home in right-wing populism). The Roman men are men of words and politics, not of meaningful action; the women are scheming, ambitious, sexually perverse, inane, and materialistic. Sura's words return as the title of the season's final episode ("Kill Them All"), now with their meaning clear: Spartacus's personal goal is the impossible and suicidal task of killing all the Romans, cleansing the world of their degenerate and corrupt bodies and culture. But even this impossible task does not represent the limits of immunitary violence.

Spartacus represents the classic immunitary problem for the peplum hero, the same one Esposito discusses in reference to Hercules: he is supposed to be a vaccine, a small dose of barbaric violence injected within the community that can defend it against the barbaric violence on the outside. This is how the gladiator has usually been understood, as a spectacular public violence that will keep the masses of the people satiated with their lot and prevent them from rebelling. What Spartacus becomes instead is something more like an antibody gone bad. It attacks everything around it, killing friends (Varro), enemies (his owner, Batiatus), neutral subjects (other gladiators in the arena), and eventually, pretty much anyone it might encounter in Capua.[16] In other words, "kill them all," precisely as Esposito argues, becomes generalized: not merely the enemy on the outside but all and sundry. Moreover, Spartacus, like many contemporary peplum heroes, finds himself in an essentially suicidal narrative arc: "kill them all" also includes one's own body. Like Conan before him, Spartacus will have no spring, no rebirth. Sura dies in front of him, the final push that allows his violence to be completely generalized and include even himself. Although Spartacus will sleep with other women, it is clear that his affective life, the possibility of being something other than a killing machine, is at an end. Indeed, both his lover and his child will be killed by the season finale ("Wrath of the Gods," 2012) of *Spartacus: Vengeance*. There is nothing left but to "kill them all," whoever they may be. Spartacus is, in psychoanalytic terms, "de-subjectified," a creature of drive—repetitious, mechanical compulsion—rather than desire, goal oriented and personally meaningful. This goes hand in hand with the biopolitical, for, of course, the show chronicles his reduction to precisely what Agamben calls "bare life" or *zōē*. He, like all Roman slaves, may be inspected, sold, beaten, used for sexual purposes, or killed on a whim.

Much of *Spartacus*—the de-saturated color palettes, the graphic-novel-style blood splatters, the green-screen filming, the protagonist who becomes a suicidal killing machine fueled by bitter resentment at being betrayed—comes from Zach Snyder's extremely influential film *300*. That film found a winning formula in depicting the honor, the personal sacrifices made in the name of duty, and the masculine camaraderie and solidarity that emerged when a small band of Spartan warriors took on a massive Persian force, knowing that they could at best delay that larger army. Yet this story of honor and sacrifice has a curiously immunitarian and biopolitical subtext. *300*'s very first shot is of a pile of infants' skulls at the bottom of a ravine; at the top of the ravine, a baby is being inspected. A voiceover explains that the Spartans habitually practiced eugenic infanticide: children who were deformed, of course, but even babies who were suspiciously small would be discarded and left to die in the pit. The film then details the horrors of Spartan childhood for those lucky enough to be "unblemished": we see a child (the baby we saw before, now perhaps five years old) forced to fight a fully grown man and punched in the face when he drops his toy sword; later, slightly older, starved and forced to fight and even (it is intimated) kill other boys for food; older still, exiled to the wilderness, fighting a wolf with nothing but a sharpened stick while he stands barefoot in the snow, wearing only a loincloth. The remarkable ideological turn that follows is that these scenes do not depict hell but rather paradise within the film's ideology—a corner of the world uncontaminated by modernity, effeminacy, civilization, tolerance, and other "pollutions."

This paradise takes its most visible form in the protagonist's exemplary body, a body that reflects the vitality of his nation, which is at risk from a degenerate foreign body, the army of Xerxes the Persian. We see the narrator, the one-eyed warrior Dilios, who explains that the Spartans and, by extension, Greece are menaced by "an army of slaves . . . ready to snuff out the world's one hope for reason and justice." The ideological sleight of hand here is jaw-dropping in its audacity, even more impressive than the slabs of manly muscle on display everywhere. "Freedom" and "reason" mean infanticide, eugenics, child abuse, and endless war. In biopolitical terms, all *bios* becomes *zōē*, or bare life, and the state of exception is made permanent. Normally, to live in the *polis* means to seek out immunity against the violence of the outside. Naturally, one incorporates a little bit of that violence as one's defense. Indeed, the pseudonymous Italian critic Wu Ming[1] describes the Spartans as "a small inoculation of a known evil" (2007, 34).[17] In

Sparta, however, the tiny inoculation of exterior violence has taken over completely; to live in this *polis* means to be subjected to a relentless Darwinian struggle for survival. Precisely what you would have assumed that society immunized you against is found here on the inside, now presented as the very definition of the community. The only certain immunity against the degenerate body outside is the constant death of the community's body inside. Although *300* wants to present the death of the Spartan warriors as a sacrifice, it is rather the natural extension of an immunitary logic that believes that the perfect male body, which stands as a bulwark against the outside, can find its absolute perfection only in death.

After the initial Bildungsroman opening of *300*, the film follows the Persian ambassador into Sparta, where he asks the Spartans only for a small sample of earth and water, a mere token submission to the great god-emperor Xerxes (he also implies that failure to comply will result in the Spartans' total destruction). Leonidas listens patiently and then explains that he will not comply, not even with a meaningless token of dirt; instead, he pushes the messenger and his men to the edge of a massive well at the entrance of the city. The messenger responds in bafflement and outrage by invoking the ancient norms that govern civilized behavior: "No man, *no* man, Persian or Greek, threatens a messenger! . . . This is blasphemy. This is madness!" He has forgotten, however, that he is speaking to a vaccine run amok. "This is Sparta!" howls Leonidas, kicking the messenger into the well, as the other Spartans slaughter the remaining Persians.[18] Sparta is blasphemy and madness. Indeed, the confrontation between Sparta and Persia is exactly what we might have expected, a scene between civilization and its violent, barbaric outside; it is simply that the sides are reversed. Barbarity must defend itself against civilization.

The film, like many peplums since the 1980s glorification of the barbarian, is not even particularly shy about this point: it was not just modernity that was a mistake; civilization itself was. The rash of barbarian and post-apocalyptic films in the 1980s, from *Conan* to the *Mad Max* franchise, all shared a common dream: the elimination of civilization that would finally allow "the real man" to re-emerge. By contrast, the Persians of *300* are multicultural and cosmopolitan. The Persian ambassador appears African (the actor who plays him is English-Canadian, of Ghanian descent), and the men who accompany him appear to be dressed as Middle Eastern . . . ninjas? When Leonidas kicks them down the well, it is clear that he is also returning their dark skin to the dark, ethnically cleansing, all-white Sparta; the point of the abject is that it is literally and etymologically thrown away as far as possible in order to preserve an image of bodily integrity.[19] Throughout the film, civilization is equated with cosmopolitanism, multiculturalism, and other forms of modern degeneracy that real manliness must defend itself from, an equation picked up by Italian political candidate Andrea De Priamo, who belongs to the neofascist Alleanza Nazionale and who used an image from Frank Miller's original graphic novel *300* in his campaign ads (figure 4.3).

When Leonidas learns that Xerxes wishes to parley, he munches on an apple while standing on top of a pile of corpses as his men go about executing any Persians who still show signs of life; he then ironically declares, "There's no reason we can't be civil, is there?" When Leonidas and Xerxes do meet, Xerxes explains that they should collaborate rather than fight in language more typical of the lib-

Figure 4.3. "Defend your values, your civilization, your neighborhood." Italian political ad using an image from *300*, 2008.

eral multiculturalism of *Star Trek* than of a demented despot: "There is much our cultures could share." Xerxes and Persia are defined by their openness to difference. But Sparta is completely determined by its immunitary logic and can offer only violence in this proposed cultural exchange. "Haven't you noticed?" Leonidas asks, grinning and gesturing at the battlefield behind him covered with dead Persian soldiers. "We've been sharing our culture with you all morning!" "Civil," "sharing," and "culture" are terms that are implicitly feminized against the values of the "real men" of Sparta, whose violence can immunize us against their infectious spread.

Most crucially, this modern cosmopolitanism involves an openness to other bodies and other sexualities; indeed, the two overlap throughout, since these other bodies are generally presented in erotic contexts. Leonidas and his men equate their perfect bodies and their perfect discipline, and they stand in stark contrast to three figures that disrupt the healthy, perfectly uniform nation-state. The first is Ephialtes, the misshapen hunchback whose weak parents foolishly failed to follow the Spartan custom of infanticide for children who were physically different. Leonidas demonstrates to this would-be warrior that he cannot hold his shield high enough to maintain the Spartans' impenetrable shield wall, and he rejects his offer to serve in the Spartan army.[20] There will be no reasonable accommodation of his difference. Ephialtes's betrayal of the Spartans is not simply political, however. It is simultaneous with, and part of, his seduction by the perverse and decadent sexual delights (we see an orgy of "other" bodies: a transgender amputee; facially scarred, nonwhite lesbians; a half man, half goat) that are offered to him by the second figure, the bisexual, androgynous, tattooed, and multiply pierced Xerxes, whom Chemers (2007) calls "an eight-foot tall RuPaul."

Xerxes's body is clearly marked as both abnormal and foreign: he is impossibly tall (digitally enlarged to make him appear eight or nine feet in height) and ethnically different (and worse, for the Spartans, racially ambiguous), speaks with an accent, and is pierced, tattooed, androgynous, and presumably bisexual (he languidly caresses Leonidas from behind as he tries to woo him on the advantages of playing for the other team). If Schwarzenegger is Conan the Republican barbarian, Xerxes represents the opposite extreme, the decadence of modern tolerance and inclusivity, presented here as a kind of slavery: the tyranny of Xerxes, the liberal urban metrosexual. The road toward decadence can be measured by how culturally developed a nation is, with eugenic infanticide and ritualized child beating at one end—the good end—and piercing, gay marriage, and arugula salads at the other. It is not enough that Xerxes be decadent; the decadence must be multiply marked as modern even for the extradiegetic spectator. Chemers (2007) also notes that the harem that seduces Ephialtes consists of "hermaphrodites, giants, amputees, transgendered people, and people with exotic deformities," and disability is indeed an almost obsessive concern of the film. It also implicitly links the disabled body to a decadence that is both an exotic Orientalism and a modern Western inclusiveness and multiculturalism. We might coin a term here and say that the Spartans are "heterophobic," defined by their shared revulsion toward difference in all its forms: racial, sexual, and corporeal.

Let me pause for a moment and consider these nonnormative bodies, in particular those that resist a clear, "natural" gender identity. Chemers (2007) notes the presence of intersected and trans bodies, and Xerxes also breaks down traditional gender identity. But we might try to think through the peplum's bodies by relying on a more capacious understanding of the term "trans," especially as applied to a biopolitical scenario. As Toby Beauchamp (2009) has argued, there is a more generalized logic of "trans" that crosses not only sexual borders but also national ones. Beauchamp claims that there is a distinctly biopolitical logic connecting apparently disparate phenomena like state surveillance, reproductive politics, medical regulations, and "transgender and gender-nonconforming populations" (356).[21] At first glance, the hyperbolically masculine figures of the peplum seem like a poor fit for a "trans" figuration, but we should note, as many have done, that there is something curiously feminine in the figure of the bodybuilder (see Dutton 2013, 155–158), perhaps in the waxed and shaved skin, the careful tanning, and the constant attention to how one is perceived by others as an object of visual pleasure. Moreover, we might look beyond the initial question of androgyny, or even gender, to the transformation that is the absolute core of bodybuilding, the cultivation and technological transformation of the exterior body to match an interior image that is somehow out of sync with external reality. Bodybuilding narratives routinely cite the way in which bodybuilding allows an internal force of will to mold and shape the body to meet an internal vision of the bodybuilder's true self; it is easy to see in this what Gill-Peterson (2014), following Stryker and Sullivan (2009), has called "the original technicity of the body" (406), that is, that "trans" is not an alteration of the true body but simply the activation of a self-shaping faculty inherent in all bodies. It will escape no one not only that bodybuilders spend countless hours and money transforming their bodies, but also that maintaining that transformation requires a constant regime of artificial hormones (which are in turn subject to biopolitical regulation, as Gill-Peterson and Beauchamp have pointed out). Without belaboring the point, we might go further still and suggest that the trans logic of the body's transformation implicitly subtends sports in general, even if it is perhaps most visible in the bodybuilder.

Here one can look at the gender transition of Caitlyn (formerly Bruce) Jenner not as an aberration within the world of sports, but as the fulfillment of a logic internal to sports in general, a full development of Gill-Peterson's "original technicity of the body." The willingness to work the body into a new, idealized form may require sex hormones (as with Schwarzenegger or Lance Armstrong), prosthetics (Oscar Pistorius), or surgery (too many Olympic athletes have had laser

Figure 4.4. Spartan bodily perfection. *300*, 2007.

eye surgery to list). The policing of sex and gender remains high, as well, as cases like Caster Semenya in 2009 and Dutee Chand in 2015 have shown. We might simply add here that perhaps the media circus that tends to surround the question of transgender and intersex bodies in sports, as well as their policing, is part of the mediatized character of biopolitics that I am calling attention to here: it is not simply a question of policies and bodies but also the images of those bodies that are at stake (see, for instance, Beauchamp's perceptive comments [2009, 359] on the Pentagon's post-9/11 screening of *The Battle of Algiers* [1965], which contains scenes of terrorists cross-dressing to escape detection). In *300*, this mediatization of the vital masculine body is particularly apparent since the inherently human "technicity of the body" appears in a different way: the bodies of the Spartan heroes are clearly digitally enhanced, just the latest trick in the arsenal of human techniques for transforming the body (figure 4.4).

The third and final figure of the bad body, the Spartan politician (not warrior) Theron, appears physically normal but is sexually perverse (he rapes Queen Gorgo, and there are indications that his desire for her is not merely cruel but queer) and is linked to the ephors, the leprosy-ridden priests who deny King Leonidas a full army with which to fight the Persians.[22] As is the case with other "abnormal" bodies in the film, it is the skin of the film that is used a marker of alterity and the failure of immunity. The ephors (whom Dilios, the narrator, calls "inbred swine . . . more creature than man") have waxen skin, covered in pustules and scales, wet and runny; Xerxes and his men are covered in piercings and include giants and dwarfs, monsters of all sorts; Ephialtes's leathery skin bulges and warps grotesquely, his teeth are all awry, and he is bent almost double.

Despite its profoundly heterophobic discourse, there is a problem in the film's rejection of these other bodies, and unsurprisingly, it is related to the immunitary logic that pervades the peplum. Referring to the approach of the massive Persian army as the approach of an animal, as well as to the king's barbaric slaughter of the Persian messenger, the film's narrator informs us that "the beast that approaches . . . it was King Leonidas himself who provoked it." The Spartans' radical heterophobia, their inability to relax their immunitary vigilance, does not permit even co-existence with alterity; the Spartans provoke their own destruction rather than admit any difference. This is made clearest in the conversation between Ephialtes and King Leonidas, where Ephialtes pleads to be allowed to fight as a Spartan. He will happily die for their cause if he is only briefly allowed to be one of them. Leonidas admits that as an individual warrior, Ephialtes's deformed body might work. "A fine thrust," he notes approvingly. But Leonidas rejects him because his body cannot be incorporated into their uniform body. "We fight as a single, impenetrable unit," explains Leonidas, invoking the Spartan ideal of *homoioi*, each equal to all the others: "Each Spartan protects the man to his left, thigh to neck." It is the idealized and uniform body that provides immunity to the body politic.

Ephialtes appears just after Leonidas asks his lieutenant whether the Spartans have found any route "through the hills to [their] back," a route that would allow the Persians to take them from behind. Xerxes also refers to it as "the hidden path that enters behind." In other words, the biopolitical organization of the Spartans warriors that makes them a giant antibody ("a single, impenetrable unit") also defends them against sexual alterity, specifically the possibility of being penetrated, especially from behind (see the earlier discussion of Theron's rape of Queen Gorgo). It will not escape the reader that here, too, the immunitary logic once again produces the very thing it is supposed to defend against: in an effort to defend themselves against sexual difference, particularly homosexuality, the Spartans have produced an absurdly camp homoerotic spectacle, a band of musclemen clad only in leather codpieces and red capes. In the world of biopolitics, the same applies: because Leonidas cannot accept the difference of Ephialtes, the hunchback goes to Xerxes and betrays the existence of the goat path that he warned Leonidas about, one that would allow the Persians to outflank them "to their back." In short, it is precisely the Spartans' inability to permit even the tiniest quantum of difference that causes them to be obliterated by difference. Once again, we see Esposito's immunitary paradigm at work.

The biopolitical character of the peplum appears, of course, in other popular genres, even in the Italian tradition—the spaghetti Western is as obsessed with the figure of the *homo sacer* as the peplum is with populations drained of vitality and forced into concentrationary spaces.[23] One of my aims in writing this chapter, however, is to call attention to the role of film in general in mediating the supposedly direct manipulation of life that characterizes modern biopolitical regimes. But the biopolitical dimension of the peplum is surprisingly deep, both within the films—their relentless tales of a people drained of life by a foreign intruder, only to be liberated by the muscular vitality of the hero—and without the march of athletes and bodybuilders through the peplum and into politics, precisely into roles in which they can once again save the health and vitality of the nation.

Notes

1. Nikolas Rose (2007), among others, has argued that biopolitics today is less a matter of the population's health and more a question of individual well-being, although Greenhalgh (2009) notes that this is perhaps true only for "advanced liberal societies of 'the West'" (207).

2. Reg Park played Hercules in four peplums: *Hercules in the Haunted World, Hercules and the Captive Women, Hercules, Prisoner of Evil* (1964), and *Hercules the Avenger* (*La sfida dei giganti*, 1965). In his autobiography *Total Recall*, Schwarzenegger mentions having seen *Hercules and the Captive Women* when he was thirteen; he loved the film because he had been "so impressed by the star's body" (Schwarzenegger and Petre 2012, 25), so this is presumably the film referenced on the magazine cover. In *Arnold: The Education of a Bodybuilder*, he says that the sight of this magazine cover inspired him to watch as many peplum films as he could, "the adventure movies of Steve Reeves, Mark Forrest, Brad Harris, Gordon Mitchell and Reg Park" (Schwarzenegger and Hall 1977, 17), and then goes on to mention *Hercules and the Vampires* (aka *Hercules in the Haunted World*) specifically. In every version of Schwarzenegger's origin story, however, it is Reg Park's body in the peplum that lies at the heart of his personal genesis.

3. Between *Hercules in New York* and *Conan the Barbarian*, Schwarzenegger also played Mickey Hargitay in the 1980 TV movie *The Jane Mansfield Story*. Hargitay had starred in two peplum films, including one with Mansfield, *Hercules vs. the Hydra* (1960), also known as *The Loves of Hercules*.

4. In *Why Arnold Matters*, Blitz and Krasniewicz (2004) list a whole series of political variations of "Conan the X" that were used in the news media, from "Conan the Deceiver" (21), a *New York Times* coinage that sounds like an authentic Howard novel or story title, to "Conan the Governor" (22), "Conan the Candidate" (26), and "Conan the Auditor" (26). Tellingly, however, they argue that although Conan was an apt symbol for a candidate challenging the state and the status quo, it was his metaphorical identity as the Terminator that allowed people to see him as a plausible governor.

5. Also within Esposito's matrix, this story is the moment at which community first breaks or ruptures because of immunity: Abel appears to have an incomprehensible privilege, the favor with which God looks on his sacrifice and that he denies to Cain. More clearly still, the community of privilege that emerges is set against the susceptibility of the family of Cain, who lives in the land of Nod (wandering) and is exposed to the risk of death and hardship in the land: bare life.

6. The Temple of Moloch and its sacrifice have been referenced on many occasions, including Fritz Lang's *Metropolis* (1927), the original *Star Trek* ("The Apple," 1967) and *Indiana Jones and the Temple of Doom* (1984).

7. Numerous scholars who have engaged with this project have asked me about the relationship between the peplum and pornography, both art pornography and mainstream porn (both straight and gay). Without attempting to universalize the category of queer (see Gerst-

ner 2013, 130–132), I maintain that the peplum's strange closeness to pornography without ever being pornography is part of what makes it queer, resistant to being collapsed into such binaries as porn/not porn and gay/straight. It is positioned after sexuality or before sexuality, but never in the "right now" temporality that Linda Williams associated with pornography; it is both strangely adult in its interest in erotic bodies and infantile in its pleasures; and it is directed (primarily) at a straight male audience but curiously reliant on images of the built male body. A movie like *300*, for instance, can be parodied as gay pornography (see Poole 2013) precisely because of its proximity to but non-union with the category. This is not to champion the peplum as queerly liberationist or as a neglected form of art. Indeed, the ambiguity the peplum displays toward sexual questions vanishes when one turns to questions of socioeconomic class: as a genre, it rejects the idea of itself as art, since art belongs to the realm of cultural elites.

8. At a screening of this film, my students giggled at the apparently unintentional homoeroticism of "his magnificent body" but really laughed when Kobrak appeared to become aware of their reaction, mirrored by Astra's reaction within the film.

9. This geographic site also had an ambiguous immunitary significance in antiquity. Most sources hold that Hercules smashed through the mountain of Atlas, dividing it in two and permitting the foreign waters of the Atlantic to flow into the Mediterranean; other sources claim, however, that Hercules pulled the strait nearly shut to prevent Atlantic sea monsters from entering the Mediterranean. In reading the death of Hercules in Greek mythology through René Girard and Vico, Esposito notes that the centaur Nessus represents not only the wild and barbaric "outside of the community" but also, more crucially, through his hybrid nature (half horse, half man), contamination itself. Hercules represents "limits and difference" (2011b, 44), but this does not help once he touches Nessus's blood: even the idealized body of Hercules cannot be immunized against "the poisoned product of immunization itself" (45). Here, too, we find an essential ambiguity in the figure of Hercules, who represents both the barrier against foreign intrusion (the strait as a blockage) and the aperture to the outside (the strait as an opening).

10. So far, this fits a fin de siècle model of degeneration: the Italian anthropologist and racial theorist Giuseppe Sergi, for example, described the origin of degeneracy as an "inferior adaptation" (Cassata 2006, 29) in the struggle for existence. Inferior adapters become leprous wretches; superior adapters become Aryan supermen. The film's immunitary logic will problematize this view, however.

11. One might think here of Italo Calvino's 1952 novel *Il visconte dimezzato* (The cloven viscount), in which the only real community is precisely a group of lepers, constituted by a cheerful openness to others and a willingness to live life fully.

12. The notion of Atlantis powered by some kind of crystal energy source comes from the American psychic Edgar Cayce, but both Cayce and Däniken were in agreement that the Atlanteans were destroyed by their own miraculous power source.

13. *The Giant of Metropolis* (also based on the Atlantis narrative) was equally clear about the transformations that a nuclear modernity itself would work on the body: "We begin the operation with a treatment of energy from radiation, which highly accelerates the rhythm of reproductive cell structure."

14. Eugen Sandow, the first bodybuilder, in the first issue of his magazine *Physical Culture*, explained that the aim of bodybuilding was "to raise the average standard of the race as a whole" (quoted in Chapman 2006, 109).

15. One of the many ways in which we see that eugenics is a fantasy is in one of the most relentlessly repeated plots in the peplum: the island of the Amazons, who plan on using the peplum hero as perfect breeding stock. From midcentury onward, hardly any peplum can resist the fantasy of the male subject at the mercy of dozens of insatiable women who wish only to use him sexually. The "fatal form" of this temptation is what permits it to remain: the hero

must reject the eugenic temptation, but reluctantly and without diminishing the erotic potential of the scenario.

16. The third season of *Spartacus* does pull back from the earlier, more totalizing genocide; Spartacus decides that killing ordinary and helpless Roman civilians, particularly women and children, would reduce him to the same moral level as the Roman oppressors. His fellow rebels do not agree, and it is not clear that the viewer is expected to either.

17. Wu Ming is both a pseudonym and a collective. When individual members of the collective write, they maintain both anonymity and individuality by using a number along with "Wu Ming." Hence Wu Ming[1], Wu Ming [2], Wu Ming[3], and so on.

18. This scene, too, is eroticized and is presented as female desire. As Leonidas weighs his decision about making this token offering, he looks about the agora at his people, and his gaze finally comes to rest on his wife. The next shot is marked as an intimate moment, the unspoken communication of spouses in sync. Slowly, deliberately (like virtually every shot without dialogue in the film, it is shot in slow motion), she nods, and Leonidas and his men attack. Here, as in *Spartacus,* there is a fantasy of a female endorsement of violence. The sense in the peplums from the 1980s onward is not only that a return to our barbarian past would restore us to traditional gender roles, but also that women, too, would be more masculine, not in body but in spirit. Women would finally understand, endorse, and even demand the desire to "kill them all." Finally, the image of Gorgo nodding in slow motion is a visual echo of an earlier scene in which Leonidas, as a child, nods in slow motion at his father (see chapter 3 on the haptic dimension of the peplum film).

19. Poole (2013) notes that one of the parodies of *300, Meet the Spartans* (2008), extended the logic of the abject (while blunting the racism of Snyder's original) by having Leonidas also toss other forms of "cultural garbage" (103–104) down the same well after the Persian messenger, including George W. Bush, Britney Spears, and the *American Idol* judges.

20. It is worth pointing out that the Spartan warriors have a fetishistic attachment to their shields: they may throw their spears or swords, but they never intentionally let go of their shields. The shield's immunitary significance is clear, particularly since this is where Ephialtes's different body falls short. He can thrust his spear well, but he cannot properly raise his shield.

21. In the context of the peplum, it is evident that the few strong women in the genre might be plausibly described as "gender nonconforming." When Kristin Beck, formerly Chris Beck, wrote her memoir, she titled it after the peplum heroine Xena: *Warrior Princess: A U.S. Navy SEAL's Journey to Coming Out Transgender* (2013).

22. Queen Gorgo is told by a city elder that she must seduce Theron if she hopes to sway the city council to send an army to her husband's aid. The next shot is a menacing point-of-view shot, typical of the horror genre, in which a predator approaches the queen from behind as she is bent over the fountain. A countershot reveals that it was Theron's gaze, our first indication that his interest is in *coitus a tergo,* or perhaps in anal intercourse. When he meets her that night to discuss her request to the council, he again approaches her from behind; when she disrobes in order to acquire his vote, he spins her around and slams her face against the wall. "This will not be over quickly," he says, thrusting into her from behind; "You will not enjoy this. I am not your king." Later, Queen Gorgo pays him back in kind by repeating his words to him after she stabs him in front of the council, but hers is a sword thrust and is delivered from the front (i.e., honorably, heterosexually). Naturally, she changes his last line to "I am not your queen." This makes no ostensible sense, since Queen Gorgo literally is his queen; it makes sense only insofar as she rectifies—i.e., renders straight—what was queer in Theron's assault: I am not to be taken like a queen, from behind. As we will see, this is also the central Spartan military fear: being taken from behind.

23. Numerous spaghetti Westerns are based on a lone figure, usually played by Tomás Milián, who can be hunted down and killed at will; what is very likely the best spaghetti Western, *The Great Silence* (1968), was directed by Sergio Corbucci, who had also directed peplums, and turns on a whole town whose entire lower class is turned into so many *homines sacri* who may be killed by the town's bounty hunter at will, with no legal consequences. Esposito (2011a) has argued that "Italian philosophy," which seems to be defined more by its resistance to notions of national character than by any national character, is in fact defined by its biopolitical character (see also Rota 2011). Italy has always been subject to the vicissitudes of the body, and this is perhaps clearest in its genre film production of the 1960s and 1970s: the peplum, the spaghetti Western, the Italian horror film or *giallo,* and its spate of exploitation and sexploitation films from *Mondo cane* to *Cannibal Holocaust.* All are body genres, not only in Linda Williams's sense but also in the biopolitical sense.

CONCLUSION
Biopolitical Fantasy

B<small>Y WAY OF</small> conclusion, I would like to return to where I began in this book. I have argued that to fully understand how the peplum works as a biopolitical genre, we also need to understand how it works to captivate its viewers. To that end, I selected three particular points of fascination: the peplum's reliance on slowed or even stopped time to accommodate the spectator's admiring and lingering gaze on the hero's muscled body; its consistently queer refusal of sexuality, situating itself in a psychic time either before or after desire; and its seductive expanse of skin, the haptic register of the peplum deployed in the service of a vision of masculinity that ranges from the violent xenophobia of *300* to a more nuanced, if still fundamentally aggrieved and melodramatic, understanding in *Spartacus: Blood and Sand*. Each of these three features of the peplum fascinates us because it constitutes a fantasy. These fantasies are, of course, fantasies of masculinity, from a hero's bodily perfection so overwhelming that time slows to a crawl to keep him in sight to the melodramatic fantasies of a masculinity founded on a loss of love and freedom. But they are also fantasies that might help explain both the surprising longevity of the genre and how the peplum might secure a hold in articulating for the viewer a relationship between politics and the stuff of life: health, vitality, hygiene. I have argued here that the peplum has been centrally and steadfastly concerned with this relationship for the past hundred years, and I have made particular use of biopolitical philosopher Roberto Esposito's immunitary paradigm to address the evolution of the peplum's biopolitical thinking.

Esposito (2008, 2011b) argues that biopolitical imperatives are modeled on an immunitary paradigm, keeping out dangerous foreign bodies and maintaining within the body an antibody that, paradoxically, reproduces the very features the body wishes to keep outside, particularly violence. That antibody, Esposito argues, inevitably turns on the body itself.[1] This same history plays out in the peplum's biopolitical fantasy. At its origin, the peplum's muscular hero is a prop that guarantees the legitimacy and flourishing of the state by disposing of foreign powers and threats (*Cabiria*) while simultaneously setting a corporeal example for young men, both those in the diegesis and those in the theater (the midcentury peplum). By the 1980s, however, the peplum increasingly began to turn to fantasies of failed states, apocalyptic scenarios in which it was no longer clear what the strongman was protecting or for whom he was setting an example. In its most recent incarnations (especially since *Gladiator*), the state is the enemy: corrupt, degenerate (in precisely the nineteenth-century sense), and weak. Against the power of an entire state, however, the protagonist, no matter how muscled, has no chance. His quest is first genocidal ("Kill them all," as Spartacus says, a motto that seems to eventually include his own band of rebel slaves as well as the corrupt Roman elites that they fight), but eventually suicidal.

In his analysis of the etymology underpinning immunity and community (2009, 3–6), Esposito looks at a number of meanings of the root word *munus*, three in particular: *onus* (burden or debt, still visible in the English term *remuneration*), *officium* (public office, as in the English word *municipal*), and *donum* (gift, as in the English *munificent*). Esposito's interest in these three semantic fields is precisely the way that they all center on the notion of a debt, obligation, or even deprivation, but I cannot help but note that Esposito does not discuss, not even implicitly, one of the most common meanings of *munus* in Roman times: *munus* can also mean a public show, a spectacle for entertainment. Indeed, this meaning of *munus* comes remarkably close to the peplum, since this public spectacle was almost invariably some form of gladiatorial combat. In short, we already find the peplum within biopolitical theory.

Does the articulation that the peplum provides between "bio" and "politics" have some wider consequences? I suggested that the peplum's mediation between the vitality of the muscled male body and the world of politics runs, somewhat surprisingly, in both directions. That is, we might expect peplum cinema to filter down certain political ideas about the management of life, and we do indeed find peplums in the midcentury extolling midcentury ideals of state power and bodily integrity, as well as a conspicuous neoliberal turn away from the state, beginning in the 1980s. Less expected, however, is the discovery that the peplum appears to have had a surprising relevance in politics, as bodies move from the world of sports to film and eventually to politics (Schwarzenegger, Mathias, Sorbo, and others have parlayed their media presence as hard-bodied heroes of antiquity into political roles). We might also ask about cinema more generally, however, as a mediator between politics and life.

Let me begin by noting that state interventions in matters of public health are not simply administrative or bureaucratic; they are also ideological (it is already ideological to presuppose the value of health and vitality) and hence are sustained and given coherence by a certain fantasy. This is true regardless of their truth-value or actual utility. No one could argue that smoking is not bad for one's health, for instance, but this does not change the profoundly ideological character of American anti-smoking campaigns, which single out this behavior as exceptionally harmful and risky, not only to the smoker but also to society as a whole. It is, however, precisely the fantasies that animate these campaigns that render visible their ideological character. They focus on melodramatic scenarios of guilt, loss, tragedy, and devastated children and families no different from public campaigns against drinking and driving.[2] Such scenarios exert a more powerful hold on the viewer than any recitation of facts about lung cancer and emphysema, which would not be enough to dispel the glamour of the cigarette; what is needed is a competing fantasy that can fascinate the viewer. In both instances, we should notice that implicit in both campaigns (against smoking and against drinking and driving) is an implicit fantasy that without such risky behaviors, life would be safe, and the family would be intact. Arguably, this is biopolitics' great unexamined ideological fantasy—that risk can be managed, contained, or even eliminated so that the body of the nation can remain endlessly and infinitely vital and healthy. It is already Esposito's immunitary paradigm.

Following Žižek's notion of "ideological fantasy" in *The Sublime Object of Ideology* (1989), I refer to this as "biopolitical fantasy." Key to both notions is the idea that exposing the ideology in a didactic or pedagogical way does not diminish its hold, precisely because one has failed to contend with the seductive power of fantasy. Ideology—or biopolitics—by itself is boring or even off-putting. In the opening to *The Impossible David Lynch*, McGowan (2007) has some insightful pages on the question of popular cinema and ideology that illuminate precisely this question. He notes, for example, that we assume the distance of popular cinema from the real world (likening a successful film to a thrill ride in a theme park, for instance) while cinema simultaneously presents us with the convincing illusion of seeing more and, perhaps more important, seeing more deeply into the hidden truth of reality itself. Both effectively work to fascinate and hold the viewer much more effectively than a Brechtian or Godardian distancing. Indeed, cynical and ironic detachment from the image is perhaps the stance that is most conducive to contemporary capitalism, he argues (9–10), allowing one to consume the image while continuing to feel free. In the teen sex comedy *EuroTrip* (2004), for instance, high school senior Cooper Harris runs away from the police who have busted a graduation party. He vaults over a fence and lands in a hot tub that contains an attractive young woman who is topless. "Well," he grins at the camera, "there's your R rating right there." This moment of Brechtian distancing (look, we all know that these scenes of female nudity are entirely gratuitous and exploitive, necessary to obtain a rating that the producers and distributors believe will maximize their market share and profit; even the characters within the diegesis know this) does absolutely nothing to diminish the exploitation and objectification of the female body or the absurd tyranny of the rating system. In fact, it does quite the opposite: the viewer may relax in his or her seat, knowing that a cynical defense of gratuitous female nudity has been presented, and that one may simply feel free to ogle the actress's body—with the proper degree of ironic distance.

The peplum as a genre, however, has never embraced irony, distance, or self-awareness (indeed, irony and self-awareness would work against the peplum's underlying populism because they are intellectual, elite, and cosmopolitan). One reason that the peplum can make viewers uncomfortable is in fact its apparent sincerity and seriousness coupled with an image that appears ironically excessive (oiled, hairless bodies bursting with muscles, clad only in leather codpieces and capes; ludicrously over-the-top Orientalist pomp and splendor). To view a peplum without irony or cynical distance is quite difficult for the contemporary viewer, but there is little question that all of the peplum's incarnations, including its current ones, intend for the viewer to do just that.[3] This is perhaps why the current affect of most peplums—a desperate, dark, and melodramatic seriousness, bordering on a kind of suicidal nihilism—has been more successful than the old-school grin-and-flex approach. Without the intense melodramatic affect, the excess of the image would predominate, permitting the viewers to see only camp rather than the biopolitical fantasy that seduces and fascinates them.

Indeed, we find the same excess of image and melodramatic intensity of affect in the public service ads (PSAs) against smoking and drunk driving. They, too, rely not only on an excessive and absolute seriousness and immediacy but also on fantasy as a scene, an implicit part of a larger narrative, and almost invariably a cinematic one. In one Mothers against Drunk Driving advertisement, we see a lifeless young woman in a graduation robe and mortarboard and clutching roses who is pushed through a sheet of glass that is simultaneously the windshield of her car and the frame of the last photograph her parents will ever have of her. This breaking-of-the-fourth-wall effect suggests that a photograph has come to life in a way typical of the interplay of still images and moving pictures. This ironic coming to life is repeated in a more direct cinematic reference in a flyer prepared for dance clubs by the Italian commune of Nettuno. In the flyer, we see the body of a young man in a white suit (slightly bloodied) stretched out on the asphalt amid broken glass and car parts in a posture that mimics John Travolta's signature move in the poster for *Saturday Night Fever* (1978), while the title of the song he danced to appears in neon at the top of the flyer: "Staying Alive." If the affect and evident seriousness were not so intense, the effect could be unintentionally comic. The world of anti-smoking PSAs shows much the same combination of cinematic fantasy and hyperbolic melodrama: the not-for-profit League against Cancer created a poster for a horror film called *Nicco Teen:* "A true story of a brutal serial killer." The poster mimics all the standard features of a modern advertising campaign, including laudatory quotes from fake newspaper movie critics and the tag line "If you don't stop him, you're next." The presence of the cinematic extends outside negative biopolitics (don't drink and drive, don't smoke) to other behaviors that are perceived as contributing to the vitality of the nation. Jessica Alba appeared in a controversial PSA encouraging young people to register to vote and not "be silent." In the ad, she is shown wearing a plastic muzzle with nails forming a grate over her mouth, and with tears running down her face. The ad was part of a series of bondage-themed PSAs encouraging voter registration for the 2008 US presidential campaign and election and draws evidently on sadomasochistic sexual scenarios, but the mask she wears is also an explicit cinematic reference, namely, to the mask worn by Hannibal Lecter in *The Silence of the Lambs* (1991). Although these advertisements are manifestly cinematic in their references, their basic features—the deployment of a melodramatic scene or fantasy and their hyperbolic affect—indicate that biopolitical discipline always relies on a certain degree of mediation to achieve its desired effects, a mediation that is closely tied to the cinematic.

In his writings about the application of power, particularly *Discipline and Punish* (1977) and *The History of Sexuality* (1978), Foucault described both direct and violent forms of coercion (public execution, imprisonment) that we tend to associate with direct political power and indirect and subtle forms of persuasive discipline (say, the architectural layout of schools and offices), which influence behavior in noncoercive ways, often simply by making a subject, such as the worker or student, visible. Missing from these accounts and from many other discussions of the effective power of biopolitical interventions, however, are other forms of visibility, such as the cinematic and the televisual. In "Ideology and Ideological State Apparatuses," Althusser (2001) describes power "hailing" an individual and transforming him into a subject when he recognizes himself in the hail with the same "obviousness" as when a friend at the door or on the phone expects to be recognized by simply saying "It's me" (117). Althusser specifically imagines a police officer on the street who yells, "Hey, you there!" (118), at which point what was an individual becomes a suspect (and more broadly, for Althusser, a subject) by recognizing himself as the subject of the call. Althusser goes on to show quite nicely that in every ideology there is an address to a "you" (as when Christ says "I died for you"), and the key to its success is that the subject must say, "Yes, it really is me!" (121). This very successful account of how ideology functions, however, also relies exclusively on spoken language as its medium, imagining (it, too, is animated by a certain fantasy scene) a series of explicit hails, calls, and addresses to the subject. There are, however, many other subtler and more unspoken ways in which a subject might recognize himself or herself, for example, in an image that is not intuitively or immediately seen as an address to the viewer, but that nonetheless captures him or her in its fantasy. In other words, my goal here is to call attention to the role of cinema (and media more generally) in the fantasies that sustain ideology in general and biopolitics in particular.

This role is double, or better, moves simultaneously in two directions. On the one hand, as I have just shown, the biopolitical discipline of the subject repeatedly relies on cinema, its genres, and its conventions. To be effective as ideology, there must be a certain quantum of affect—disgust at those who do not wash their hands after using the restroom, the melodramatic tears for the daughter who died on graduation night, the fear of nicotine as a serial killer—and cinema is a superb vehicle for delivering emotion. Although it is perhaps subtler in the examples I have cited previously, this aspect of the relationship between biopolitical initiatives and film can become surprisingly explicit. As Susan Jeffords (1994) and others noted years ago, the Reagan administration drew amply on images from cinema to suggest that the president was a source of masculine strength and vitality, perhaps never more famously than in calling the Strategic Defense Initiative "Star Wars," an initiative that would protect the nation from an "Evil Empire." At the same time, however, we can also detect a countercurrent: film can also draw on those same biopolitical initiatives. Science fiction has a particular penchant for drawing on biopolitical scenarios, especially in its dystopian register. *Logan's Run* (1978), for example, depicts an apparently utopian post-apocalyptic society living in a dome, but one in which each citizen voluntarily commits suicide on reaching the age of thirty as a way to manage overpopulation. More recently, *The Hunger Games* (2012) and the ensuing franchise dramatized not only a vampiric elite that enjoys perfect health, comfort, and safety at the expense of a populace doomed to illness, hunger, and precariousness, but also the mediatization of that exploitation: members of this precarious proletariat are forced to fight each other to the death on national television both for a chance at a lifetime of free food and as a reminder that the elites still hold the power of life and death. In a climactic sequence in the second film, *The Hunger Games: Catching Fire* (2013), the protagonist, Katniss, finds an unexpected way to bring down both the arena where they fight and the television broadcast. President Snow watches in stupefaction as the screens showing the television broadcast go dark one by one, and we hear the voice of one of the technicians offscreen: "We've lost power." This comment, of course, refers not only to the loss of electricity but also simultaneously (especially insofar as it comes from offscreen and cannot be attributed to any particular subject) to a larger loss of political power. It cements the relationship between political control over life and the ability of the state to mediate that control through moving images.

The larger point here is that a full (or at least fuller) understanding of the relationship between biopolitics and cinema requires that we also consider the fundamentally psychoanalytic dimension of fantasy for the subject: how do we find a place for ourselves within a dramatic scene, a scenario that we find irresistibly compelling? For the current generation of undergraduates that I teach, *The Hunger Games* has (and has had for several years now) a particular resonance. It is hard to say—and herein is perhaps the secret of its success as a compelling fantasy scenario—which aspect of the film is the factor that most seduces the contemporary viewer. Is it the fantasy of a struggle against a world of neoliberal precariousness produced by the privileges of an elite (the left-wing fantasy)? Or is it a struggle by the honest and hardworking poor of West Virginia against a cosmopolitan and sexually ambiguous elite (the right-wing fantasy)? A masochistic fantasy of self-sacrifice and suffering, or the narcissistic fantasy of being everyone's object of attention? The now-commonplace fantasy predominantly aimed at women and largely popularized by the *Twilight* franchise of the girl who chooses between two equally but differently compelling men? Or the post-feminist fantasy, perhaps aimed equally at both men and women, of a woman who is beautiful but strong and competitive, unhindered by any notions of conventional gender roles but successful at performing her biological gender? One could go on: celebrity culture, reality television, love in the time of the apocalypse, the decaying vampiric blood fetish of President Snow—fantasies that range from the seductive to the horrific, all of which produce the effect of Hollywood glamour. But we should understand that glamour not as a superficial sheen that indicates a lack of depth of core meaning, but in its older sense of an enchantment, a spell that subjugates and controls while also creating an illusion. The larger point here is that this spell ties us not simply to "mere entertainment" but to a certain vision of the world.

In the case of *The Hunger Games,* the widespread success of the franchise is also tied to its ideological fluidity and ambivalence. As I suggested, the political oppression and the concomitant revolution it depicts remain open to both left- and right-wing understandings, and its underlying fantasies of gender also have elements that appeal to a wide variety of spectators. In the case of the contemporary peplum, however, both its ideology (ranging from a vague, anti-elite populism to nearly fascist xenophobia, as in *300's* endorsement of Spartan infanticide and eugenics) and its fantasies of gender (an aggrieved and wounded masculinity that has no place in a degenerate modernity) have an appeal that is undoubtedly narrower but perhaps makes up in intensity for what it lacks in breadth. In going into detail about three of the peplum's most perennial points of fascination—slowed and stopped time, the avoidance of the time of sexuality, and the camera's richly detailed exploration of the idealized male body's skin, muscles, and viscera—I have tried not only to elaborate how a certain kind of beguiling fantasy is created for the spectator of these films, but also to show how those fantasies play into the peplum's biopolitical work, namely, the muscular male body in mythological antiquity as a guarantee of the nation's health, strength, and vitality. In short, looking at how cinema mediates the management of life and health for its spectators requires that we also examine its underlying fantasies, the alluring scenarios that make cinema rise above the pedagogical and didactic. If a film like *300,* for example, dispensed with its lingering, contemplative slow time, its ambiguous and deferred sexuality, and its exploration of the ideal male body as constituted by perfect skin and taut musculature that conceal a wounded and melodramatic interior, its appeal as a didactic text about the dangers of the Middle East and the virtues of Western masculinity would be limited to those already convinced. We need, I am suggesting, something like a psycho-biopolitics if we are to understand the role that film plays in helping shape our ideas about the politics of life.[4]

Notes

1. For Esposito, this is not a contingent event but follows necessarily from the original decision to base a community (etymologically, a shared burden) on immunity (an exclusion in which some do not share the communal burden).

2. Perversely, many American anti-smoking ads demonstrate how deadly the vice is by likening it to a gun: a revolver loaded with cigarettes or a hand holding a cigarette that casts a shadow of a hand clutching a pistol. What makes it clear that such ads, despite their generally truthful character, are always pure ideology is that none of them can mention the vast death toll caused by the ready access to firearms in the United States. Such a public service announcement or ad campaign is almost inconceivable, despite the fact that the number of gun-related deaths each year in the United States is approximately three times that of drunk driving. Indeed, when I typed "ads against guns" into Google, it suggested instead "ads against gun control."

3. There are, of course, a handful of exceptions: a few midcentury peplums (such as *Colossus and the Amazon Queen* and *Hercules in the Valley of Woe*) were clearly meant to be understood as parodic or comic, and many of the 1980s barbarian peplums were clearly meant to be enjoyed with a cynical detachment—but not the most influential of them, *Conan the Barbarian*. Of the contemporary peplums, *The Legend of Hercules* (2014) and *Hercules* (2014) are both characterized, rather awkwardly, by a desperate seriousness punctuated by occasional moments of campy, ironic detachment. Elsewhere, however (*300, 300: Rise of an Empire, Immortals, Spartacus: Blood and Sand, Pompeii*), the seriousness is pervasive even in spite of the apparent camp excess of the imagery. Reich argues that after Mussolini took power, the silent-era Maciste films also shed "much of the irony and comedic tone of the previous films" (2015, 19).

4. Hilary Neroni's *The Subject of Torture* (2015) brings together psychoanalysis and biopolitics in a series of perceptive and persuasive readings of torture in contemporary film and television, but primarily in order to show what psychoanalysis can perceive in torture that biopolitics cannot (the desire of the subject). Certainly, both theoretical approaches have their blind spots, but my hope for this book, as well as future work, is that the two might be complementary rather than antagonistic in their relations.

Filmography

For foreign-language titles that are significantly different from their English titles or were never translated, I offer a literal translation in roman (not italic) type in parentheses immediately following the foreign-language title.

Maciste and Silent-Era Peplum Films

Cabiria. 1914. Giovanni Pastrone. Italy.
Maciste. 1915. Giovanni Pastrone. Italy. Released in the USA as *Marvelous Maciste.*
Maciste all'inferno. 1926. Guido Brignone. Italy. Released in the USA as *Maciste in Hell.*
Maciste alpino (Alpine Maciste). 1916. Giovanni Pastrone. Italy. Released in the USA as *The Warrior.*
Maciste contro la morte (Maciste against death). 1920. Carlo Campogalliani. Italy. See also *La trilogia di Maciste.*
Maciste contro lo sceicco (Maciste vs. the sheik). 1926. Mario Camerini. Italy. Released in the USA as *Maciste in Africa.*
Maciste imperatore (Emperor Maciste). 1924. Guido Brignone. Italy.
Maciste innamorato (Maciste in love). 1919. Luigi Romano Borgnetto. Italy.
Maciste in vacanza (Maciste on vacation). 1921. Luigi Romano Borgnetto. Italy.
Maciste medium. 1918. Vincenzo Denizot. Italy.
Maciste nella gabbia dei leoni (Maciste in the lions' cage). 1926. Guido Brignone. Italy. Released in English as *The Hero of the Circus.*
Maciste und der Tochter des Silberkönigs (Maciste and the silver king's daughter). 1922. Luigi Romano Borgnetto. Germany, Italy.
Maciste und die Javanerin (Maciste and the Javanese woman). 1922. Uwe Jens Krafft. Germany.
Mister Radio. 1924. Nunzio Malasomma. Germany.
Quo vadis? 1913. Enrico Guazzoni. Italy.
Sansone e la ladra di atleti (Samson and the athlete thief). 1919. Amedeo Mustacchi. Italy.
Spartaco. 1913. Giovanni Enrico Vidali. Italy. Released in the USA and the UK as *Spartacus.*
Testamento di Maciste, Il (Maciste's last will and testament). 1920. Carlo Campogalliani. Italy. See also *La trilogia di Maciste.*
Trilogia di Maciste, La (The Maciste trilogy). 1920. Carlo Campogalliani. Italy. This consists of three shorter films that make one continuous narrative arc: *Il viaggio di Maciste, Maciste contro la morte,* and *Il testamento di Maciste.*
Ultima fatica di Ercole, La (The last labor of Hercules). 1918. Emilio Graziani Walter. Italy.
Unüberwindliche, Der (The invincible). 1928. Max Obal. Germany.

Viaggio di Maciste, Il (Maciste's journey). 1920. Carlo Campogalliani. Italy. See also *La trilogia di Maciste*.

Midcentury Peplum Films

Atlas in the Land of the Cyclops. Original title: *Maciste nella terra dei ciclopi*. 1961. Antonio Leonviola. Italy. Also released as *Atlas against the Cyclops* and *Monster from the Unknown World* (UK).

Attila. 1954. Pietro Francisci. Italy, France. Also released as *Attila the Hun*. UK, Australia.

Avenger, The. Original title: *La leggenda di Enea* (The legend of Aeneas). 1962. Giorgio Venturini (as Giorgio Rivalta). Italy, France, Yugoslavia. Also released as *War of the Trojans*.

Colossus and the Amazon Queen. Original title: *La regina delle Amazzoni* (The queen of the Amazons). 1960. Vittorio Sala. Italy. Also released as *Colossus and the Amazons*.

Colossus of the Arena. Original title: *Maciste, il gladiatore più forte del mondo* (Maciste, the strongest gladiator in the world). 1962. Michele Lupo. Italy.

Conqueror of Atlantis. Original title: *Il conquistatore di Atlantide*. 1965. Alfonso Brescia. Italy, Egypt.

Conquest of Mycene. Original title: *Ercole contro Moloch* (Hercules against Moloch). 1963. Giorgio Ferroni. Italy, France. Also released as *Hercules against Moloch* and *Hercules Attacks* (UK).

Devil of the Desert against the Son of Hercules. Original title: *Anthar l'invincibile* (Anthar the invincible). 1964. Antonio Margheriti (as Anthony Dawson). Italy, Spain, France.

Duel of the Titans. Original title: *Romolo e Remo* (Romulus and Remus). 1961. Sergio Corbucci. Italy, France.

Fabiola. 1949. Alessandro Blasetti. Italy, France. Also released as *The Fighting Gladiator* (UK).

Fire Monsters against the Son of Hercules. Original title: *Maciste contro i mostri* (Maciste against the monsters). 1962. Guido Malatesta. Italy, Yugoslavia. Also released as *Colossus of the Stone Age* and *Land of the Monsters* (UK).

Giant of Metropolis, The. Original title: *Il gigante di Metropolis*. 1961. Umberto Scarpelli (as R. Nichols). Italy.

Goliath and the Barbarians. Original title: *Il terrore dei barbari* (The terror of the Barbarians). 1959. Carlo Campogalliani. Italy.

Goliath and the Dragon. Original title: *La vendetta di Ercole* (The revenge of Hercules). 1960. Vittorio Cottafavi. Italy, France. Also released as *Vengeance of Hercules*.

Goliath and the Sins of Babylon. Original title: *Maciste, l'eroe più grande del mondo* (Maciste, the greatest hero in the world). 1963. Michele Lupo. Italy.

Goliath and the Vampires. Original title: *Maciste contro il vampiro* (Maciste against the vampire). 1961. Sergio Corbucci, Giacomo Gentilomo. Italy. Also released as *Goliath and the Island of Vampires, Maciste vs. the Vampire, Samson vs. the Vampires,* and *The Vampires*.

Hercules. Original title: *Le fatiche di Ercole* (The labors of Hercules). 1958. Pietro Francisci. Italy, Spain.

Hercules against the Mongols. Original title: *Maciste contro i Mongoli*. 1963. Domenico Paolella. Italy.

Hercules against the Moon Men. Original title: *Maciste e la regina di Samar* (Maciste and the queen of Samar). 1964. Giacomo Gentilomo. Italy, France.

Hercules against the Sons of the Sun. Original title: *Ercole contro i figli del sole*. 1964. Osvaldo Civirani. Italy, Spain.

Hercules and the Captive Women. Original title: *Ercole alla conquista di Atlantide* (Hercules conquers Atlantis). 1961. Vittorio Cottafavi. Italy, France. Also released as *Hercules and the Haunted Women* and *Hercules Conquers Atlantis* (UK).

Hercules and the Treasure of the Incas. Original title: *Sansone e il tesoro degli Incas* (Samson and the treasure of the Incas). 1964. Piero Pierotti. West Germany, Italy, France. Also released as *Lost Treasure of the Incas* and *Lost Treasure of the Aztecs*.

Hercules and the Tyrants of Babylon. Original title: *Ercole contro i tiranni di Babilonia* (Hercules against the tyrants of Babylon). 1964. Domenico Paolella. Italy.

Hercules in New York. 1969. Arthur Seidelman. USA.

Hercules in the Haunted World. Original title: *Ercole al centro della terra* (Hercules at the center of the earth). 1961. Mario Bava. Italy. Also released as *Hercules vs. the Vampires, The Vampires vs. Hercules, With Hercules to the Center of the Earth*, and *Sword and Sandal* (Australia).

Hercules in the Valley of Woe. Original title: *Maciste contro Ercole nella valle dei guai* (Maciste against Hercules in the valley of woe). 1961. Mario Mattoli. Italy. Also released as *Hercules in the Vale of Woe*.

Hercules, Prisoner of Evil. Original title: *Ursus, il terrore dei Kirghisi* (Ursus, terror of the Kyrghyz). 1964. Antonio Margheriti (as Anthony M. Dawson). Italy. Also released as *Terror of the Kirghiz*.

Hercules, Samson and Ulysses. Original title: *Ercole sfida Sansone* (Hercules challenges Samson). 1963. Pietro Francisci. Italy.

Hercules the Avenger. Original title: *La sfida dei giganti* (The challenge of the giants). 1965. Maurizio Lucidi (as Maurice A. Bright). Italy.

Hercules Unchained. 1959. Pietro Francisci. Original title: *Ercole e la regina di Lidia* (Hercules and the queen of Lydia). Italy, France, Spain.

Hercules vs. the Hydra. Original title: *Gli amori di Ercole* (The loves of Hercules). 1960. Carlo Ludovico Bragaglia. Italy, France. Also released as *The Loves of Hercules* and *Hercules and the Hydra*.

Minotaur, the Wild Beast of Crete, The. Original title: *Teseo contro il minotauro* (Theseus vs. the Minotaur). 1960. Silvio Amadio. Italy. Also released as *The Minotaur* and *Warlord of Crete*.

Mole Men against the Son of Hercules. Original title: *Maciste, l'uomo più forte del mondo* (Maciste, the strongest man in the world). 1961. Antonio Leonviola. Italy.

My Son, the Hero. Original title: *Arrivano i titani* (The Titans are coming). 1962. Duccio Tessari. Italy, France. Also released as *The Titans* and *Sons of Thunder* (UK).

Quo vadis? 1951. Mervyn LeRoy. USA, Italy.

Robe, The. 1953. Henry Koster. USA.

Samson against the Sheik. Original title: *Maciste contro lo sceicco*. 1962. Domenico Paolella. Italy.

Samson and Delilah. 1949. Cecil B. DeMille. USA.

Samson and the Seven Miracles of the World. Original title: *Maciste alla corte del Gran Khan* (Maciste at the court of the Great Khan). 1961. Riccardo Freda. Italy, France. Also released as *Maciste at the Court of the Great Khan* (UK).

Samson and the Slave Queen. Original title: *Zorro contro Maciste* (Zorro against Maciste). 1963. Umberto Lenzi. Italy, Spain.

Samson in King Solomon's Mines. Original title: *Maciste nelle miniere di re Salomone.* 1964. Piero Regnoli (as Martin Andrews). Italy. Also released as *Maciste in King Solomon's Mines.*

Son of Samson. Original title: *Maciste nella valle dei re* (Maciste in the valley of the kings). 1960. Carlo Campogalliani. Italy, France, Yugoslavia. Also released as *Maciste the Mighty.*

Spartacus. 1960. Stanley Kubrick. USA.

Three Stooges Meet Hercules, The. 1962. Edward Bernds. USA.

Triumph of Maciste. Original title: *Il trionfo di Maciste.* 1961. Tanio Boccia (as Amerigo Anton). Italy, France. Also released as *Triumph of the Son of Hercules.*

Ulysses against the Son of Hercules. Original title: *Ulisse contro Ercole.* 1962. Mario Caiano. Italy, France. Also known as *Ulysses against Hercules* (UK).

Ursus. 1961. Carlo Campogalliani. Italy, Spain.

Vengeance of Ursus, The. 1961. Original title: *La vendetta di Ursus.* Luigi Capuano. Italy. Also released as *Revenge of Ursus* (USA) and *The Mighty Warrior* (UK).

Vulcan, Son of Jupiter. Original title: *Vulcano, figlio di Giove.* 1962. Emimmo Salvi. Italy.

Witch's Curse, The. Original title: *Maciste all'inferno* (Maciste in hell). 1962. Riccardo Freda (as Robert Hampton). Italy.

The Barbarian Peplum

Adventures of Hercules, The. 1985. Original title: *Le avventure dell'incredibile Ercole* (The adventures of the incredible Hercules). Luigi Cozzi (as Lewis Coates). Italy, USA.

Ator, the Fighting Eagle. Original title: *Ator l'invincibile.* 1982. Joe d'Amato (as David Hills). Italy. Also released in Italy as *Ator, l'aquila battante.*

Barbarian Queen. 1985. Héctor Olivera. USA, Argentina. Also released as *Queen of the Naked Steel.*

Barbarian Queen II: The Empress Strikes Back. 1989. Joe Finley. USA, Mexico.

Barbarians, The. 1987. Ruggero Deodato. Italy, USA. Also released as *The Barbarian Brothers.*

Beastmaster, The. 1982. Don Coscarelli. USA, West Germany.

Clash of the Titans. 1982. Desmond Davis. USA, UK.

Conan the Barbarian. 1982. John Milius. USA.

Conquest. 1984. Lucio Fulci. Italy, Spain, Mexico.

Deathstalker. 1983. James Sbardellati (as John Watson). Argentina, USA.

Deathstalker II: Duel of the Titans. 1987. Jim Wynorski. Argentina, USA.

Deathstalker and the Warriors from Hell. 1988. Alfonso Corona. USA, Mexico. Also released as *Deathstalker III.*

Deathstalker IV: Match of Titans. 1991. Howard R. Cohen. USA.

Gor. 1988. Fritz Kiersch. USA.

Gunan, King of the Barbarians. Original title: *Gunan il guerriero.* 1982. Franco Prosperi (as Frank Shannon). Italy. Also released as *The Invincible Barbarian.*

Hercules. 1983. Luigi Cozzi (as Lewis Coates). USA, Italy.

Ironmaster. Original title: *La guerra del ferro: Ironmaster.* The war of iron: Ironmaster). 1983. Umberto Lenzi (as Humphrey Milestone). Italy, France.

Outlaw of Gor. 1989. Bud Cardos. USA. Also released as *Gor II.*

Quest for the Mighty Sword. 1990. Joe d'Amato (as David Hills). Italy. Also released as *Ator III: The Hobgoblin, The Hobgoblin, Troll 3,* and *The Lord of Akili* (Italy).

Red Sonja. 1985. Richard Fleischer. Netherlands, USA.

She. 1982. Avi Nesher. Italy.

Sword of the Barbarians, The. Original title: *Sangraal, la spada di fuoco.* 1982. Michele Massimo Tarantino (as Michael E. Lemick). Also released as *Barbarian Master.*

Throne of Fire, The. Original title: *Il trono di fuoco.* 1983. Franco Prosperi. Italy.

Warrior and the Sorceress, The. John Broderick. USA, Argentina.

Yor, the Hunter from the Future. Original title: *Il mondo di Yor* (Yor's world). 1983. Antonio Margheriti (as Anthony M. Dawson). Italy, Turkey.

Peplum Television

BeastMaster. 1999–2002. Australia, Canada, USA.

Conan and the Young Warriors. 1994. USA.

Conan the Adventurer. Animated. 1992–1993. USA, Canada.

Conan the Adventurer. Live Action. 1997–1998. Germany, USA, Mexico.

He-Man and the Masters of the Universe. 1983–1985. USA.

Hercules: The Legendary Journeys. 1995–1999. USA, New Zealand.

Mighty Hercules, The. 1963–1966. Canada.

She-Ra: Princess of Power. 1985. USA.

Spartacus: Blood and Sand. 2010. USA.

Spartacus: Vengeance. 2012. USA.

Spartacus: War of the Damned. 2013. USA.

Thundarr the Barbarian. 1980–1982. USA.

Xena: Warrior Princess. 1995–2001. New Zealand.

Young Hercules. 1998–1999. USA.

The Contemporary Peplum

Alexander. 2004. Oliver Stone. Germany, USA, Netherlands, France, UK, Italy.

Amazons and Gladiators. 2001. Zachary Weintraub. USA, Germany.

Clash of the Titans. 2010. Louis Leterrier. USA.

Gladiator. 2000. Ridley Scott. USA, UK.

Hercules. 2014. Brett Ratner. USA.

Immortals. 2011. Tarsem Singh. USA.

Legend of Hercules, The. 2014. Renny Harlin. USA.

Pompeii. 2014. Paul W. S. Anderson. Canada, Germany, USA.

Scorpion King, The. 2002. Chuck Russell. USA, Germany, Belgium.

300. 2007. Zach Snyder. USA.

300: Rise of an Empire. 2014. Noam Murro. USA.

Troy. 2004. Wolfgang Petersen. USA, Malta, UK.

Wrath of the Titans. 2012. Jonathan Liebesman. USA, Spain.

Other Films

Aliens. 1986. James Cameron. USA, UK.

Battle of Algiers, The. Original title: *La battaglia d'Algeri*. 1965. Gillo Pontecorvo. Italy, Algeria.

Ben-Hur. 1959. William Wyler. USA.

Birds, The. 1963. Alfred Hitchcock. USA.

Blade Runner. 1982. Ridley Scott. USA, Hong Kong, UK.

Cannibal Holocaust. 1980. Ruggero Deodato. Italy.

chien andalou, Un. 1929. Luis Buñuel. France.

Day After, The. 1983. Nicholas Meyer. USA.

Detour. 1945. Edgar G. Ulmer. USA.

1860. 1934. Alessandro Blasetti. Italy.

Empire Strikes Back, The. 1980. Irvin Kershner. USA. *Escape from New York*. 1981. John Carpenter. UK, USA.

EuroTrip. 2004. Jeff Schaffer. USA, Czech Republic.

Factory of Gestures, The: Body Language in Film. 2008. Oksana Bulgakowa. USA.

Falling Down. 1993. Joel Schumacher. France, USA, UK.

Fight Club. 1999. David Fincher. USA, Germany.

Germany Year Zero. Original title: *Germania: Anno zero*. 1948. Roberto Rossellini. Italy.

Great Silence, The. Original title: *Il grande silenzio*. 1968. Sergio Corbucci. Italy, France, Germany.

History of the World: Part I. 1981. Mel Brooks. USA.

Hunger Games, The. 2012. Gary Ross. USA.

Hunger Games, The: Catching Fire. 2013. Francis Lawrence. USA.

Indiana Jones and the Temple of Doom. 1984. Steven Spielberg. USA.

Jane Mansfield Story, The. 1980. Dick Lowry. USA.

Life of Brian. 1979. Terry Jones. UK.

Logan's Run. 1976. Michael Anderson. USA.

Maltese Falcon, The. 1941. John Huston. USA.

Marnie. 1964. Alfred Hitchcock. USA.

Matrix, The. 1999. The Wachowskis. USA.

Meet the Spartans. 2008. Jason Friedberg, Aaron Seltzer. USA.

Metropolis. 1927. Fritz Lang. Germany.

Miracle in Milan. Original title: *Miracolo a Milano*. 1951. Vittorio De Sica. Italy.

Mondo cane. 1962. Paolo Cavara, Gualtiero Jacopetti, Franco Prosperi. Italy.

Night of the Comet. 1984. Thom Eberhardt. USA.

1990: The Bronx Warriors. Original title: *1990: I guerrieri del Bronx*. 1982. Enzo Castellari. Italy.

Once upon a Time in the West. Original title: *C'era uno volta il West*. 1968. Sergio Leone. Italy, USA, Spain.

Open City. Original title: *Roma: Città aperta*. 1946. Roberto Rossellini. Italy.

Paisan. Original title: *Paisà*. 1946. Roberto Rossellini. Italy.

Pride and Prejudice. 1940. Robert Leonard. USA.

Pulp Fiction. 1994. Quentin Tarantino. USA.

Rear Window. 1954. Alfred Hitchcock. USA.

Road Warrior, The. 1981. George Miller. Australia. Also released as *Mad Max 2: The Road Warrior.*

Rocky. 1976. John G. Avildsen. USA.

Run Lola Run. Original title: *Lola rennt.* 1998. Tom Tykwer. Germany.

Saturday Night Fever. 1978. John Badham. USA.

Scipio Africanus: The Defeat of Hannibal. Original title: *Scipione l'africano.* 1937. Carmine Gallone. Italy.

The Silence of the Lambs. 1991. Jonathan Demme. USA.

Single Man, A. 2009. Tom Ford. USA.

Spellbound. 1945. Alfred Hitchcock. USA.

Star Wars. 1977. George Lucas. USA.

Street of Crocodiles. 1986. Stephen Quay, Timothy Quay. UK.

Sunset Boulevard. 1950. Billy Wilder. USA.

Toy Story. 1995. John Lasseter. USA.

Transformers. 2007. Michael Bay. USA.

2019: After the Fall of New York. Original title: *2019—Dopo la caduta di New York.* 1983. Sergio Martino (as Martin Dolman). Italy, France.

2047—Sights of Death. 2014. Alessandro Capone. Italy.

Vertigo. 1958. Alfred Hitchcock. USA.

Warriors of the Wasteland. Original title: *I nuovi barbari* (The new barbarians). 1982. Enzo Castellari. Italy, USA. Also released as *The New Barbarians: Warriors of the Wasteland.*

World War Z. 2013. Marc Forster. USA, Malta.

Works Cited

Agamben, Giorgio. 1995. *Homo sacer: Il potere sovrano e la nuda vita.* Turin: Einaudi.

———. 1998. *Homo Sacer: Sovereign Power and Bare Life.* Translated by Daniel Heller-Roazen. Stanford, CA: Stanford University Press.

Althusser, Louis. 2001. "Ideology and Ideological State Apparatuses." In *Lenin and Philosophy, and Other Essays,* translated by Ben Brewster, 127–186. New York: Monthly Review Press.

Anzieu, Didier. 1989. *The Skin Ego.* Translated by Chris Turner. New Haven, CT: Yale University Press.

Arnold, Martin. 2002. "Book Parties with Togas." *New York Times,* July 11. http://www.nytimes.com/2002/07/11/books/making-books-book-parties-with-togas.html. Accessed August 20, 2015.

Aziza, Claude. 1998. "Le mot et la chose." *CinémAction* 89: 7–11.

Baker, George. 2008. "Photography's Expanded Field." In *Still Moving: Between Cinema and Photography,* edited by Karen Beckman and Jean Ma, 175–188. Durham, NC: Duke University Press.

Barker, Jennifer. 2009. *The Tactile Eye: Touch and the Cinematic Experience.* Berkeley: University of California Press.

Barthes, Roland. 1981. *Camera Lucida: Reflections on Photography.* Translated by Richard Howard. New York: Hill and Wang.

Bazin, André. 1960. *Qu'est-ce que le cinéma?* Paris: Les Editions du Cerf.

———. 1967–1971. *What Is Cinema?* Translated by Hugh Gray. 2 vols. Berkeley: University of California Press.

"BeastMaster" (TV Series). *Wikipedia: The Free Encyclopedia.* https://en.wikipedia.org/wiki/BeastMaster_(TV_series). Accessed October 1, 2013.

Beauchamp, Toby. 2009. "Artful Concealment and Strategic Visibility: Transgender Bodies and US State Surveillance after 9/11." *Surveillance and Society* 6.4: 356–366.

Beck, Kristin, and Anne Speckhard. 2013. *Warrior Princess: A US Navy SEAL's Journey to Coming out Transgender.* Advances Press.

Bellour, Raymond. 2008. "Concerning 'the Photographic.'" Translated by Chris Darke. In *Still Moving: Between Cinema and Photography,* edited by Karen Beckman and Jean Ma, 253–276. Durham, NC: Duke University Press.

Bendery, Jennifer. "Paul Ryan, 'Hercules' Rally House Republicans." *Huffington Post,* September 20, 2012. http://www.huffingtonpost.com/2012/09/20/paul-ryan-hercules_n_1900586.html. Accessed March 25, 2016.

Benjamin, Walter. 1968. "The Work of Art in the Age of Mechanical Reproduction." In *Illuminations,* edited by Hannah Arendt and translated by Harry Zohn, 219–253. New York: Harcourt, Brace and World.

Berenstein, Rhona. 1990. "Mommie Dearest: *Aliens, Rosemary's Baby* and Mothering." *Journal of Popular Culture* 24.2: 55–73.

Bertellini, Giorgio. 2003. "Colonial Autism: Whitened Heroes, Auditory Rhetorics, and National Identity in Interwar Italian Cinema." In *A Place in the Sun: Africa in Italian Colonial Culture from Post-unification to the Present,* edited by Patrizia Palumbo, 255–278. Berkeley: University of California Press.

Berton, Mireille. 2012. "A Subjectivity Torn between Stasis and Movement: Still Image and Moving Image in Medical Discourse at the Turn of the 20th Century." In *Between Still and Moving Images,* edited by Laurent Guido and Olivier Lugon, 47–58. Bloomington: Indiana University Press.

Blanshard, Alastair, and Shahabudin, Kim. 2011. *Classics on Screen: Ancient Greece and Rome on Film.* Bristol: Bristol Classical Press.

Blitz, Michael, and Louise Krasniewicz. 2004. *Why Arnold Matters: The Rise of a Cultural Icon.* New York: Basic Books.

Brunetta, Gian Piero. 2004. *Cent' anni di cinema italiano.* Vol. 2, *Dal 1945 ai giorni nostri.* Bari: Laterza.

Buchanan, Andrew. 2008. "'Good Morning, Pupil!' American Representations of Italianness and the Occupation of Italy, 1943–45." *Journal of Contemporary History* 43.2: 217–240.

Burke, Edmund. 1998. *A Philosophical Enquiry into the Origins of the Sublime and Beautiful: And Other Pre-Revolutionary Writings.* New York: Penguin.

Burke, Frank. 2011. "The Italian Sword-and-Sandal Film from *Fabiola* to *Hercules and the Captive Women.*" In *Italian Popular Cinema,* edited by Flavia Brizio-Skov, 17–51. London: I. B. Tauris.

Butler, Judith. 1993. *Bodies That Matter: On the Discursive Limits of Sex.* New York: Routledge.

Calvino, Italo. 1952. *Il visconte dimezzato* (The cloven viscount). Turin: Einaudi.

Cammarota, Domenico. 1987. *Il cinema peplum: La prima guida critica ai film di Conan, Ercole, Goliath, Maciste, Sansone, Spartaco, Thaur, Ursus.* Rome: Fanucci.

Cassata, Francesco. 2006. *Molti, sani e forti: L'eugenetica in Italia.* Turin: Bollati Boringhieri.

Chapman, David. 2002. *Retro Stud: Muscle Movie Posters from around the World.* Portland, OR: Collector's Press.

———. 2006. *Sandow the Magnificent: Eugen Sandow and the Beginnings of Bodybuilding.* Urbana: University of Illinois Press.

Chemers, Michael M. 2007. "With Your Shield, or on It: Disability Representation in *300.*" *Disability Studies Quarterly* 27.3. http://dsq-sds.org/article/view/37/37. Accessed September 6, 2012.

Classen, Constance. 2012. *The Deepest Sense: A Cultural History of Touch.* Urbana: University of Illinois Press.

Clover, Carol. 1992. *Men, Women, and Chain Saws: Gender in the Modern Horror Film.* Princeton, NJ: Princeton University Press.

Connor, Steven. 2004. *The Book of Skin.* Ithaca, NY: Cornell University Press.

Conway, Gerry (writer), and J. L. García López and Wally Wood (artists). 1975. "Hercules Unbound!" *Hercules Unbound,* no. 1 (October–November). New York: National Periodical Publications [DC Comics].

Cornelius, Michael G. 2011. "Introduction—Of Muscles and Men: The Forms and Functions of the Sword and Sandal Film." In *Of Muscles and Men: Essays on the Sword and Sandal Film,* edited by Michael G. Cornelius, 1–14. Jefferson, NC: McFarland.

Cowie, Elizabeth. 1997. *Representing the Woman: Cinema and Psychoanalysis*. Minneapolis: University of Minnesota Press.

Cyrino, Monica Silveira. 2005. *Big Screen Rome*. Malden, MA: Blackwell Publishing.

Dall'Asta, Monica. 1992. *Un cinéma musclé: Le surhomme dans le cinéma muet italien (1913–1926)*. Translated by Franco Arnò and Charles Tatum. Crisnée, Belgium: Editions Yellow Now.

Dalle Vacche, Angela. 1992. *The Body in the Mirror: Shapes of History in Italian Cinema*. Princeton, NJ: Princeton University Press.

———. 2008. *Diva: Defiance and Passion in Early Italian Cinema*. Austin: University of Texas Press.

D'Amelio, Maria Elena. 2014. "The Hybrid Star: Steve Reeves, Hercules and the Politics of Transnational Whiteness." *Journal of Italian Cinema and Media Studies* 2.2: 259–277.

Dayan, Daniel. 1974. "The Tutor-Code of Classical Cinema." *Film Quarterly* 28.1: 22–31.

Deleuze, Gilles. 1985. *Cinema 2: L'image-temps*. Paris: Editions de Minuit.

———. 1995. *Cinema 2: The Time Image*. Minneapolis: University of Minnesota Press.

Della Casa, Stefano. 2001. "L'estetica povera del peplum." In *Storia del cinema italiano*, vol. 10, *1960–1964*, edited by Giorgio De Vincenti, 306–318. Venice: Marsilio.

Della Casa, Stefano, and Marco Giusti. 2013. *Il grande libro di Ercole: Il cinema mitologico in Italia*. Roma: Edizioni Sabinæ.

Doane, Mary Anne. 2002. *The Emergence of Cinematic Time: Modernity, Contingency, the Archive*. Cambridge, MA: Harvard University Press.

Dutton, Kenneth. 2013. "The Self-Contained Body: The Heroic and Aesthetic/Erotic Modes of Representing the Muscular Body." In *Critical Readings in Bodybuilding*, edited by Adam Locks and Niall Richardson, 151–165. New York: Routledge.

Dyer, Richard. 1997. *White*. New York: Routledge.

Ebert, Roger. 2000. "Gladiator." *Chicago Sun Times*, May 5. http://www.rogerebert.com/reviews/gladiator-2000. Accessed November 18, 2013.

Edelman, Lee. 2004. *No Future: Queer Theory and the Death Drive*. Durham, NC: Duke University Press.

Esposito, Roberto. 1998. *Communitas: Origine e destino della comunità*. Turin: Einaudi.

———. 2002. *Immunitas: Protezione e negazione della vita*. Turin: Einaudi.

———. 2004. *Bíos: Biopolitica e filosofia*. Turin: Einaudi.

———. 2008. *Bíos: Biopolitics and Philosophy*. Translated by Timothy Campbell. Minneapolis: University of Minnesota Press.

———. 2009. *Communitas: The Origin and Destiny of Community*. Translated by Timothy Campbell. Stanford, CA: Stanford University Press.

———. 2011a. "Fortuna e politica all'origine della filosofia italiana." *California Italian Studies* 2.1. http://escholarship.org/uc/item/5ht7n7p4. Accessed November 18, 2013.

———. 2011b. *Immunitas: The Protection and Negation of Life*. Translated by Zakiya Hanafi. Malden, MA: Polity Press.

Falkof, Nicky. 2013. "Arnold at the Gates: Subverting Star Persona in *Conan the Barbarian*." In *Conan Meets the Academy: Multidisciplinary Essays on the Enduring Barbarian*, edited by Jonas Prida, 123–143. Jefferson, NC: McFarland.

Farassino, Alberto. 1983. "Anatomia del cinema muscolare." In *Gli uomini forti*, edited by Alberto Farassino and Tatti Sanguineti, 28–49. Milan: Mazzotta.

Foucault, Michel. 1977. *Discipline and Punish*. Translated by Alan Sheridan. New York: Vintage.

———. 1978. *The History of Sexuality, Vol. 1: An Introduction*. Translated by Robert Hurley. New York: Vintage.

———. 2003. *"Society Must Be Defended": Lectures at the Collège de France, 1975–1976*. Translated by David Macey. New York: Picador.

Fradley, Martin. 2004. "Maximus Melodramaticus: Masculinity, Masochism, and White Male Paranoia in Contemporary Hollywood Cinema." In *Action and Adventure Cinema*, edited by Yvonne Tasker, 235–251. New York: Routledge.

Freud, Sigmund. 1953–1974a. *Beyond the Pleasure Principle*. In *Standard Edition of the Complete Psychological Works of Sigmund Freud*, edited and translated by James Strachey, 18:1–64. London: Hogarth Press.

———. 1953–1974b. "The Dissolution of the Oedipus Complex." In *Standard Edition of the Complete Psychological Works of Sigmund Freud*, edited and translated by James Strachey, 19:172–179. London: Hogarth Press.

———. 1953–1974c. *The Interpretation of Dreams*. In *Standard Edition of the Complete Psychological Works of Sigmund Freud*, edited and translated by James Strachey, vols. 4–5. London: Hogarth Press.

———. 1953–1974d. "Some Psychological Consequences of the Anatomical Distinction between the Sexes." In *Standard Edition of the Complete Psychological Works of Sigmund Freud*, edited and translated by James Strachey, vol. 19, 248–258. London: Hogarth Press.

Galt, Rosalind. 2011. *Pretty: Film and the Decorative Image*. New York: Columbia University Press.

Gerstner, David A. 2013. "Choreographic Homosexual Desire in Philippe Vallois's *Johan*." *Camera Obscura* 28.3: 124–157.

Ghigi, Giuseppe. 1977. "Come si spiegano le fortune dei pepla, su cui sembra si torni a puntare." *Cineforum* 17.2: 733–746.

Gill-Petersen, Julian. 2014. "The Technical Capacities of the Body: Assembling Race, Technology and Transgender." *TSQ: Transgender Studies Quarterly* 1.3: 402–418.

Giordano, Michele. 1998. *Giganti buoni: Da Ercole a Piedone (e oltre); Il mito dell'uomo forte nel cinema italiano*. Rome: Gremese.

Greenhalgh, Susan. 2009. "The Chinese Biopolitical: Facing the Twenty-First Century." *New Genetics and Society* 28.3: 205–222.

Gregori, Cecilia. 2009. "I codici di genere nei manifesti del cinema 'peplum.'" *Acme: Annali della facoltà di lettere dell'Università degli Studi di Milano* 62.1: 215–252.

Grell, Mike (writer and artist). 1976. "Arena of Death." *The Warlord* 1.2 (March–April). New York: National Periodical Publications [DC Comics].

Guido, Laurent. 2012a. "Introduction: Between Deadly Trace and Memorial Scansion; The Frozen Image in Film." In *Between Still and Moving Images*, edited by Laurent Guido and Olivier Lugon, 225–243. Bloomington: Indiana University Press.

———. 2012b. "Introduction: The Paradoxical Fits and Starts of the New 'Optical Unconscious.'" In *Between Still and Moving Images*, edited by Laurent Guido and Olivier Lugon, 9–22. Bloomington: Indiana University Press.

Guido, Laurent, and Olivier Lugon. 2012. *Between Still and Moving Images*, Bloomington: Indiana University Press.

Gunning, Tom. 1986. "The Cinema of Attraction: Early Film, Its Spectator and the Avant-Garde." *Wide Angle* 8.3–4: 63–70.

———. 2012. "The 'Arrested' Instant: Between Stillness and Motion." In *Between Still and Moving Images*, edited by Laurent Guido and Olivier Lugon, 23–31. Bloomington: Indiana University Press.

Günsberg, Maggie. 2005. *Italian Cinema: Gender and Genre*. New York: Palgrave.

Hark, Ina Rae. 1993. "Animals or Romans: Looking at Masculinity in *Spartacus*." In *Screening the Male: Exploring Masculinities in Hollywood Cinema*, edited by Steven Cohan and Ina Rae Hark, 151–172. New York: Routledge.

Hay, James. 1987. *Popular Film Culture in Fascist Italy: The Passing of the Rex*. Bloomington: Indiana University Press.

Heath, Steven. 1977–1978. "Notes on Suture." *Screen* 18.4: 48–76.

Ipsen, Guido. 2012. "Conan the Blueprint: The Construction of Masculine Prototypes in Genre Films." In *The Handbook of Gender, Sex, and Media*, edited by Karen Ross, 135–156. Malden, MA: Wiley-Blackwell.

Jameson, Fredric. 1998. *The Cultural Turn: Selected Writings on the Postmodern, 1983–1998*. New York: Verso.

Jay, Martin. 1993. *Downcast Eyes: The Denigration of Vision in Twentieth-Century French Thought*. Berkeley: University of California Press.

Jeffords, Susan. 1987. "'The Battle of the Big Mamas': Feminism and the Alienation of Women." *Journal of American Culture* 10.3: 73–84.

———. 1994. *Hard Bodies: Hollywood Masculinity in the Reagan Era*. New Brunswick, NJ: Rutgers University Press.

Lacan, Jacques. 1991. *The Seminar of Jacques Lacan. Book I: Freud's Papers on Technique, 1953–1954*. Translated by John Forrester and edited by Jacques-Alain Miller. New York: W. W. Norton.

———. 2007. "The Mirror Stage as Formative of the *I* Function as Revealed in Psychoanalytic Experience." In *Écrits: The First Complete Edition in English*, translated by Bruce Fink, 75–81. New York: W. W. Norton.

LaCapra, Dominick. 1999. "Trauma, Absence, Loss." *Critical Inquiry* 25.4: 696–727.

Lannut, Karine. 1998. "Le péplum fantastique." *CinémAction* 89.4: 72–74.

Leamer, Laurence. 2005. *Fantastic: The Life of Arnold Schwarzenegger*. New York: St. Martin's Press.

Lee, Chris. 2012. "'Conan' Producer: Arnold's Aging Barbarian Faces Self-Doubt." *LA Times*, December 3. http://herocomplex.latimes.com/movies/conan-producer-arnolds-aging-barbarian-faces-self-doubt/. Accessed September 3, 2013.

Loewald, Hans W. 2000. "The Waning of the Oedipus Complex." *Journal of Psychotherapy Practice and Research* 9.4: 239–249.

Lowe, Dunstan. 2009. "Playing with Antiquity: Videogame Receptions of the Classical World." In *Classics for All: Reworking Antiquity in Mass Culture*, edited by Dunstan Lowe and Kim Shahabudin, 64–90. Newcastle upon Tyne: Cambridge Publishing Group.

Marks, Laura. 2000. *The Skin of the Film: Intercultural Cinema, Embodiment, and the Senses*. Durham, NC: Duke University Press.

Martinelli, Vittorio. 1983. "Lasciate fare a noi, siamo forti." In *Gli uomini forti*, edited by Alberto Farassino and Tatti Sanguineti, 9–46. Milan: Mazzotta.

Mathias, Bob, and Bob Mendes. 2001. *A Twentieth Century Odyssey: The Bob Mathias Story*. Champaign, IL: Sports Publishing.

McDowell, Deborah. 1997. "Pecs and Reps: Muscling in on the Subject of Race and Masculinities." In *Race and the Subject of Masculinities,* edited by Michael Uebel and Harry Stecoupoulas, 361–385. Durham, NC: Duke University Press.

McGowan, Todd. 2007. *The Impossible David Lynch.* New York: Columbia University Press.

Merleau-Ponty, Maurice. 1964. *Le visible et l'invisible.* Paris: Gallimard.

———. 1968. *The Visible and the Invisible.* Translated by Alphonso Lingis and edited by Claude Lefort. Evanston: Northwestern University Press.

Mulvey, Laura. 1987. "Visual Pleasure and Narrative Cinema." In *Narrative, Apparatus, Ideology: A Film Theory Reader,* edited by Bruce Rosen, 198–209. New York: Columbia University Press.

———. 2006. *Death 24× a Second: Stillness and the Moving Image.* London: Reaktion Books.

Muñoz, José Esteban. 2009. *Cruising Utopia: The Then and There of Queer Futurity.* New York: New York University Press.

Neale, Steve. 1993. "Masculinity as Spectacle: Reflections on Men and Mainstream Cinema." In *Screening the Male: Exploring Masculinities in Hollywood Cinema,* edited by Steven Cohan and Ina Rae Hark, 9–22. New York: Routledge.

Neroni, Hilary. 2015. *The Subject of Torture: Psychoanalysis and Biopolitics in Television and Film.* New York: Columbia University Press.

Newman, Paul S. (writer, uncredited), and Reed Crandall and George Evans (artists, uncredited). 1960. *Hercules Unchained.* Dell Four Color Movie Classics 1121. New York: Dell Comics.

Nietzsche, Friedrich. 1989. *On the Genealogy of Morals.* Translated by Walter Kaufmann. New York: Vintage Books.

———. 2003. *Twilight of the Gods.* Translated by R. J. Hollingdale. New York: Penguin.

O'Brien, Daniel. 2014. *Classical Masculinity and the Spectacular Body on Film: The Mighty Sons of Hercules.* New York: Palgrave Macmillan.

O'Hara, Helen. 2009. "Exclusive: Tarsem on *War of the Gods.*" *Empire Online,* January 29. Accessed March 12, 2016.

Oudart, Jean-Pierre. 1977–1978. "Cinema and Suture." *Screen* 18.4: 35–47.

Paolella, Domenico. 1965. "La psychanalyse du pauvre." *Midi-minuit fantastique* 12: 1–8.

Paterson, Mark. 2007. *The Senses of Touch: Haptics, Affects and Technologies.* New York: Berg.

Poole, Ralph J. 2013. "'Everybody Loves a Muscle Boi': Homos, Heroes and Foes in Post-9/11 Spoofs of *The 300 Spartans.*" In *Ancient Worlds in Film and Television: Gender and Politics,* edited by Almut-Barbara Renger and Jon Solomon, 95–122. Boston: Brill.

Reich, Jacqueline. 2011. "Slave to Fashion: Masculinity, Suits, and the *Maciste* Films of Italian Silent Cinema." In *Fashion in Film,* edited by Adrienne Munich, 236–259. Bloomington: Indiana University Press.

———. 2013. "The Metamorphosis of Maciste." *Film History* 25.3: 32-56.

———. 2015. *The Maciste Films of Italian Silent Cinema.* Bloomington: Indiana University Press.

Ricci, Steven. 2008. *Cinema and Fascism: Italian Film and Society, 1922–1943.* Berkeley: University of California Press.

Richardson, Niall. 2010. *Transgressive Bodies: Representations in Film and Popular Culture*. Burlington, VT: Ashgate.

Roberts, Dorothy. 2011. *Fatal Invention: How Science, Politics, and Big Business Re-create Race in the Twenty-First Century*. New York: New Press.

Rose, Nikolas. 2007. *The Politics of Life Itself: Biomedicine, Power, and Subjectivity in the Twenty-First Century*. Princeton, NJ: Princeton University Press.

Rota, Emanuel. 2011. "No Future for You: Italy between Fictional Past and Postnational Future." *California Italian Studies* 2.1. http://escholarship.org/uc/item/1np7n8ss. Accessed November 18, 2013.

Rushing, Robert A. 2008. "Gentlemen Prefer Hercules: Desire | Identification | Beefcake." *Camera Obscura* 69.3: 158–191.

Savran, David. 1998. *Taking It like a Man: White Masculinity, Masochism, and Contemporary American Culture*. Princeton, NJ: Princeton University Press.

Schenk, Irmbert. 2006. "The Cinematic Support to National(istic) Mythology: The Italian Peplum, 1910–1930." In *Globalization, Cultural Identities, and Media Representations*, edited by Natascha Gentz and Stefan Kramer, 153–168. Albany: State University of New York Press.

Schubart, Rikke. 2007. *Super Bitches and Action Babes: The Female Hero in Popular Cinema, 1970–2006*. Jefferson, NC: McFarland.

Schwarzenegger, Arnold, and Douglas Kent Hall. 1977. *Arnold: The Education of a Bodybuilder*. New York: Simon and Schuster.

Schwarzenegger, Arnold, and Peter Petre. 2012. *Total Recall: My Unbelievably True Life Story*. New York: Simon and Schuster.

Scott, A. O. 2007. "Battle of the Manly Men: Blood Bath with a Message." *New York Times*, March 9. Accessed March 13, 2016.

Shahabudin, Kim. 2009. "Ancient Mythology and Modern Myths: *Hercules Conquers Atlantis* (1961)." In *Classics for All: Reworking Antiquity in Mass Culture*, edited by Dunstan Lowe and Kim Shahabudin, 196–216. Newcastle upon Tyne: Cambridge Publishing Group.

Shukin, Nicole. 2009. *Animal Capital: Rendering Life in Biopolitical Times*. Minneapolis: University of Minnesota Press.

Silverman, Kaja. 1983. *The Subject of Semiotics*. New York: Oxford University Press.

Simmons, David. 2011. "'By Jupiter's Cock!' *Spartacus: Blood and Sand*, Video Games and Camp Excess." In *Of Muscles and Men: Essays on the Sword and Sandal Film*, edited by Michael G. Cornelius, 144–153. Jefferson, NC: McFarland.

Sobchack, Vivian. 1992. *The Address of the Eye: A Phenomenology of Film Experience*. Princeton, NJ: Princeton University Press.

Solomon, Jon. 2001. *The Ancient World in the Cinema*. Rev. and exp. ed. New Haven, CT: Yale University Press.

Sontag, Susan. 1966. "Notes on Camp." *Against Interpretation, and Other Essays*. New York: Farrar, Straus & Giroux.

Sorlin, Pierre. 1996. *Italian National Cinema, 1896–1996*. New York: Routledge.

Spackman, Barbara. 1996. *Fascist Virilities: Rhetoric, Ideology, and Social Fantasy in Italy*. Minneapolis: University of Minnesota Press.

Späth, Thomas, and Margit Tröhler. "Muscles and Morals: Spartacus, Ancient Hero of Modern Times." Translated by Mark Kyburz. In *Ancient Worlds in Film and*

Television: Gender and Politics, edited by Almut-Barbara Renger and Jon Solomon, 41–64. Boston: Brill.

Spinazzola, Vittorio. 1963. "Ercole alla conquista degli schermi." In *Film 63,* edited by Vittorio Spinazzola, 75–111. Milan: Feltrinelli.

Stevens, Kyle. 2013. "Dying to Love: Gay Identity, Suicide, and Aesthetics in *A Single Man.*" *Cinema Journal* 52.4: 99–120.

Stewart, Garrett. 1999. *Between Film and Screen: Modernism's Photo Synthesis.* Chicago: University of Chicago Press.

Stryker, Susan, and Nikki Sullivan. 2009. "King's Member, Queen's Body: Transsexual Surgery, Self-Demand Amputation, and the Somatechnics of Sovereign Power." In *Somatechnics: Queering the Technologisation of Bodies,* edited by Nikki Sullivan and Samantha Murray, 49–61. Farnham: Ashgate.

Tasker, Yvonne. 1993. "Dumb Movies for Dumb People: Masculinity, the Body, and the Voice in Contemporary Cinema." In *Screening the Male: Exploring Masculinities in Hollywood Cinema,* edited by Steven Cohan and Ina Rae Hark, 230–244. New York: Routledge.

Theodorakopoulos, Elena. 2010. *Ancient Rome at the Cinema: Story and Spectacle in Hollywood and Rome.* Liverpool: Liverpool University Press.

Tomkins, Calvin. 1967. "Profiles: The Very Rich Hours of Joe Levine." *New Yorker,* September 16, 55–136.

Turner, Susanne. 2009. "'Only Spartan Women Give Birth to Real Men': Zach Snyder's *300* and the Male Nude." In *Classics for All: Reworking Antiquity in Mass Culture,* edited by Dunstan Lowe and Kim Shahabudin, 128–149. Newcastle upon Tyne: Cambridge Publishing Group.

Usai, Paolo Cherchi. 1986. *Giovanni Pastrone: Gli anni d'oro del cinema a Torino.* Turin: UTET.

Väliaho, Pasi. 2014. *Biopolitical Screens: Image, Power, and the Neoliberal Brain.* Cambridge, MA: MIT Press.

Vitali, Valentina. 2010. *Hindi Action Cinema: Industries, Narratives, Bodies.* Bloomington: Indiana University Press.

Von Däniken, Erich. 1969. *Chariots of the Gods.* Translated by Michael Heron. New York: Penguin.

Wagstaff, Christopher. 1996. "Cinema." In *Italian Cultural Studies: An Introduction,* edited by David Forgacs and Robert Lumley, 216–232. New York: Oxford University Press.

Wall, Stephen. 2013. "Fandom and the Nostalgia of Masculinity." In *Conan Meets the Academy: Multidisciplinary Essays on the Enduring Barbarian,* edited by Jonas Prida, 174–192. Jefferson, NC: McFarland.

Weineck, Silke-Maria. 2014. *The Tragedy of Fatherhood: King Laius and the Politics of Paternity in the West.* London: Bloomsbury.

Willemen, Paul. 2009. "Fantasy in Action." In *World Cinemas, Transnational Perspectives,* edited by Nataša Ďurovičová and Kathleen Newman, 245–284. New York: Routledge.

Williams, David. E. 2007. "Few against Many." *American Cinematographer* 88.6: 52–65.

Williams, Linda. 1991. "Film Bodies: Gender, Genre, Excess." *Film Quarterly* 44.4: 2–13.

Wu Ming¹. 2007. "Allegoria e guerra in *300.*" *La Valle dell'Eden (Dossier: Americana. Cinema e televisione negli Stati Uniti dopo l'11 settembre)* 18: 11–36.